NIETZSCHE ON TRUTH
AND PHILOSOPHY

NIETZSCHE ON TRUTH AND PHILOSOPHY

MAUDEMARIE CLARK
Colgate University

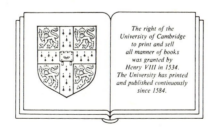

The right of the
University of Cambridge
to print and sell
all manner of books
was granted by
Henry VIII in 1534.
The University has printed
and published continuously
since 1584.

CAMBRIDGE UNIVERSITY PRESS

CAMBRIDGE

NEW YORK   PORT CHESTER   MELBOURNE   SYDNEY

Published by the Press Syndicate of the University of Cambridge
The Pitt Building, Trumpington Street, Cambridge CB2 1RP
40 West 20th Street, New York, NY 10011, USA
10 Stamford Road, Oakleigh, Melbourne 3166, Australia

© Cambridge University Press 1990

First published 1990

Printed in the United States of America

Library of Congress Cataloging-in-Publication Data
Clark, Maudemarie.
Nietzsche on truth and philosophy / Maudemarie Clark.
p.   cm. – (Modern European philosophy)
Includes bibliographical references.
ISBN 0-521-34368-2. – ISBN 0-521-34850-1 (pbk.)
1. Nietzsche, Friedrich Wilhelm, 1844–1900 – Contributions in
concept of truth.   2. Truth.   I. Title.   II. Series.
B3318.T78C55   1990
121'.092 – dc20   90-36094
                                                          CIP

British Library Cataloguing in Publication Data
Clark, Maudemarie
Nietzsche on truth and philosophy. – (Modern European
philosopy).
1. Epistemology. Truth. Theories of Nietzsche, Friedrich
1844–1900
I. Title   II. Series
121

ISBN 0-521-34368-2 hardback
ISBN 0-521-34850-1 paperback

To the memory of my father, Vincent M. Clark
(1918–1968)
and of my friend and student, Bruce P. Cooper
(1956–1987)

On the origin of scholars. – . . . If one has trained one's eye
to recognize in a scholarly book or scientific treatise the
scholar's intellectual *idiosyncrasy* . . . one will almost always
discover behind it the scholar's "pre-history," his family,
and especially their occupations and crafts.

 . . . The son of an advocate will be an advocate as a
scholar, too; he wants in the first place to prove his case right,
in the second, perhaps, that it be right. The sons of Protes-
tant ministers and school teachers may be recognized by
their naive certainty when, as scholars, they consider their
case proved when they have merely stated it with vigor and
warmth; they are thoroughly used to being *believed,* as that
was part of their fathers' job. A Jew, on the other hand . . . is
least of all used to being believed. Consider Jewish scholars
in this light: All of them have a high regard for logic, that is
for *compelling* agreement by force of reasons; they know with
that they are bound to win even when they encounter race
and class prejudices and where one does not like to believe
them. For nothing is more democratic than logic; it is no
respecter of persons and makes no distinction between
crooked and straight noses. (Notice by the way that Europe
owes the Jews no small thanks for making people think more
logically and for establishing *cleaner* intellectual habits . . .
Wherever Jews have won influence, they have taught human beings to make finer distinctions, more rigorous infer-
ences, and to write in a more luminous and cleanly fashion;
their task was ever to bring a people "to listen to *raison.*")

The Gay Science, 348.

CONTENTS

vii

PREFACE

Nietzsche says much about truth that is interesting and quite influential. As I argue in Chapter 1, it is also problematic and perhaps even self-contradictory. In this study I attempt to make sense of it, and I emphasize aspects of the problem of truth that bear on Nietzsche's view of the role of philosophy. Throughout I try to make the best case for what I take him to be saying. More accurately, as far as Nietzsche's texts allow, I avoid attributing to him positions against which there are obvious objections. As will be clear from Chapter 3, this approach does not ensure the defensibility of his claims. I argue that Nietzsche's early position on truth is vulnerable to fatal objections, although it is the position that has recently won him disciples and considerable influence. I also argue that Nietzsche himself eventually rejected this now influential position and suggest that some of his greatest thinking was called forth by his attempt to understand what was wrong with it and the source of its hold on him.

I will be happy if my work contributes to efforts to show that Nietzsche was a great thinker. Of course, he was much more than that; he was a great writer. He could do incredible things with language, things that most of us may be better off not even trying to imitate. I barely touch on that aspect of his work and genius here. While I make no attempt to reproduce the effect of

ix

reading Nietzsche, I hope my approach shows that one need not take the life out of his thought by concentrating on arguments, objections, and other truth-related matters. That life should be evident if one gets at Nietzsche's thinking, and at what he has left for us to think about. I hope this study also supplies some basis for appreciating the high compliment that Ernest Jones tells us Freud paid to Nietzsche, that he had a greater self-knowledge than any man who ever lived, or is ever likely to live.

This book began as a chapter on truth that I planned to add to my dissertation on Nietzsche's critique of morality when I revised it for publication. Despite my continuing belief in the importance of Nietzsche's thinking about morality, I found that the material on truth soon outgrew my original format and took over the project. Although this book therefore contains none of the material from my dissertation, it has benefited greatly from the attention bestowed on its predecessor by the members of my dissertation committee at the University of Wisconsin: Ivan Soll, William H. Hay, Robert Ammerman, and Max Bäumer. I am very grateful to them for their criticisms, suggestions, and encouragements. I am also grateful to the members of the Philosophy Department at the University of California at San Diego for the opportunity to present to them a chapter of my dissertation. The questions they asked made clear to me the necessity of reworking the dissertation project in terms of Nietzsche's development, and the present book carries out the same lesson in relation to Nietzsche's view of truth.

I wrote the first version of the last chapter of this book while I was still a graduate student, and am grateful to Claudia Card of the University of Wisconsin for her help and encouragement with that early version. I read that version at Columbia University, Indiana University, Iowa State University, and the University of Illinois at Champaign-Urbana, and am grateful to the members of the philosophy departments at these schools for many helpful comments and criticisms received on those occasions.

But, above all else, this book bears the stamp of the time I spent in the Philosophy Department at Columbia University. It was conceived and largely written while I was teaching at Columbia, and I am very grateful for ideas, inspiration, criticisms, and encouragements from many colleagues and students, and for the influence of countless philosophers who presented colloquia at Columbia.

It would be a poorer book, and in some cases, a very different one, if I had not been influenced at close range by the thought of Arthur Danto, Isaac Levi, Sidney Morgenbesser, and Charles Parsons, and if I had not had to try to deal with some difficult questions concerning truth posed to me by Charles Larmore and Norbert Hornstein. And without many conversations on truth with Sue Larson, and great encouragement from Mary Mothersill and Hidé Ishiguro, I am sure it would not have been written.

My colleagues in the Department of Philosophy and Religion at Colgate University provided an especially supportive environment in which to finish the book. I am very grateful for that, and for their helpful comments on material from Chapters 5 and 8.

As will be evident, I also owe a tremendous debt of gratitude to many Nietzsche scholars whose work has made mine possible. I am particularly grateful for the support given me by the community of North American Nietzsche scholars. The North American Nietzsche Society gave me the opportunity to try out early versions of many of the ideas in this book on audiences of such scholars, and I have learned much on these occasions. The early versions were published as "On 'Truth and Lie' in the Extra-Moral Sense" in *International Studies in Philosophy* 16, no. 2 (1984), "Nietzsche's Perspectivist Rhetoric" in *International Studies in Philosophy* 18, no. 2 (1986), and "Nietzsche's Doctrines of the Will to Power" in *Nietzsche-Studien* 12 (1983). I am grateful to the editors of these journals for permission to make use of revised versions of this material in Chapters 3, 5, and 7. I am also grateful to John Wilcox and Kenneth Westphal for their lengthy comments on the manuscript at various stages of its composition, and to Bernd Magnus, Alexander Nehamas, and Richard Schacht for their generous encouragement of the project at times when I most needed it.

Finally, I want to thank Raymond Geuss, the editor of the series, for his indispensable support and comments on the manuscript, and Connie Jones, who has discussed all of its material with me over many years and many more walks in Riverside Park.

NOTE ON TEXTS AND CITATIONS

In order to minimize footnotes and to eliminate the inconvenience of endnotes, I have incorporated almost all references to secondary sources into the text, citing only the author's name (unless it is clear from the context), the page number of the work, and the publication date (unless I cite only one work by that author). The works cited are listed in the Bibliography.

For Nietzsche's works, I have used *Sämtliche Werke. Kritische Studienausgabe in 15 Bänden,* edited by G. Colli and M. Montinari (Berlin: de Gruyter, 1980). I generally follow the excellent translations listed below, and the alterations I have made are usually minor. I cite Nietzsche's works by the initials of their English titles and the section number. In the case of "Truth and Lie in the Extra-Moral Sense," I have supplied page numbers because of the absence of a convenient division into sections. I give the page of the English translation first, followed by the corresponding page of Volume 1 of the *Studienausgabe.* Chapter 1, section 5, supplies my justification for the choice of the specific works on which I base my interpretation.

I list here the abbreviations used in the text and the works to which they refer, followed by the publication date of the first edition. If Nietzsche did not himself publish the work (in the case of A and EH only because his insanity kept him from seeing the finished work through the publication process), I supply instead the year in which he finished working on it. The dates of works in this second group are marked with asterisks. "P" always refers to the preface of the cited work.

A   *Der Antichrist (The Antichrist)* 1888*
        Translated by Walter Kaufmann in *The Portable Nietzsche*.
        New York: Viking Penguin, 1954.

BG   *Jenseits von Gut und Böse (Beyond Good and Evil)* 1886
        Translated by Walter Kaufmann in *Basic Writings of Nietzsche*. New York: Random House (Modern Library),
        1968.

BT   *Der Geburt der Tragödie (The Birth of Tragedy)* 1872
        Translated by Walter Kaufmann in *Basic Writings of Nietzsche*.

D   *Morgenröte (Dawn)* 1881
        Translated by R. J. Hollingdale as *Daybreak*. Cambridge University Press, 1982.

EH   *Ecce Homo* 1888*
        Translated by Walter Kaufmann in *Basic Writings of Nietzsche*.

GM   *Zur Genealogie der Moral (On the Genealogy of Morals)* 1887
        Translated by Walter Kaufmann and R. J. Hollingdale in *Basic Writings of Nietzsche*.

GS   *Die fröhliche Wissenschaft (The Gay Science)* 1882
        Part 5 of GS 1887
        Translated by Walter Kaufmann. New York: Random House (Vintage), 1974.

HA   *Menschliches, Allzumenschliches* (Human, All-Too-Human) 1878
        Translated by R. J. Hollingdale. Cambridge University Press, 1986.

TL   "*Über Wahrheit und Lüge im aussermoralischen Sinne*" ("Truth and Lie in the Extra-Moral Sense") 1873*
        Translated by Daniel Breazeale in *Truth and Philosophy: Selections from Nietzsche's Notebooks of the 1870's*. Atlantic Highlands, N. J.: Humanities Press, 1979.

TI   *Götzen-Dämmerung (Twilight of the Idols)* 1889
        Translated by Walter Kaufmann in *The Portable Nietzsche*.

WP   *Der Wille zur Macht (The Will to Power)* Notes from the
1880's*
Translated by Walter Kaufmann and R. J. Hollingdale.
New York: Viking, 1968.

Z   *Also Sprach Zarathustra (Thus Spoke Zarathustra)* 1883–85
Translated by Walter Kaufmann in *The Portable Nietzsche.*

—⇥ ⇤—

INTERPRETING NIETZSCHE
ON TRUTH

Nietzsche's philosophy has recently generated a significant amount of interest and excitement, much of it centered around his position on truth. Considerable hope exists, and much conviction, that Nietzsche has something important to say about truth. This study begins with the problem that confronts anyone with such hopes, namely, that Nietzsche's claims about truth seem hopelessly confused and contradictory. This chapter sets out the problem and gives an overview of the four most influential ways in which those sympathetic to Nietzsche have tried to solve it. After explaining why these solutions seem unsatisfactory, it sketches a solution to the problem that will be defended in the remainder of this book. This solution stresses the development in Nietzsche's position. It will be argued that Nietzsche's position was contradictory in its early and middle formulations, but that he progressed toward and finally arrived at a coherent and defensible position in the works of his final two years.

1. The problem of truth

Nietzsche's position on truth seems to amount to a denial that any human belief is, or could be, true. He proclaims, for example, that "truths are illusions we have forgotten are illusions" (TL 84; WL 880–1), that "truth is the kind of error without which a certain kind of being could not live" (WP 493), and that there are "no facts," but "only interpretations" (WP 481). Although these clearest statements of Nietzsche's denial of truth are all from the *Nachlass*, the works he published contain many statements apparently designed to make the same point. He denies, for instance, that we have any organ for knowledge or "truth" (GS 354), claiming that we engage in a "constant falsification of the world by means of numbers" (BG 4) and that even physics is "only an interpretation" (BG 14). He suggests that science at its best keeps us in a "*simplified,* thoroughly artificial, suitably constructed and suitably falsified world" (BG 24) and that the world that concerns us is a "fiction" (BG 34). Finally, in his polemic against the ascetic ideal (GM III), he offers a detailed analysis of the belief in truth as the latest expression of that ideal.

Such claims have made Nietzsche, once associated with the political right, a rallying point for the epistemological left – for those who attack with revolutionary fervor traditional beliefs and attitudes concerning truth, science, philosophy, and the roles of argument and theory. Many assume that Nietzsche has demonstrated that there are no facts and no truths, but "only interpretations," or "different perspectives" on reality. It is therefore apparently a mistake to attempt to give the correct interpretation of anything, including, if not especially, of Nietzsche's own philosophy. Only the misguided, it seems, will even take Nietzsche to be offering arguments or theories, since that would make him captive of the belief in truth that he rejected. His writings can only be supposed to offer a model of what lies on the other side of philosophy – the liberated intellect playing joyfully with itself, rather than engaged in the ascetic activity of offering arguments and theories, or even attempting to say something true.

While this view of Nietzsche and truth may be embraced only by the most radical of contemporary intellectuals, Nietzsche's claims about truth have undoubtedly exerted great influence in more respectable circles. Richard Rorty, whose recent essays (1982 and 1986) emphasize his agreement with Nietzsche's denial of truth, even suggests that we think of the history of twentieth-century Continental philosophy not in terms of the distinctions and transitions between such movements as phenomenology, existentialism, structuralism, and post-structuralism, but as a series of attempts to come to terms with Nietzsche's claim that truth, like God, is dead. Although the history of twentieth-century Anglo-American philosophy would reveal no comparable Nietzschean influence, striking resemblances between Nietzsche's view of truth and that of the early American pragmatists have been noted (by Danto, e.g.), as well as resemblances to Wittgenstein and such contemporary philosophers as Quine, Sellars, Goodman, and Putnam (by West, e.g.). Furthermore, there can be no question that Nietzsche's epistemological and anti-metaphysical views have exerted enormous influence on the contemporary intellectual scene in both Europe and the United States, perhaps especially among literary critics, to such an extent that he is plausibly regarded as "the central figure of postmodern thought in the West" (West, 242).

The problem with this influential view of truth is that it seems to lead Nietzsche into hopeless self-contradiction. There is, first of all, the problem of self-reference. If it is supposed to be true that there is no truth, then there is apparently a truth after all; and if it is not supposed to be true, it seems that we have no reason to take it seriously, that is, accept it or its alleged implications. I shall not at this point consider attempts to meet this objection, for even if it can be met, an equally (or even more) important objection would remain. Despite the recent emphasis on his claims about truth, few would deny that Nietzsche's ultimate importance is connected to what he has to say about values, especially to the challenge he offers to received values. His challenge to received values, and received opinion about values, seems to rest on such claims as the following: that morality is an expression of resentment and of the negation of life; that life itself is will power; that philosophy, religion, and morality are among the more refined forms of this will; that Western civilization is in grave danger from the death of God and the nihilism bound to grow out of it. It is not my concern here to explain exactly how such claims challenge received values, but it seems clear that they cannot do so unless they are taken to be true. Nietzsche explicitly grounds his denial of morality on the claim that morality is based on error (D 103), and bases his demand that the philosopher "take his stand beyond good and evil and leave the illusion of moral judgment *beneath* himself" (TI VII, 1) on the claim that moral judgment involves illusion. But if truths are illusions, the illusion involved in moral judgment can hardly give us reason to abandon it, assuming, as we must, that Nietzsche does not demand that we abstain from judgment altogether. Nietzsche's apparent nihilism in regard to truth thus threatens the coherence of his critique of morality, and of his entire philosophy – insofar as the latter commits Nietzsche to certain truths while at the same time it denies that there are any truths. Nietzsche's own practice is apparently at odds with his theory.

A related inconsistency between theory and practice threatens his critique of metaphysics. Although his first book, *The Birth of Tragedy* (1872), seems committed to Schopenhauer's metaphysics, Nietzsche's enormous influence on twentieth-century Continental philosophy is inseparable from the rejection of metaphysics he announced in *Human, All-Too-Human* (1878) and developed in later works. His passionate claims as to the importance of overcoming metaphysics and its often hidden remnants set him apart from most other critics of metaphysics and account for much of his abiding influence. Yet his own doctrines of eternal recurrence and will to power seem obviously "metaphysical" on any reasonable construal of that term. Nietzsche's mature philosophy seems to make claims to metaphysical truth while at the same time rejecting all such claims.

The obvious conclusion to draw is that there is something seriously wrong with Nietzsche's philosophy. At the very least, it seems that we must reject either his general claim about truth or the specific claims (especially regarding values) that have established him as a thinker to be reckoned with. An interpreter who holds that Nietzsche has something important to teach us about both truth and values must explain how this is possible in the face of the apparently self-contradictory nature of his position on truth. Two main strategies seem available: to show that the self-contradiction is only apparent, or to admit the contradiction but to argue that its presence in Nietzsche's work teaches us something about truth. We find both of these strategies in the literature on Nietzsche. But we also find two very different views of truth attributed to Nietzsche. Since each of the strategies can be coupled with either view of truth, we find four basic approaches in dealing with the problems posed by the apparent contradictions in his position.[1]

1. The suggestion is that all interpretations that offer a solution to the problem under consideration can be situated in relation to the four categories of interpretation set up here, not that each fits neatly into one of them. In particular,

2. Traditional interpretations:
Kaufmann and Heidegger

Traditional interpretations attribute to Nietzsche the traditional understanding of truth as correspondence to reality, and the belief that his own views are true in this sense. The two most important traditional interpretations are the empiricist version advanced by Kaufmann and defended more recently by Wilcox, and Heidegger's metaphysical version. Twenty years ago, it could be said that Kaufmann's interpretation was "almost completely dominant in America" (O'Brien, 5), whereas Heidegger's dominated Continental discussion of Nietzsche. Although this dominance has ended, the state of Nietzsche interpretation today owes much to these two interpretations and has been inspired in large part by the desire to find an alternative to them.

Kaufmann's strategy is to show that the contradiction in Nietzsche's position is merely apparent, that Nietzsche does not deny the existence of truth, and that he does not put forward any metaphysical theories. Taking Socrates as Nietzsche's ideal, Kaufmann emphasizes those passages in which Nietzsche seems committed to both the existence and the overriding value of truth. He attempts to explain away Nietzsche's apparent denial of truth as a denial of what Nietzsche called the "true world," the supersensuous and eternal world of the Platonic forms or the Kantian thing-in-itself. Kaufmann's Nietzsche denies the possibility of transcendent or metaphysical truth, which would be correspondence to the way things are in themselves, but affirms the existence of empirical truth. To affirm the existence of truth is simply to say that some statements, propositions, sentences, or utterances are true. According to Kaufmann's interpretation, then, Nietzsche denies that any metaphysical statements are true but accepts many empirical statements as true. Kaufmann can deny any inconsistency between Nietzsche's theory and his practice, for he interprets Nietzsche as putting forward his own views, including the doctrines of eternal recurrence and will to power, as empirical truths. He stresses Nietzsche's claim that the

two important recent interpretations, those of Richard Schacht and Alexander Nehamas, attempt to combine the advantages of two or more of the interpretations I distinguish, which is also my own approach. I sketch my approach later in this chapter, and deal with Schacht and Nehamas at length in Chapters 5 and 7.

eternal recurrence is "the most *scientific* of all possible hypotheses" (WP 55), and interprets the will to power as an unfortunate extension of an empirical hypothesis regarding human motivation (see Chapter 7). Finally, Kaufmann handles the problem posed by Nietzsche's analysis of the faith in truth as an expression of the ascetic ideal by insisting that Nietzsche accepts both the ascetic ideal and the faith in truth (see Chapter 6).

A number of factors have made it difficult for recent interpreters to accept Kaufmann's interpretation. In the first place, if one interprets will to power and eternal recurrence in traditional terms – as straightforward claims about the nature of reality, as claims that are supposed to correspond to reality – it seems implausible to deny their metaphysical character (see Chapters 7 and 8). Further, in many passages Nietzsche clearly rejects much more than metaphysical truth or the thing-in-itself. He appears to deny that there are even any things and to insist that all of our so-called truths are therefore really illusions since they presuppose, state, or imply the existence of things (Megill, 207 ff.). Kaufmann's interpretation does not therefore seem consistent with the Nietzschean texts. Its insistence that Nietzsche embraces both the belief in truth and the ascetic ideal also seems to make it incapable of explaining Nietzsche's belief in the radical character of his position on truth. From beginning to end, Nietzsche's writings convey his belief that he is saying something about truth that is of the utmost importance for understanding human life and that sets him at odds with the whole philosophical tradition (GM III, 23–8, e.g.).

Wilcox defends an interpretation that is very close to Kaufmann's, but actually gives us reason to look for an alternative. In the first place, he admits that he cannot explain away all of the passages in which Nietzsche appears to deny the existence of truth. He argues that, on balance, we have more evidence that Nietzsche accepts the existence of empirical truths than that he rejects all truth. Secondly, although Wilcox agrees with Kaufmann that much of Nietzsche's apparent denial of truth is only a rejection of the "true" world, that is, of metaphysics, he thinks that it has another source in Nietzsche's view that concepts always falsify reality. I will argue in Chapter 4 that Wilcox here makes an important contribution to the understanding of Nietzsche's position. However, it also gives us reason to reject the view, which Wilcox shares with Kaufmann, that Nietzsche allows for the possibility of obtaining empirical truth, since such truth is obtainable only by means of concepts. If Nietzsche believes that concepts always falsify reality, it is difficult to see how we can explain away his denial of truth.

Heidegger offers a version of the traditional interpretation insofar as he insists that Nietzsche's claims about truth presuppose the correspondence theory of truth (1961, I, 621) and that the doctrines of eternal recurrence and will to power are put forward as truths in this traditional sense (I, 621–55). But his reading is not vulnerable to the objections raised above to Kaufmann's. In the first place, he rejects an empiricist construal of the will to power and the eternal recurrence. Although he considers Nietzsche the great critic of metaphysics, he believes that these central Nietzschean doctrines are themselves metaphysical, that they are answers to the traditional questions of metaphysics concerning the essence and existence of what is. Secondly, rather than attempting to explain away Nietzsche's denial of truth, he presents it as the ultimate consequence of Nietzsche's acceptance of the "metaphysical" conception of truth as correspondence to reality (*Einstimmigkeit mit dem Wirklichem*). Finally, Heidegger has perhaps done more than anyone to bring out the radical character of Nietzsche's claims about truth through his attempt to show their connection to nihilism and to the modern "technological" attitude towards the world.

Yet, Heidegger escapes the difficulties of the empiricist interpretation only at the cost of doing nothing to dissolve the apparent contradictions in Nietzsche's positions on truth and metaphysics. His Nietzsche remains caught in the net of the correspondence theory of truth, and of metaphysics in general, even while he delivers his fatal objections to them. This does not give us sufficient reason to reject Heidegger's interpretation, since he does not claim that Nietzsche's position is internally consistent. But it does give us reason to be very careful since Heidegger has so little incentive to look for an account that would dissolve the apparent contradictions in Nietzsche's philosophy. His use of Nietzsche's philosophy to support his own depends on interpreting it so that Nietzsche's claims about truth and metaphysics are inconsistent with his practice.

Heidegger's later philosophy is directed toward a recovery of the sense of Being, the acknowledgement of Being as Being. This acknowledgement, he tells us, "means allowing Being to reign in all its questionableness . . . ; it means persevering in the question of Being" (II, 338; trs. 201). His early philosophy had already insisted that Being had been forgotten or suppressed within the metaphysical tradition of previous philosophy. Metaphysics might seem to be concerned exclusively with Being, since it asks not about a particular kind of being (or about some aspect of such), but about beings as such, that is, the Being of beings. Heidegger claimed, however, that in their efforts to ascertain the Being of beings, philosophers have covered up the prior question as to what Being itself is. They had taken for granted an understanding of Being – for example, as enduring presence – which they failed to recognize as such.

Heidegger presents the phenomenological analysis of *Being and Time* as preparation for a "fundamental ontology" that would provide the missing account of Being itself by uncovering the original experiences of it that have been covered up in and by the philosophical tradition. That this project is abandoned, or at least transformed, in Heidegger's later philosophy is indicated by his insistence that "any discussion of 'Being itself' must always remain interrogative" (II, 338; trs. 201). Rather than giving an account of Being, Heidegger now insists only on keeping alive the question of Being, which includes promoting the recognition that the question can never be closed, that thinking must remain open to the possibility that more primordial or new determinations of Being may always be disclosed. Of course, this presupposes that some determination of Being has been disclosed. Heidegger agrees, claiming that metaphysics is itself the history of Being, a history in which Being discloses itself as withdrawn or concealed. Through his reading of the history of philosophy as the history of Being, Heidegger aims at a recovery of the sense or mystery of Being, which is at the very least a sense of a power that cannot be brought under human control or domination. Such a recovery would also involve a recovery of the original and nonmetaphysical sense of truth as the unconcealment of Being, and a conception of human beings (*Dasein*) as shepherds of the mystery of Being, keepers of the house of Being – that is, as ones whose role it is to let Being be, to let the Being of beings disclose itself, instead of insisting on the domination or mastery of beings, in accord with the spirit of technology that Heidegger considers the fulfillment of metaphysics.

Since Nietzsche calls Being an "empty fiction" (TI III, 2), he would seem more likely to consider Heidegger's position nonsensical than to offer support for it. Things look somewhat different, however, once Nietzsche's positions are taken to be contradictory in the way Heidegger claims. If the great critic of metaphysics was himself a metaphysician, something about the nature of metaphysics must have escaped him. If Nietzsche's denial of truth is the ultimate consequence of his acceptance of the correspondence theory of truth (I, 622), and yet he cannot refrain from presenting his own doctrines as true, we need a different conception of truth. These points open the door for Heidegger to present his own account of metaphysics as an explanation for Nietzsche's blindness, and his own attitude towards Being and conception of truth as the direction in which Nietzsche points us.

Heidegger suggests that Nietzsche's blindness concerning truth and metaphysics is the blindness to Being characteristic of metaphysicians. Nietzsche's understanding and rejection of metaphysics is itself metaphysical, according to Heidegger, for it ignores Being and understands metaphysics instead in terms of values. That is, Nietzsche understands metaphysics as the acceptance of a true or transcendent world that devalues this world, and eventually leads to nihilism, when the values protected by metaphysics are devalued. Nietzsche aims to overcome nihilism by overcoming metaphysics, apparently by means of his doctrines of the eternal recurrence, which rules out a transcendent world, and of the will to power, which provides the principle for a new valuation. However, Heidegger insists that these doctrines are themselves metaphysical since they offer Nietzsche's answer to the question concerning the Being (will to power as the essence, eternal recurrence the mode of existence) of beings. Since one might defend Nietzsche, as Kaufmann does, by claiming that will to power and eternal recurrence do not have the features of metaphysics to which Nietzsche objects – the acceptance of a transcendent world which devalues this world – Heidegger needs a deeper reason for considering Nietzsche's doctrines metaphysical. He offers such a reason by claiming that Nietzsche's doctrine of the will to power reduces Being to the status of a value, and is therefore part and parcel of the metaphysics of subjectivity initiated by Descartes.

According to Heidegger, with Descartes the human being or *Dasein* is transformed into the subject – the substance or underlying support, that which lies at the foundation of beings. Given the procedure of doubt followed in the first *Meditation,* the decision as to what is to count as a being comes to rest with human beings: only what can be presented to them as indubitable counts as a being; only what they can be certain of is true. Human beings are thus established "in a position of dominance" in relation to everything that is (II, 146; trs. 100). Since Nietzsche attacks Descartes' subject as a fiction of logic, he would hardly seem to be a follower in this regard. According to Heidegger, however, he does follow Descartes in that he makes human beings the subject or foundation of things, the difference being only that the Nietzschean subject is not a spiritual ego, but the body, interpreted as a center of drives and affects, that is, as will to power. Like its Cartesian counterpart, this Nietzschean subject disposes over the whole of beings, providing the "measure for the beingness [*Seiendheit*] of every individual being" (II, 171; trs. 121). The will to power is the other side of the metaphysical coin of Nietzsche's claims about truth. In positing error as the essence of truth (i.e., in claiming that truths are illusions), according to Heidegger, Nietzsche "fashions for the subject an absolute power to enjoin what is true and what is false," and thus what is and what is not a being (II, 199; trs. 145). In other words, Nietzsche regards truths as illusions insofar as, in accord with the doctrine of the will to power, he denies that the Being of things places any limitation on what is true. Instead, what allows anything to count as true is that it serves the interests of the subject, or is posited as true by the subject in accord with its essence as will to power. By means of the doctrine of the will to power, therefore, Being is degraded to the status of a value, "a condition of the preservation and enhancement of the will to power" (II, 232; trs. 176).

   The doctrine of the will to power thus leads directly not only to the claim that truths are illusions, but also to Nietzsche's characterization of Being as "an empty fiction," "the last smoke of evaporating reality" (TI II, 2, 4). This is why Heidegger considers it the completion of metaphysics: by reducing Being to a value, the doctrine of the will to power makes the nihilism of the metaphysical tradition, the assumption that Being itself is nothing, a matter of principle. Heidegger understands the nihilism Nietzsche wanted to overcome – the sense of emptiness and purposeless, the devaluation of the highest values and devotion to frenzied consumption – as a loss of any sense of Being and the consequent focus on beings, ultimately as the withdrawal of Being itself.

   Heidegger also regards the feature of metaphysics to which

Nietzsche most obviously objected, the acceptance of a transcendent world, as due to the withdrawal of Being. Insofar as a question is raised concerning the Being of beings, it is presupposed that beings are not their own foundation, that they are to be explained in terms of something beyond themselves. But in the absence of a sense of Being, the request for a ground of beings could only lead philosophers to another being, though it had to be a special kind of being, a transcendent being – for example, the Platonic ideas, on the side of essence, and a first cause, God or absolute spirit, on the side of existence. According to this account, the aspect of metaphysics that Nietzsche most obviously rejects – the acceptance of a transcendent or true world – derives from a more fundamental feature that Nietzsche's own philosophy exemplifies: the loss of a sense of, the withdrawal of, Being. According to Heidegger, Nietzsche understands Being in terms of values because Being has totally withdrawn. And he thus brings to completion metaphysics, the history of Being in its withdrawal.

Already in *Being and Time* (section 44), Heidegger treats the correspondence theory of truth as a symptom of the withdrawal (there, the forgetfulness) of Being, a covering over of the idea of truth as the unconcealment of Being. He is therefore able to treat it in *Nietzsche* as part and parcel of the metaphysical understanding that finds its completion in the denial of Being, which makes truths in the sense of correspondence impossible, in Nietzsche's terms, "errors" or "illusions."

The contradictions in Nietzsche's account of truth and metaphysics thus allow Heidegger to give Nietzsche a place in his history of metaphysics, and to view him as pointing the way to Heidegger's own philosophy. Heidegger's is a powerful interpretation that has understandably exerted tremendous influence on those working within the Continental tradition. However, as I explain in the next section, interpreters have become increasingly unwilling to draw Heideggerian lessons from the apparent contradictions in Nietzsche's philosophy.

3. Nontraditional interpretations: the "new Nietzsche"

The weaknesses in Kaufmann's interpretation and the search for an alternative to Heidegger's have contributed to the rise of the "new Nietzsche," a Nietzsche with nontraditional ideas concerning truth. I classify as radical or nontraditional interpreters who take Nietzsche's claim that truths are illusions to state his ultimate position on truth, and who deny that he accepted the traditional understanding of truth as correspondence, or regarded his own doctrines as true in this sense. Like the traditionalist, the radical interpreter has two basic options for dealing with the apparent contradiction in Nietzsche's position on truth: to explain it away or to insist that we can learn something from it. Danto's analytic approach exemplifies the former option, whereas the deconstructionist readings of Derrida and his students embody the latter.

The analytic approach rests on the distinction between theories or conceptions of truth, that is, competing sets of beliefs about the nature of truth. The major options available (see Chapter 2 for a detailed discussion) are the correspondence, pragmatic, and coherence theories of truth. The idea is to dissolve the apparent contradiction in Nietzsche's position by saying that he denies the existence of truth in the sense of denying that human beliefs correspond to reality, but he affirms the truth of his own claims in the sense specified by the pragmatic or coherence theories. Danto does remove some of the appearance of contradiction in this way (see Chapter 2). His Nietzsche calls truths "illusions" because he denies that our truths correspond to reality, yet he affirms the truth of certain theories and beliefs in the pragmatic sense of truth, which, according to Danto, means only that they "facilitate life" (71). However, even if Nietzsche is a pragmatist in this sense about empirical theories (see Chapter 2 for reason to doubt this), Danto himself admits that he is not when it comes to the doctrines of eternal recurrence and will to power. These doctrines, Danto makes clear, are metaphysical doctrines and are supposed to correspond to reality (96 ff.). Danto makes no attempt to show how this can be reconciled with Nietzsche's critique of metaphysics. Danto's interpretation thus seems to warrant Rorty's conclusion that "James and Nietzsche made parallel criticism of nineteenth-century thought," but that "James' version is preferable, for it avoids the 'metaphysical' elements in Nietzsche which Heidegger criticizes, and, for that matter, the 'metaphysical' elements in Heidegger which Derrida criticizes" (1982, xviii).

Bernd Magnus has done more than any other proponent of the analytic strategy to avoid construing Nietzsche as a metaphysician. Interpreting the eternal recurrence as an imperative and a myth (see Chapter 8), and the will to power as a meta-philosophical doctrine about the nature of philosophy and theory, Magnus avoids construing either as a metaphysical doctrine. But he admits that his account does not remove all appearance of contradiction, since Nietzsche would still have to regard the will to power as simply true (1978, 201) – that is, as corresponding to the nature of philosophy and theory. Since this seems inconsistent with Nietzsche's denial of truth, the analytic strategy seems unable to explain away the apparent contradictions in his position.

The deconstructionist strategy admits the contradictions, but denies that they pose a problem. Derrida formulates the basis for this strategy as follows:

> There is no sense in doing without the concepts of metaphysics in order to attack metaphysics. We have no language – no syntax and no lexicon – which is alien to that history [of metaphysics]; we cannot utter a single destructive proposition which has not already slipped into the form, the logic, and the implicit postulation of precisely what it seeks to contest (1978, 280).

Derrida here responds to Heidegger's interpretation. If metaphysical assumptions are built into our grammar and vocabulary, and we cannot therefore utter a single proposition without presupposing them, Nietzsche could not reject metaphysics without at the same time being caught up in it. This implies that it is only to be expected that Nietzsche's critique of metaphysics would involve him in self-contradiction, but that this does not indicate his failure to think deeply enough about the nature of metaphysics, or the need to go beyond Nietzsche to Heidegger.

Equating Nietzsche's "critique of metaphysics" with "the critique of the concepts of Being and truth" (1978, 280), Derrida evidently thinks Nietzsche criticizes as metaphysical any belief that is presented as the truth or that attributes to the world a stable being or presence. Since this seems to make metaphysics coextensive with rational-discursive thought in general, it seems clear why Nietzsche could not simply reject or abandon metaphysics. The idea seems to be that the world is a ceaseless flux of becoming in which nothing is anything long enough to allow true beliefs about it. That metaphysics is built into our language thus amounts to the claim that our language is not suitable for portraying this Hericlitean world, that it always introduces stability and the presumption of truth. But why not conclude, then, that Nietzsche was simply confused when he tried to reject metaphysics, that we are simply stuck with metaphysics in the widened sense in which the term is used here? Deconstructionists respond that Nietzsche's writings show us that we can reject metaphysics, by undermining it from within.

Paul de Man has offered one of the most persuasive accounts of how Nietzsche can consistently reject metaphysics by deconstructing it, subverting it from within.[2] He seems to rely on an implicit distinction between what a statement literally asserts and what it does or shows. We find in Nietzsche's writings statements with obvious metaphysical content, and if we are only concerned with what is literally asserted, we must interpret Nietzsche as a metaphysician who was unable to remain consistent with his own critique of metaphysics. If we concentrate instead on what is being done by means of language, de Man suggests, we discover that these metaphysical statements actually undermine their own authority and reveal their own inadequacy. Statements are thus able to show what they cannot literally assert without falling into self-contradiction: for example, that all language is metaphorical (based in rhetoric rather than logic) and that statements are therefore unable to correspond to anything nonlinguistic (or, in Nietzsche's terminology, are "illusions"), contrary to what metaphysics would require (see Chapter 3). De Man seems to think that we can show the limits of rational-discursive thought by revealing its origin in rhetoric or metaphor, but that this origin cannot simply be asserted because the assertion would presuppose the validity or autonomy of rational-discursive thought. The apparent contradictions between Nietzsche's theory and practice of metaphysics do not, therefore, reveal any inadequacy in his philosophy, since only by means of such contradictions can the illusions of metaphysics be exhibited.

But we should not take this to mean that Nietzsche, or we

2. See Clark, 1987, for an attempt to show the plausibility of de Man's approach, as well as reasons for rejecting it, in the case of BT. My forthcoming paper, "Language and Deconstruction," attempts to strengthen the case against de Man's deconstructive approach by combining the argument of the 1987 paper with the one I give against de Man's interpretation of TL in Chapter Three of this study.

ourselves, can therefore possess the truth. If we could, Nietzsche would be wrong when he claims that truths are illusions. And Nietzsche's own situation would once again be inconsistent with his assertions: he would possess the truth while claiming that we are all caught in error. To avoid thereby rendering Nietzsche's philosophy inconsistent, de Man insists that Nietzsche remains caught in the same errors he exposed. Nietzsche himself inevitably claims to possess the truth (including, I presume, when he claims that truths are illusions). His own work therefore remains steeped in the errors it denounces, but it thereby remains internally consistent. Thus, according to de Man, the "allegory of errors" we find in Nietzsche's writings is "the very model of philosophical rigor" (118).

Sarah Kofman, also writing under Derrida's influence, suggests a way of making Nietzsche's rejection of metaphysics consistent with his practice without accusing him of error when she denies that his apparently metaphysical doctrines are supposed to be true. She denies metaphysical status to the doctrine of the will to power, for instance, on the grounds that it is not designed to give us "the truth of Being" (136) but is instead a metaphorical expression, based on a political model, of a method of dealing with interpretations (136–7), one which treats them as symptoms of instincts, sets of values, and, finally, of health or illness. The doctrine of the will to power is a hypothesis about interpretations and is therefore itself an interpretation rather than the assertion of a truth. Yet we cannot consider it merely "one hypothesis among others" (203) because Nietzsche clearly regards it as superior to other interpretations or hypotheses. But according to Kofman, this is not because it represents the truth, but because it permits the greatest "enrichment and embellishment of life" (202). The will to power is therefore "not a revelation but a justification of Being" (201), in the sense that it affirms life in its fullness, that is, in the multiplicity of its possible interpretations. It does this by allowing every interpretation its own place and justification in the overall economy of life, as the expression of some particular set of instincts or constellation of life. Kofman can therefore say that Nietzsche's preference for the hypothesis of the will to power is based on his belief that it affirms life and is indicative of the fullness of life, just as she has earlier said this about his preference for the metaphorical over the "demonstrative" (rational-discursive) style:

the metaphorical style indicates the fullness of life, just as the "demonstrative" style indicates its poverty. To deliberately use metaphor is to affirm life, in the same way that favoring concepts reveals a will to nothingness, an adherence to the ascetic ideal (33; trs. 210).

On Kofman's interpretation, Nietzsche's practice, his use of the will to power, is consistent with his theory that there are no truths but only interpretations precisely because Nietzsche does not regard it as a truth. And Kofman makes this plausible, at least initially, because she supplies a reason Nietzsche would have for preferring the will to power to other interpretations without committing him to its truth. On her account, it is not a privileged hypothesis – it's just like all the others, a symptom of a set of instincts, values, and ultimately, health or illness, rather than a revelation of Being. But this does not deprive Nietzsche of a basis for preferring it to other interpretations, because he prefers life-affirming interpretations, ones expressing health rather than illness.

There are, however, problems with Kofman's account. As David Hoy (1981) has argued, it makes the will to power a second-order principle that explains and demands the multiplication of first-order interpretations, but evidently rules out any way of distinguishing between better and worse first-order interpretations. According to Kofman, Nietzsche prefers the will to power because it calls for the acceptance and multiplication of all interpretations and thereby affirms life, unlike interpretations that impoverish life by ruling out other interpretations. But if Nietzsche's affirmation of life requires him to accept all first-order interpretations, it is inconsistent with preferring one first-order interpretation to any other, for example, an interpretation of nihilism or of morality. Yet, he clearly prefers the interpretations of nihilism and depression offered in GM to the religious interpretations (in terms of sin) of the same phenomena.

Kofman might insist that Nietzsche can consistently prefer one first-order interpretation to another, namely, as long as he does so in terms of health rather than truth. But, on her account, Nietzsche's only basis for regarding an interpretation as healthy appears to be that it encourages the multiplication of interpretations. Kofman might respond that an interpretation is healthy if it is life-affirming. But the judgment that one interpretation is more life-affirming than another seems to require for its justification claims presented not simply as life-affirming, but also as true. Nietzsche regards his own philosophy as life-affirming because he believes it promotes the affirmation of life, the ability to find value in human life (Chapter 8 discusses this at length). But this interpretation of his philosophy seems to rest upon many claims he regards as true. Among these, I will argue later (Chapters 7 and 8) are claims about depression and the ability to affirm life. He cannot prefer his own claims about the psychological prerequisites for affirming life simply on the grounds that they are life-affirming, since unless he knows the truth about what is required for the affirmation of life, he can have no basis for considering an interpretation more life-affirming than another. Therefore, Kofman gives us no basis for denying what otherwise seems obvious: that Nietzsche regarded, for instance, his interpretation of depression in terms of the will to power not only as more life-affirming than an account in terms of sin, but also as truer. In this (and in many other cases), the will to power is used to offer a first-order interpretation that competes with and therefore rules out other such interpretations rather than demanding the proliferation of interpretations.

A final problem is that Kofman evidently puts forward her own interpretation as true of Nietzsche's philosophy, for example, that Nietzsche's preference for the will to power hypothesis is based on the belief that it affirms and justifies life, not that it represents the truth about it. But if we can have a correct interpretation of Nietzsche's philosophy, why not a correct account of Being or life? If there is a truth about Nietzsche's philosophy, why not about the rest of the world? De Man seems more successful with this problem. As Nietzsche remains caught in the errors he denounces, de Man suggests that his own blindness (which would certainly include the assumption that he has the truth) will be revealed by other interpreters, whose errors will need to be exposed by still others.

Derrida offers a somewhat different solution to the same problems when he treats all of Nietzsche's writings on a par with the following sentence included in Nietzsche's *Nachlass:* " 'I have forgotten my umbrella.' " Since there is no context to provide help in interpreting this fragment, Derrida can plausibly conclude that its meaning is undecidable, and that it is undecidable whether it has any (other than surface) meaning. But he also treats this fragment as a model for the totality of Nietzsche's writings (1979, 133). On the interpretation Derrida thereby suggests, Nietzsche's philosophy remains consistent with his denial of truth since we have no way of deciding what the truth about it is, or even whether there is any truth about it. In the latter case, Nietzsche's writings would be what Derrida describes elsewhere as "the joyous affirmation of the play of the world and the innocence of becoming, the affirmation of a world of signs without fault, without truth" (1978, 292). Finally, Derrida himself remains faithful to Nietzsche's denial of truth since he suggests that what he himself is saying is undecidable – and that there may be no true interpretation of it.

But even if it suggests how Nietzsche and Derrida can remain consistent with Nietzsche's denial of truth, Derrida's fragment seems a bad model for the interpretation of Nietzsche's published writings. Unlike a single sentence cut off from any connection to others, each section of Nietzsche's published works is embedded in a very rich context constituted by other sections of the same work, and, usually, by earlier and later works. This context provides a basis for checking interpretations that is completely missing for Derrida's umbrella fragment. Derrida insists that no matter how far we have carried out a conscientious interpretation, we cannot reject the hypothesis that the totality of Nietzsche's writings *might* be of the type "I have forgotten my umbrella" (1979, 133). If this is true, it is because no matter how good our interpretation, we cannot have the kind of certainty Descartes demanded concerning its truth. But we can find in Nietzsche's writings strong reason to deny the hypothesis that the totality *is* of the type "I have forgotten my umbrella." A denial of certainty rules out neither the possibility of truth, nor the right to claim one has discovered it (see Chapter 2).

Some will think that I am missing the point in worrying about the truth of the undecidability thesis, that the appropriate question concerns its value rather than its truth (e.g., Draine, 434). Derrida would probably base the value of the undecidability thesis on the same grounds Kofman offers in support of the will to power: that it offers us greater freedom to play with the text – as exemplified, for instance, by his own very playful readings of Nietzsche in *Spurs* – and encouragement to produce readings and misreadings that will give rise to more of the same, thereby keeping the game of interpretation alive. I see two serious problems with this. In the first place, it is not at all clear that the undecidability thesis makes a greater contribution to the game of interpretation than would the reverse belief. New generations always seem to come up with new interpretations, despite their "belief in truth," and the motivation to offer new interpretations may well depend on the belief that they are closer to the truth than previous ones.

Secondly, even if the proliferation of playful interpretations (ones unconcerned with truth) would be encouraged by the undecidability thesis, we would be left with the question as to why playing with the text is more valuable than attempting to discover the truth about it. The assumption as to the greater value of playful interpretation rests to a large extent, I believe, on the acceptance of Nietzsche's critique of the belief in truth as an expression of the ascetic ideal (see Chapter 6), which he considers a life-negating ideal that threatens the human race with nihilism. Those attracted to Derrida's undecidability thesis and playful interpretations seem to assume that they reform intellectual practice in the manner demanded by Nietzsche's critique of the belief in truth as an expression of the ascetic ideal. Playing with the text is supposed to be an unascetic or anti-ascetic activity, the opposite of looking for the truth, or pretending to have found it. Thus Derrida's abundant use of erotic elements and imagery in his playful interpretations of Nietzsche, for the erotic seems opposed to the ascetic.

I believe that this is the new Nietzscheans' underlying objection to Heidegger's interpretation of Nietzsche: that it is too ascetic, and takes insufficient account of both the playful elements in Nietzsche and of his critique of the ascetic ideal. Under the influence of Heidegger, these interpreters have discovered that Nietzsche's claims about metaphysics and the belief in truth capture what is wrong with previous philosophy, and, in some cases, what is amiss in Western civilization. But they regard Heidegger's idea of letting Being be or becoming shepherds of Being – his vision of those who have left metaphysics behind and with it the obsession with mastery and technology that drives our civilization – as too ascetic a response, and promote as their alternative the more Nietzschean vision of playing with the text instead of attempting to discover the truth about it (e.g., Derrida, 1978, 278–93; 1982, 109–36).

There is, then, a great deal at stake in the opposition to

Heidegger's interpretation of Nietzsche. In their playful, nonar-
gumentative, often erotic and outrageous interpretations of
Nietzsche, many of the new Nietzscheans suppose that they offer
a model for a better, less ascetic, and therefore more Nietzschean
response than the one Heidegger offers to the problems of Western civilization and for an affirmative attitude toward life that
they think may be our only chance to keep from extinguishing
life on earth altogether. However, if my understanding of its
underlying assumptions is correct, their position is vulnerable to
the same objections I have already raised against Kofman. It
presupposes, in the first place, that they have interpreted correctly Nietzsche's claims about the ascetic ideal, its relation to the
problems of Western civilization, and its implications regarding
the reform of intellectual practice; and, in the second, that Nietzsche's claims concerning the ascetic ideal, its relation to the decay
of Western civilization and to the belief in truth and intellectual
practice, are true. Only on the basis of these presuppositions can
the deconstructionists explain Nietzsche's (and their own) belief
in the importance of his attacks on truth and metaphysics. Even
if it is possible to avoid making any claim to truth for their own
interpretations or for Nietzsche's claims, it would be at the cost
of depriving both of their interest and importance.

The same claim can plausibly be made of de Man's interpretation. In line with the rest of his interpretation, de Man denies
that there is any progress from blindness to insight (or truth)
over the course of Nietzsche's writings, insisting (118) that their
structure "resembles the endlessly repeated gesture of the artist"
Nietzsche himself described as "one who does not learn from
experience and always falls again in the same ditch" (TL 91, WL
890). But then what is the value or importance of the kind of
intellectual activity in which Nietzsche engages? I believe de Man
thinks that Nietzsche's practice can be life-affirming only if his
writings repeat the same errors rather than making progress
toward truth. In part, at least, this is because Nietzsche analyzes
both the desire for an ultimate end and the desire for truth as
expressions of the ascetic ideal (see Chapter 6), and characterizes
the eternal recurrence as the highest formula for the affirmation
of life (see Chapter 8). But if these considerations underlie his
interpretation, de Man is presupposing both that there is a truth
about Nietzsche's writings and that they teach us something true.

I do not therefore believe that the deconstructionists have offered a convincing alternative to Heidegger's interpretation of Nietzsche. Although I agree that Heidegger does not take sufficient account of Nietzsche's critique of the ascetic ideal and that the lessons he would have us draw from Nietzsche are too ascetic, I do not see how these charges can be made openly without admitting that sometimes, at least, Nietzsche is making ordinary assertions, that is, presenting something as the truth and not merely for the purpose of contradicting or deconstructing it. It has therefore not been shown how one can escape the implication of Heidegger's interpretation: that Nietzsche's philosophy is contradictory on the topic of truth in a way that shows the need to go beyond him. And for anyone who does not find Heidegger's philosophy plausible, the deconstructionists have not even shown that Nietzsche's claims about truth are worth taking seriously.

4. Sketch of a combined interpretation

Although my own approach to Nietzsche differs greatly from the new Nietzscheans', it follows in their footsteps in a number of ways. It is, to begin with, another attempt to contribute to the continuing debate between Nietzsche and Heidegger and another attempt to defend Nietzsche against Heidegger. I will argue that Nietzsche's ultimate position on truth and metaphysics is defensible and coherent, and that it is not undermined by his own practice. Unlike the deconstructionists, I separate sharply Nietzsche's critique of metaphysics and his denial of truth. I argue that Nietzsche rejects metaphysics and eventually overcomes it in his own work, but that he ultimately affirms the existence of truths, and therefore does not undermine his own theory when he claims truth for his own positions.

In this defense of Nietzsche, I attempt to combine the advantages of the interpretations discussed above. My general strategy for rendering Nietzsche's mature position on truth consistent with his practice follows Kaufmann and Wilcox. I take Nietzsche to reject the existence of metaphysical truth – correspondence to the thing-in-itself – but not truth itself. This allows Nietzsche to put forward as truths the kind of claims about history, philosophy, the ascetic ideal, and the affirmation of life that can give him the claim on our interest that the new Nietzscheans think he deserves. To defend this strategy, however, I must explain the following better than Kaufmann did: 1) the passages in which

Nietzsche claims to deny all truth, 2) Nietzsche's belief in the radical character and importance of his claims about truth, and 3) the compatibility between Nietzsche's critique of metaphysics and his doctrines of eternal recurrence and will to power. For help with these issues, I make use of elements suggested by nontraditional interpreters.

My proposed solution to the first problem involves paying closer attention than previous interpreters to the development in Nietzsche's position on truth. It also makes use of Danto's distinction between different theories of truth. The development of this distinction in Chapter 2 provides much of the philosophical basis for my interpretation and allows me to argue in later chapters that when Nietzsche rejects metaphysical truth in his early and middle works, he rejects not merely a kind of truth, but truth itself. This is because he accepts a theory of truth such that all truth is metaphysical, that is, is correspondence to things as they are in themselves. In Chapter 3, I show that Nietzsche's early denial of truth results from his acceptance of this metaphysical correspondence theory, the conception of truth as correspondence to the thing-in-itself. I also argue that Nietzsche's early position on truth was internally inconsistent and that he had reason to reject it in his later works. In Chapter 4, I explain that he is nevertheless forced to retain his early metaphysical conception of truth in works up to and including *Beyond Good and Evil* because of his continued acceptance of a representational view of knowledge. This explains one of the factors that otherwise counts against Kaufmann's interpretation: that Nietzsche continued his denial of truth even in works in which he rejects as incoherent the very idea of the thing-in-itself. I argue that without the thing-in-itself, he has no basis for denying truth, but that he recognizes this clearly only after *Beyond Good and Evil*. This explains why he continued to deny truth when he had lost all basis for doing so and why there are no signs of such a denial in the books after *Beyond Good and Evil*. In Chapter 5, I argue that Nietzsche's mature perspectivism gives him an alternative to the representational model of knowing and thereby allows him to affirm the existence of truth while denying metaphysical truth.

If I seem to be saying that what appears as radical in Nietzsche's position on truth is actually mistaken or confused and that it disappears from his later philosophy, this is in fact what I believe about much of what has generated the greatest amount of recent excitement about Nietzsche. But I agree that even in his late works, Nietzsche writes as if his position on truth is radical (in the sense of setting him apart from others in the philosophical tradition) and important. If he has guessed any riddles, he suggests, it is in his analysis of the belief in truth as the latest expression of the ascetic ideal (GM III, 24). In Chapter 6, I therefore attempt to account for the radical character and importance of Nietzsche's later position on truth (and thus to solve the second problem listed above) in terms of his analysis of the relation between metaphysics, truth, philosophy, and the ascetic ideal.

As I interpret him, Nietzsche rejects metaphysics not simply because it lacks truth, but because it expresses the nihilistic ascetic ideal. In rejecting metaphysical truth and the thing-in-itself, therefore, he rejects not merely a theory of truth, but also a life-devaluing ideal and set of valuations that he claims constitute a threat to human life. This is why Nietzsche still screams at us to the end to pay attention to what he has to say about truth. Not because he thinks there is no truth, but because if we understand why philosophers have been caught up in the dream of metaphysical truth, we understand something he thinks important for our future. In fact, I will argue that according to Nietzsche's analysis of the ascetic ideal, his own earlier denial of truth is one of its expressions. If my analysis is correct, the new Nietzscheans are still too caught up in what Nietzsche later rejected as an expression of the ascetic ideal. According to this analysis, the denial of truth, not its affirmation, is life-devaluing or ascetic. The Nietzschean ideal of affirmation does not require us to abandon logic, argument, or the commitment to truth, nor to embrace contradiction or metaphor as the only cognitive modes.

However, when Nietzsche analyzes the "belief in truth" as "the latest expression of the ascetic ideal," he cannot mean the belief in metaphysical truth, for he has already rejected metaphysics as an earlier expression of the ascetic ideal. I interpret him as claiming that the commitment to truth – which his own work exemplifies, and which has led to atheism and the denial of metaphysics – is itself the latest expression of the ascetic ideal. The radical character of Nietzsche's thought is also evident here, when he so consistently applies his analysis of the philosophical tradition to his own work. I will argue, however, that his analysis requires him to abandon neither his belief in the existence of truth, nor his commit-ment to truth. The upshot of his analysis is instead that we need a new ideal, that philosophers must supply and come to philoso-phize in the name of a new ideal, an alternative to the ascetic ideal.

My solution to the third problem – how to account for the doctrines of eternal recurrence and will to power in the light of Nietzsche's rejection of metaphysics – borrows once again from the nontraditionalists. I admit that the doctrines in question would have to be interpreted as metaphysical if they are put forward as truths – if Nietzsche asserts that the world is will to power recurring eternally in its exact configurations. But I deny that Nietzsche asserts this, and, therefore, that these "doctrines" are supposed to correspond to reality. I think we can learn from radical interpreters to read Nietzsche better, to recognize the masks he uses, and to see that he is not always doing something as straightforward and traditional as making assertions or de-fending philosophical claims.

Two important recent interpreters (Nehamas, 1985, and Mag-nus, 1988) who have learned such lessons from the nontradi-tionalists use them to deny that Nietzsche offers us an ideal (see Chapter 6). I argue, to the contrary, that learning to read Nietz-sche better allows us to recognize that he defends the doctrines of eternal recurrence and will to power not on the grounds of their truth, but rather on the grounds that they offer a new ideal, the needed alternative to the ascetic ideal (see Chapters 7 and 8). What makes them able to offer this new ideal is, at least in part, that they are life-affirming. But it would be a mistake to extend this kind of interpretation to all of Nietzsche's claims, to suppose that Nietzsche's justification for his positions is always that they are life-affirming, and never that they are true. For the claim that these doctrines are life-affirming is itself supposed to be true, and it is accepted by Nietzsche on the basis of other alleged truths.

Despite my heavy borrowings from their approaches, many nontraditionalists will consider my interpretation of Nietzsche too concerned with traditional questions and argumentative forms of persuasion, and will accuse me of "betraying the new by cloaking it in the garb of the old" (Zanardi, 69). But the real issue between radical interpretations and my combined approach con-cerns what actually is new in Nietzsche's thought, and what is a betrayal of it. If I am correct, the nontraditionalists have not caught up with Nietzsche, and are betraying the self-analysis and insight of his later thought by their emphasis on early positions he himself overcame and considered expressions of the ascetic ideal. The only way to decide between these competing interpretations, as far as I can see, is in terms of the *kind* of textual and philosophical considerations I put forward in the rest of this book.

5. The role of the *Nachlass*

Most interpretations of Nietzsche's philosophy rely heavily on the notes and fragments that make up his *Nachlass*, especially on those collected by Nietzsche's sister and others under the title of *The Will to Power*. Some assume, following Heidegger, that the *Nachlass* is superior to the books Nietzsche published as a source of his final philosophy, whereas others seem to agree with Derrida's suggestion that the two sources are of equal value. I assume, to the contrary, following Kaufmann, Alderman, and Magnus, that Nietzsche's published writings (the books he published or prepared for publication, as in the cases of *The Antichrist* and *Ecce Homo*) are far superior sources of his philosophy, and I rely on them almost exclusively for my interpretation.

Kaufmann argued for the relative importance of the published writings on the grounds that they are surely more reliable indicators of what Nietzsche believed than are notebooks containing much that he rejected and nothing he specifically approved for publication. Magnus has recently added a persuasive argument that by the end of 1888, Nietzsche had given up any intention of publishing a work called, or bearing any resemblance to, *The Will to Power*, and that the work he earlier planned to publish under that title is very different from the one of which interpreters make such use (1988, 218–35). Magnus points out that Kaufmann himself relied heavily on *The Will to Power* and argues that he would have had little basis for interpreting the eternal recurrence and will to power as truths about the universe if he had not.

Those wishing to justify use of the *Nachlass* might respond to these arguments by agreeing that the published writings are a superior basis for the interpretation of Nietzsche's philosophy, although insisting that the unpublished writings can be used when the published ones do not tell us enough. Or they may insist that because the task is to interpret a body of texts, and the author's intentions have no privileged status when it comes to deciding which are the important ones, Kaufmann and Magnus fail to show why we should emphasize the published works. I therefore offer two further reasons for greater restraint in the use of the *Nachlass*. In the first place, it seems a good idea to hold off on the use of the *Nachlass* as long as possible since the published writings provide much more of a context for specific passages and therefore many more checks on the accuracy of interpretations. Kuenzli's view (106) seems plausible, that interpreters have relied so heavily on the *Nachlass* precisely because they "could quite easily reproduce their own self-reflection in these rearrangeable notes. The labyrinthians have found their labyrinth, the systematizers their system." The mass of material combined with the paucity of order and arrangement prevent the *Nachlass* from offering the many checks on interpretations provided by the published works. The latter may be used in the same way, of course – as notes or fragments with no context that need be taken into consideration – and this is often done, as Kaufmann never tired of complaining. But I find it difficult to see how anyone who did not place high value on the *Nachlass* could find this a plausible procedure.

A second reason for confining attention largely to the published works (as Alderman [6] also suggests) is philosophical. I believe that where Nietzsche's notes suggest a position different from that suggested by the published writings, it is usually a philosophically weaker one. I obviously cannot argue for such a large claim in advance of my interpretation. This whole study attempts to supply part of what is necessary by defending on both philosophical and textual grounds an interpretation of the texts Nietzsche actually published. I therefore give the *Nachlass* a very secondary status, using it only when it provides the foundation for an interpretation against which I am arguing or when it helps to support an interpretation of a specific passage in the published writings for which the latter also provide evidence (e.g., my interpretation of GS 354 in Chapter 4, section 4). It may be that Nietzsche's notes should not be relegated to this secondary status. However, we can determine this only if we have an interpretation of Nietzsche's books with which to compare ones that give the *Nachlass* equal or superior status. I attempt only the first task here. But if I succeed in making a convincing case for the claim that there is a development to a defensible and consistent position in Nietzsche's published writings, the plausibility of granting equal or superior status to Nietzsche's notes should be greatly lessened.

—❧ ❧—

NIETZSCHE AND THEORIES OF TRUTH

As my first chapter suggests, much of the disagreement regarding Nietzsche's position on truth stems from differences in the philosophical views of his interpreters. Heidegger provides only the most obvious example. Philosophical views affect not only the texts interpreters draw from, but also the way in which they interpret them. Finding the nihilism with which they sympathize in Nietzsche's early works and the *Nachlass*, nontraditionalists interpret his later books in terms of it. Those with more traditional sympathies, on the other hand, can find in Nietzsche's later work a commitment to both the existence and value of truth, and therefore minimize the importance of the *Nachlass*.

There is nothing regrettable about this situation. Reasonable interpretation clearly demands that we attribute to a text the best position compatible with the relevant evidence about its meaning. But only what the interpreter takes to be true or reasonable can function as the standard for the best position.[1] Appeal to the interpreter's own standards will be necessary not only when

---

1. Davidson argues for a much more radical principle of charity, namely, that interpretation can take place only if we regard most of the beliefs of the person being interpreted as true. For philosophical texts, this may not be necessary, because usually only beliefs that are "up for grabs," i.e., that are not among the "most" we must consider true, are under consideration.

there are two equally plausible interpretations of a given text, but also for the purpose of selecting which texts to interpret or consider as evidence. No interpretation can take explicitly into account every preserved sentence Nietzsche wrote. Interpreters can choose passages to consider in terms of their centrality to Nietzsche's main points, of course, and should also consider passages that appear to conflict with their interpretations. But this means that the choice of passages upon which to base an interpretation is informed by what one takes to be reasonable, if not correct, positions on questions dealt with in the text.[2]

Unfortunately, Nietzsche's interpreters too often confine themselves to assembling passages to support a particular interpretation and fail to make explicit the philosophical commitments that motivate the selection and interpretation of these passages. Although we may not be able to make all of our principles explicit, adequate evaluation of interpretations and the existence of productive – or even meaningful – disagreement among interpreters seems impossible without efforts to make explicit the philosophical commitments underlying interpretations (cf. Westphal, 343–4).

In this chapter I therefore endeavor to make explicit the position on truth I consider the most defensible one we can attribute to Nietzsche, given certain general and largely uncontroversial aspects of his philosophy. My considerations center around the correspondence theory of truth, which three of the four interpretations discussed in Chapter 1 claim Nietzsche rejects or shows why we should reject. I argue that we can defend Nietzsche's position (his apparent denial of truth) only if we distinguish a

2. I take a major principle of selection for relevant passages to be that they cohere so as to suggest a position on some issue that the interpreter finds worthy of our serious consideration – either because it seems reasonable and may indeed be a correct account, or because it is very different from our own views, but not easy to combat, and therefore may force a rethinking of these views, or because it seems obviously wrong, but well worth combating for any number of reasons. There may be many other bases for finding a view worthy of serious consideration – and different bases may, of course, be combined, as in Heidegger's *Nietzsche* – but it seems that they must all involve some evaluation of the position in relation to what one takes to be at least reasonable, and perhaps correct, answers to the relevant questions. In the best cases, one's beliefs will be changed through one's interaction with the text and the position one finds in it, but this seems most likely to happen (given that one is interpreting a rich and important text) precisely when one self-consciously uses as principles of selection and interpretation one's own beliefs concerning the issues with which the text deals.

metaphysical from a common sense version of the correspondence theory and take him to reject only the former. This gives us what I call a neo-Kantian understanding of truth, which is the conception I attribute to Nietzsche on textual grounds in the remainder of this study.

The first section below argues that Nietzsche must accept the common sense version of the correspondence theory, the second section uses contemporary discussions of realism to formulate the metaphysical version of the theory he could plausibly reject, and the final section puts his rejection of the metaphysical correspondence theory into the context of the debate between Descartes and Kant and justifies considering Nietzsche's position on truth neo-Kantian. I claim not that Nietzsche accepted this position from the beginning, but that he moved toward it and unambiguously embraced it in his final six books. Although later chapters will offer textual evidence for this interpretation, my selection and interpretation of passages is greatly influenced by my belief that Nietzsche could reach an acceptable position on truth – given his early position and certain other aspects of his philosophy – only by arriving at the one I attribute to him. In this chapter I defend that belief.

The fact that I present this philosophical chapter first should not be taken as an indication that I came to Nietzsche's texts with the neo-Kantian conception of truth presented here fully hatched. The conception was worked out in a dialectic with Nietzsche's texts, as I tried to make sense of his position and to see what was defensible in it, in accord with the philosophical views I held at that time. I present the philosophical results of this dialectic in abstraction from a consideration of Nietzsche's texts both for ease of organization and because I believe that most disagreements with my interpretation of these texts will stem from disagreement with the philosophical points discussed in this chapter. By presenting it in this way, I hope to bring the philosophical issues that separate interpreters of Nietzsche into the foreground and into better focus.

1. Nietzsche's commitment to truth as correspondence

Arthur Danto's influential interpretation comes closest to providing the standard account of Nietzsche's denial of truth (cf. Wilcox, 1986). Danto interprets this denial as a misleadingly stated rejection of the correspondence theory. He recognizes only one version of the correspondence theory, which he identifies as the conventional understanding of truth as "expressing what is the case" (75). According to his interpretation, Nietzsche accepts the pragmatic theory that truth is nothing more than "facilitation of life" (72), but believes that "nothing is true and everything is false" if we use "true" in the conventional (i.e., correspondence) sense (75). Because Nietzsche therefore denies not that any beliefs are true, but only that our true beliefs (i.e., those that facilitate life) correspond to reality, Danto intends his interpretation to save Nietzsche's denial of truth from the most obvious objections. But the view he attributes to Nietzsche seems indefensible.

According to the pragmatic theory Danto attributes to Nietzsche, truth is what works, in the sense of what satisfies practical interests such as survival or happiness. But why couldn't a false belief make us happier than a true one? Nietzsche, in fact, insisted repeatedly that knowledge of the truth may conflict with the satisfaction of practical interests (e.g., GS 121, 344; BG 11). Danto interprets such passages as awkward attempts to reject the correspondence theory in favor of the pragmatic, to say that true beliefs need not correspond to what is the case. But since this apparently means that "God exists" might be true, even if God does not exist, the position Danto attributes to Nietzsche would violate the principle that expresses our surest intuition regarding truth, namely, the equivalence principle derived from Tarski's Convention T (the requirement that an adequate definition of truth entail all sentences of the following form): sentence "S" is true in language L if and only if (iff) S.

The equivalence principle tells us that we can state the conditions under which any sentence is true in a particular language by simply removing the quotation marks from that sentence, or, following Davidson here, by providing in the metalanguage an interpretation of the sentence from which we have removed the quotation marks. Thus, "snow is white" is true in English iff snow is white, and "es regnet" is true in German iff it is raining. Equivalences of this form seem trivially true for anyone who knows the language(s) involved, and it is difficult to see how one can reject them and still claim to share our concept of truth (i.e., to use "true" or "wahr" as do speakers of standard English or German). Therefore, if, in accord with Danto, Nietzsche equates truth with what satisfies our practical interests, this does not give us a new theory of truth, a new account of what we are doing when we pick out certain beliefs as true (or, of what the beliefs so picked out are supposed to have in common). Instead, it discards the very concept of truth, that is, proposes that we use "true" or "*wahr*" in a different way than do speakers of standard English or German.

Müller-Lauter and Grimm would both accept this emendation of Danto's interpretation. Both claim that Nietzsche considers true any belief that satisfies a particular practical interest, that of increasing the feeling of power (e.g., Müller-Lauter, 1971, 95–115, esp. 110–11). Unlike Danto, however, they do not suggest that this merely gives us a different theory of what we now mean by "truth." They think that Nietzsche discards our ordinary concept of truth and replaces it with a new use of "true" and "false." However, unless Nietzsche has a reason to reject our ordinary use of "true," his new use would seem to reflect only an arbitrary linguistic decision of no philosophical interest.

His reason is supposed to be that if we use "true" in the ordinary (i.e., correspondence) sense, then there is no truth. But this is implausible if we accept the equivalence principle as governing the ordinary use of "true." Nietzsche cannot consistently make any claims at all unless he would admit to considering them true in our ordinary sense.

According to some interpreters (especially those influenced by Derrida), Nietzsche rejects our ordinary concept of truth because of its metaphysical nature. But if the equivalence principle governs this concept, it is difficult to see how it is metaphysical in any sense in which Nietzsche would consider this an objection (unless one accepts Heidegger's analysis [see Chapter 1], which Derrida rejects). Because Nietzsche denies that we can have Cartesian certainty, some assume he thinks we should put forward claims only as hypotheses and therefore not as certainties or truths. But our beliefs may lack certainty and still be true. Nontraditionalists who consider truth metaphysical seem to interpret Nietzsche as denying that we are justified in claiming truth for our beliefs if they lack the certainty that only a metaphysical system could provide. But we cannot require certainty of truth claims if we do not require it of other types of assertions. No one seriously believes that the absence of the kind of certainty provided by metaphysics requires Nietzsche to refrain from asserting that resentment plays a major role in moral evaluation. In accord with the equivalence principle, if Nietzsche asserts 1) "resentment plays a role in moral judgment," he must accept 2) " 'resentment plays a role in moral judgment' is true." But if the assertion of 1) is justified, and 1) entails 2), then the assertion of 2) must also be justified. We can justify claiming that an assertion is true to the same extent that we can justify making the assertion. Since lack of certainty does not prohibit us from making assertions, it cannot give us a reason against regarding assertions as true (cf. Putnam, 1978, 2–3).

To attribute a reasonable position to Nietzsche, we must therefore follow Danto's suggestion that Nietzsche rejects a particular theory of truth and does not deny the truth of all beliefs. But the theory of truth Nietzsche accepts cannot contradict the equivalence principle. We therefore need an alternative to the crude pragmatic theory Danto apparently attributes to him.

The most likely candidate would seem to be the coherence theory, which takes truth to consist in a relation among beliefs or representations, rather than a relation between beliefs and the world. The coherence theory should be compatible with the equivalence principle, since the latter concerns the relationship between two kinds of sentences. If we accept a sentence of type 1) above, we must also accept the corresponding sentence of type 2), and vice versa. But this tells us nothing about the relation between sentences and the world (cf. Davidson, 51).

Further, it is difficult to see how correspondence could function as our criterion for truth. We cannot directly compare our beliefs to the world to see if they correspond. It may seem that we can in some cases, simply by looking. But most philosophers would not deny that reality is ever simply "given" to us. We cannot even confirm the simple belief that it is raining just by looking out the window. We would, for instance, need a different explanation for our observation of falling water if we believed the sky was completely clear. Sense experience thus fails to give the sort of access to reality unmediated by our other beliefs that would allow us to compare beliefs directly to reality. In Quine's classic formulation, "our statements about the external world face the tribunal of sense experience not individually but only as a corporate body" (41). Insofar as sense experience justifies a belief, it does so only "indirectly through considerations of equilibrium [coherence] affecting the field [the system of beliefs] as a whole" (Quine, 43).* It seems plausible to go even further, following Davidson, and say that it is only in the form of beliefs – the belief that I see rain falling outside the window, for example – that the testimony of the senses can provide justification for other beliefs. From this it follows that "nothing can count as a reason for holding a belief except another belief" (Davidson in Henrich, 426), that there is no foundation outside of our beliefs that could justify them. This means that our only possible test for truth is coherence: how the belief fits in with other beliefs we accept.

This anti-foundationalist argument constitutes a major source of sympathy with Nietzsche's putative rejection of the correspondence theory. One might agree, however, that coherence is our *criterion* of truth, while insisting that correspondence to reality constitutes the *nature* of truth. Coherence theorists can respond by asking how we can justify claiming that our beliefs correspond to reality if we cannot compare the two. Blanshard argues that the mere fact of coherence among our representations or beliefs does nothing to "prove that anything precisely corresponding to them exists 'out there,' " and therefore provides no basis for assuming such correspondence (268). Since coherence does not guarantee correspondence, the nature of what the criterion of coherence measures – namely, truth – apparently consists in nothing more than coherence with other beliefs.

But the same argument can be turned against the coherence theory. The coherence theorist must grant, argues Rescher, "certainly not the premise of the correspondence theory that truth *means* correspondence to fact, but merely its consequence, that truths must correspond to the facts" (28). But since coherence does not guarantee correspondence, coherence is only a "generally effective test" that authorizes us to affirm the truth of a statement but does not guarantee it. Coherence cannot therefore constitute the nature of truth.

Coherence theorists may respond to Rescher's defense of the correspondence theory by denying that there is a distinct realm of fact to which sentences could correspond. They must admit, of course, that "it is snowing" is true only if it is snowing. But there are difficulties (described later in this section) for considering that it is snowing a fact in the sense of a distinct entity to

* I have added the material in brackets.

which "it is snowing" could correspond. These difficulties constitute the major reason philosophers have given against the correspondence theory and a major source of the tendency for sympathetic interpreters to think that Nietzsche rejects it.

John Austin offered one of the last defenses of the view that truth is correspondence to the facts. As a standard piece of English, he wrote (121), it can hardly be wrong to say that a statement is true "when it corresponds to the facts," but it can be misleading. We are misled, he claimed, if we infer either that "fact" is only an alternative expression for "true statement," or that "for every true statement there exists 'one' and its own precisely corresponding fact" (123). In the first case, we follow coherence theorists in their "failure to appreciate the trite but central point that truth is a matter of the relationship between words and world" (130). According to Austin, facts are situations in the world, states of affairs which are *toto mundo* distinct from the true statements they make true, as we see in the "great gulf fixed" between saying, however truly, that I am feeling sick and feeling sick (124). However, if we assume a one-to-one correspondence between facts and truths, we will "grossly overpopulate" the world with linguistic *Doppelgänger* such as negative and general facts (123).

The problem for Austin's defense of facts is brought out by Davidson's argument that if a statement corresponds to one fact, it will correspond to all facts. To vary his example slightly, consider the statement that New York is east of Chicago. This obviously corresponds to the fact that New York is east of Chicago. But it also seems to correspond to the fact that Chicago is west of New York, and therefore to the fact that Chicago is west of Detroit and Detroit is west of New York, as well as the fact that Chicago is west of the largest city in the United States. It becomes difficult to resist the conclusion that our original statement corresponds to all facts when we recognize that New York satisfies the following description: it is the largest city in the United States, and such that Springfield is the capital of Illinois (Davidson, 42).

Thus, if we say that true statements correspond to the facts, we must submit that they all correspond to the same facts, to the "Great Fact," as Davidson puts it. This forces us to abandon the intuitive idea that different truths are made true by different states of affairs. We could avoid this by insisting that a statement corresponds only to the fact that the same words express – for example, the true statement that New York is east of Chicago corresponds only to the fact that New York is east of Chicago. But then we return to the situation Austin wanted to avoid, overpopulating the world with linguistic *Doppelgänger*. We can avoid this situation only by admitting that talk of the "facts" does not pick out distinct entities to which truths could correspond, but only constitutes another way of talking about truths. If we agree with Austin that the business of philosophy is "to prise the words off the world and keep them off it" (124), we should agree with Strawson that we thereby "prise the facts off it too; but the world would be none the poorer" (197).

Contrary to Strawson, however, these considerations are compatible with retaining a conception of truth as correspondence. If we are to have correspondence, rather than mere coherence among beliefs or representations, there must be something ontologically distinct from the latter to which they can correspond. In *Individuals,* Strawson affirms just this kind of ontological distinction between the world and subjects who experience it. Gareth Evans explains Strawson's idea of an "objective" or "non-solipsistic" world as the idea of "an experience's being of something distinct from it, and therefore the idea of something which is capable of existing independently of any experience of it" (Van Stratten, 78, for Strawson's concurrence, 274). Here we find the sense in which something distinct from true representations must exist if we are to talk sensibly of correspondence: there must be something the existence of which is not reducible to these representations, something that could exist without them. Strawson rejects the conception of truth as correspondence because he believes that the facts are the only plausible candidate for this role, but that, for the reasons given above, they cannot play it. Facts cannot play the role of such ontological distinct entities without multiplying beyond plausibility. One who wishes to defend the correspondence conception can reply, however, that the distinct entity to which truths correspond is precisely Strawson's "objective world," constituted, as he would agree (198), by the things and events in it.

Strawson resists this move by insisting that "we *never* say that a statement corresponds to the thing, person, etc. it is about. What 'makes the statement' that the cat has mange 'true,' is not the cat, but the *condition* of the cat, i.e., the fact that the cat has mange" (195). I agree that what makes our sentences true is not the world or the things in it, but the condition of these things, in Davidson's words, "how the world is arranged" (in Henrich, 425). And this does lead to the problems associated with an ontology of individualized facts if we "include in the entity to which a true sentence corresponds not only the objects the sentence is about . . . but also whatever it is the sentence says about them" (Davidson, 49). To avoid these problems, a defender of correspondence could deny that what makes statements true – the condition of the world, how it is arranged – is a distinct entity to which a true sentence could correspond. Even if we do not now say that true statements correspond to things or events, we have every reason to say it. After all, the idea of agreement with the object, or adequacy to things, also expresses the correspondence conception of truth. The world (or the things in it) is well suited to play the required role of an entity that is distinct from true representations, an entity with which true statements can therefore agree, to which they can correspond or be adequate. That is perfectly compatible with saying that what makes a sentence true (or adequate) is something about the entity (the world) to which it corresponds: its condition, what it is like, that is, what predicates or descriptions it satisfies.

In this way we can have correspondence without overpopulating the world with linguistic *Doppelgänger*. To talk about the facts, the way the world is, the predicates it satisfies, is to talk not about an entity in the world, but about what is true of the world. Yet, we can say without redundance that true beliefs are ones that correspond to reality or the world, since the point is that there are entities ontologically distinct from true beliefs, and that what these distinct entities are like (what is true of them, what predicates they satisfy) determines whether or not our beliefs are true. We may even continue to say that truth is correspondence to the way the world is (or to the facts), if we are careful to avoid confusion and do not imply that these facts are ontologically distinct from truths.

In addition to an acceptance of the equivalence principle, therefore, an understanding of truth as correspondence requires the rejection of subjective idealism. By "subjective idealism," I mean the view usually associated with Berkeley, that to be is to be perceived (or a perceiver), that nothing exists except ideas or representations (and representors). We can also include as a more contemporary form of idealism the claim that there is nothing beyond language, that is, no nonlinguistic reality. Although it is not clear that anyone actually holds this position, some enthusiasts of Nietzsche's claims about truth certainly sound as if they do when they repeat without qualification Derrida's dictum that "there is nothing outside the text." They may mean simply that language always mediates our access to what lies outside the text (the physical world, for example). But it often sounds as if they mean that there is only the representation (taken to be linguistic rather than mental, the sign rather than the idea), and nothing represented.

Subjective idealism would provide a basis for defending the coherence theory of truth. If nothing exists beyond representations or text, there is nothing to which they could correspond. Coherence remains as the only reasonable candidate for the nature of truth. But if one rejects such idealism – thereby accepting the common sense realism Paul Guyer (20) has recently called "ontological realism" ("realism" for short, to be distinguished from metaphysical realism below), it becomes difficult to see what basis would remain for rejecting the correspondence conception of truth. Consider Putnam's account of its intuitive basis:

> However puzzling the *nature* of the "correspondence" may be, the naturalness of the idea is undeniable. There is a world out there; and what we say or think is "true" when it gets it *the way it is* and "false" when it doesn't correspond to *the way it is* (1978, 1).

That "there is a world out there" is not a comment about the world's spatiality. Its point seems to be that the world – that about which we have beliefs – exists independently of us in the sense that we cannot reduce its existence to acts of knowledge or the occurrence of representations. Contrary to subjective idealism, it is not the case that *esse* is *percipi*. The world has its own, extra-mental existence, and therefore does not need God or any other mind to be thinking of it in order to continue in existence. But if our beliefs are about an independently existing world, it seems clear that they can be true only if they correspond to it, that is, get it "the way it is." Far from being puzzling, the relation of correspondence between beliefs and the world – given the assumption that beliefs are about an independently existing world – seems to amount to no more than the equivalence principle. Given the world's independent existence, "snow is white" corresponds to the world iff snow is white.

Nietzsche would therefore have reason to reject an understanding of truth as correspondence in favor of the coherence theory only if he embraced subjective idealism. But Nietzsche scholars agree almost unanimously that he rejects all forms of idealism (and I shall argue in Chapters 4 and 5 that his later works reject subjective idealism). If he is consistent, then, Nietzsche must accept a correspondence conception of truth.

American interpreters under the influence of Richard Rorty (Magnus and Nehamas, e.g.) have recently tried to avoid attributing to Nietzsche any theory of truth at all. I do not disagree with the spirit of these attempts. The conception of truth I attribute to Nietzsche certainly does not count as a "theory" in a very strong sense. It consists merely in a number of connected assertions about truth which I find implicit in Nietzsche's later works as well as in our ordinary beliefs about truth. In Austin's words, this common sense "theory of truth" is a series of truisms. Making these truisms explicit serves mainly to make clear that we have no need to develop – or to attribute to Nietzsche – an alternative conception of truth: say a coherence or pragmatic theory. The articulation of this "minimal correspondence theory" also helps us to clarify the nature of the theory of truth Nietzsche has reason to reject.

2. Against the metaphysical correspondence theory

I interpret Nietzsche as rejecting what I call the "metaphysical correspondence theory." Later chapters give textual grounds for this interpretation. This section arrives at the same conclusion by considering what version of the correspondence theory Nietzsche could most plausibly reject.

I examine the arguments offered by three different critics of the correspondence theory, William James, Richard Rorty, and Hilary Putnam. All three seem to accept the two points that I have claimed commit Nietzsche to understanding truth as correspondence, namely, the equivalence principle (that "grass is green" is true, for instance, iff grass is green) and common sense realism (the claim that the world exists independently of our representations of it). Following Putnam, I call what these critics reject "metaphysical realism" (abbreviated realism$_m$): the doctrine that reality is something-in-itself, that its nature is determinately constituted independently of us (a notion I make more precise below). When we combine this claim about the nature of reality with the correspondence theory I attribute to Nietzsche, we get the claim that truths must correspond to the world (or reality) as it is *in itself*. Thus, we have two different conceptions of truth as correspondence: the minimal version, which combines the equivalence principle with common sense or ontological realism, and the metaphysical version, which combines the minimal version with metaphysical realism.

Since they reject subjective idealism, the critics of the correspondence theory discussed here should distinguish the two versions and claim to reject only the metaphysical one.[3] If they equate correspondence with correspondence to things-in-themselves, they imply that the common sense realism they accept (a claim about the ontological distinctness of the world and our representations of it) entails metaphysical realism (a claim about what we can know or conceive of). They thus give the game away to the realist$_m$. They also make it appear that they reject a view of truth supported by common sense, rather than a philosophical theory that they think enlightened common sense should consider nonsense.

I examine four slightly different arguments critics have given against the metaphysical correspondence theory. In each case, they accuse the metaphysical realist of trying to pass off as truth something of which we have only a contradictory concept, or no concept at all. They argue that, contrary to the realist$_m$, we have no concept of truth beyond that of _____. The difference between the four versions of anti-realism$_m$ consists in how they fill in this blank. In each case, the anti-realist$_m$ connects truth to the notion of rational acceptability (used here interchangeably with "warranted assertability," "justifiability," and "verifiability"),

3. Rorty actually suggests something very close to this in "The World Well Lost," (1982, 14–15, and note 13), but otherwise writes as if belief in correspondence is always a bad thing. The same point should be made about his objection to the idea of representation. The problems Rorty is trying to avoid by getting rid of representations arise, I believe, from the assumptions that 1) what is represented is ontologically distinct from the representation, and 2) that situations in the world or facts are what is represented. This leads to the same ontology of facts against which I have argued above. Once it is denied that facts are ontologically distinct entities to which truths could correspond, saying that truths represent the world correctly seems as harmless as saying that a statement is true when it corresponds to the world.

the notion of what we are justified in believing or asserting. But there are important differences in how they understand this connection.

Rorty sometimes seems to accept what I consider the weakest version of anti-realism$_m$: that truth equals rational acceptability. Rorty disparages attempts to "make truth something more than what Dewey called 'warranted assertability': more than what our peers will, *ceteris paribus*, let us get away with saying" (1979, 176). On the other hand, he denies that "assertible" gives the meaning of "true," and apparently means only to follow Dewey in refusing to talk about anything more than "warranted assertability." But since Rorty does not want to give up talk of truth, he seems to be proposing that we use "true" as equivalent to "assertible." This suggests that he thinks realists$_m$ correct about our ordinary concept of truth, but that he considers that concept incoherent. A coherent notion of truth evidently requires us to think of "true" only as a "compliment paid to sentences that seem to be paying their way and that fit in with other sentences that are doing so" (1982, xxv). In other words, Rorty believes we have no coherent notion of truth beyond the notion of what we currently believe justified.

That only our current standards of rational acceptability can function as our criterion of truth seems the strongest point in favor of this first version of anti-realism$_m$. But we cannot accept this version if we want to admit that our currently justified beliefs might turn out to be false. If we used "true" as equivalent to "acceptable," we could no longer say that the belief that the earth was flat was once justifiable, though it was never true. We could not insist that the truth of a belief does not change just because its acceptability does. But far from ridding our language of an incoherence, this change would impoverish language by depriving it of a convenient way to mark the distinction between changes in the situation of knowers and changes in the world of which they have knowledge.

James' identification of truth with what we can verify in the long run (430, 438) offers a second, and more promising, version of anti-realism$_m$. James actually suggests two different versions of anti-realism$_m$. He sometimes seems to mean that the truth is whatever we *in fact* verify in the long run, that is, whatever we justifiably believe if and when inquiry comes to an end. This implies, counterintuitively, that if no intelligent life exists elsewhere, human beings could insure the truth of their currently justified beliefs simply by destroying life on earth, thereby bringing inquiry to an end.

At other times, James seems to make the more plausible claim usually identified with Peirce that truth equals what we would have justification for believing at the ideal limit of inquiry. This third version of anti-realism$_m$ also coincides with the version Putnam seems to offer.

Although Putnam denies that truth equals rational acceptability, he believes that the former is an idealization of the latter – that truth is what would be rationally acceptable under "epistemologically ideal conditions" for beings like ourselves (ones with our current capacities for observation, conceptualization, calculation, and reasoning). Since Putnam does little to specify the nature of these conditions, critics object that he explicates the relatively clear notion of truth in terms of a much fuzzier notion of ideal conditions for inquiry. Some deny that we have any such notion. Rorty, who once embraced this Peircian version of anti-realism$_m$, now agrees with Williams that we have no idea of what it would be for a theory to be "ideally complete and comprehensive" or for inquiry to have an end (LePore, 337–8; Williams, 269).

Putnam answers the former objection by asserting that once we get beyond the triviality of the equivalence principle, the concept of truth is not all that clear. Consider the important connection that obtains between our concepts of truth and rational acceptability. We call a belief "true" precisely when we believe it meets our standards for rational acceptability. " 'S' is true" is assertible (rationally acceptable), therefore, if "S" is rationally acceptable. If this does not make the two concepts identical, it certainly makes it imperative for those who deny this identity (e.g., metaphysical realists) to say how truth differs from acceptability. If they cannot explain the difference – that is, explain what it means to say that a belief is false though fully acceptable – we can hardly consider the concept of truth to be so clear.

Putnam claims that to consider a fully acceptable belief possibly false is to suppose that under better conditions for inquiry we might justifiably reject it. We can make no plausible objection to this use of "better conditions for inquiry" simply on the grounds of fuzziness. If we need the concept of "better conditions for inquiry" to differentiate truth and acceptability, then we need it to clarify the concept of truth. We cannot regard truth as the clearer concept. A problem of circularity would arise, of course, if we need the concept of truth to clarify the idea of better conditions for inquiry. The following considerations suggest that we do not.

Conditions for inquiry could be better in two main ways. On the one hand, the world could be different in such a way as to make available to us more information relevant to answering our questions about it. For instance, better conditions for inquiry into a particular life would obtain if protective relatives had not burned all of the person's letters and personal papers. If we believe we have uncovered the basic truth about this life even without this data, we believe that our basic beliefs about it would still be rationally acceptable if we recovered the lost data. On the other hand, our own cognitive resources – our capacities and theories – might differ in such a way as to make possible better answers to our questions.

The crucial point here concerns the standards by which answers are to be judged "better." Putnam apparently does not restrict to current ones the standards in terms of which currently justified beliefs might turn out to be false. He includes those standards that we will adopt in the course of inquiry, as we acquire more information, sharpen our capacities, and change our theories. He claims that we are able to make sense of the idea that a currently justified belief is false only by supposing that we could in principle arrive at a point in inquiry where it would be rational to reject it. A belief is true if it is rationally acceptable and no better conditions for inquiry exist under which human beings could justifiably reject it. It follows that we have no concept of truth beyond what we would be justified in accepting even at the ideal limit of (under ideal conditions for) inquiry – because the ideal limit represents just that point at which we cannot, even in principle, attain better conditions for inquiry. The notion of "ideal conditions" therefore involves no greater obscurity than the notion of "better conditions." Putnam need not say that ideal conditions for inquiry actually exist. Nor need he posit a unique set of such conditions, much less an obligation to attain them. To have a basis for rejecting Putnam's account of truth as an idealization of rational acceptability, critics therefore need an argument against his central claim: that we cannot make sense of the idea of a false belief that we could not, even in principle, have justification to consider false.

Colin McGinn describes the realist$_m$ position opposed to Putnam's as the thesis that "truth (falsity) is an epistemologically unconstrained property of a sentence," that "there is nothing in the concept of truth to exclude the possibility that a sentence be unknowably true (false)." He takes this thesis to reflect the "realist[$_m$] conviction that the world, or a given sector of it, is determinately constituted quite independently of any limitation on our capacity to come to know truths concerning it" (Platts, 19). The common sense realism already discussed posits the world's existence as independent of, in the sense of ontologically or numerically distinct from, knowers and their representations, and therefore as capable of existing without them. Realism$_m$, in contrast, holds that the world's nature, essence, or character – and therefore the truth about it – is independent of knowers. Realism$_m$ may seem to follow from common sense realism. Whether it does follow depends on how we understand "independent" and "knowers" in the above formulation.

If it means that the nature of the world is independent of the actual *existence* of knowers and representations, then realism$_m$ does follow from ontological realism. If the world exists whether or not there is any knowledge of it, it must have a nature or constitution whether or not anyone actually knows what it is. To deny this is to insist on the possibility of a world that exists without characteristics, a blank slate waiting for a knower to give it its character. However, realism$_m$ does not claim merely that the world's constitution is independent of the existence of representations. It also holds that the world's nature is independent of what *can be known of it*. The knower's best theory might be false, or the truth might be such that the knower could never have the information necessary to warrant accepting it. The realist$_m$ insists that there is no basis in our concept of truth for denying this possibility. This does not preclude the possibility that the world is in fact constituted so as to guarantee the truth of the knower's best theory,[4] but this guarantee cannot follow, contrary to Putnam, simply from our concept of truth. Philosophers must therefore look to theories about the actual constitution of reality if they are to answer the challenge of skepticism.

But who is the "knower" in question? In the first quotation

---

4. Nor does this preclude that it is a matter of necessity – that of God's nature, for instance, as in Descartes – that the world is so constituted.

above from McGinn, he seems to mean that truth might differ from what any possible knower would have reason to believe. In the second quote, however, he clearly regards truth as independent only of possible *human* knowers – independent of the best possible human theory, not of any theory. The difference between these two interpretations is of great importance. Given the first, we can dismiss metaphysical realism with relative ease. As Michael Dummett has written: "it is difficult to resist the idea that any intelligible statement could if it were true, be known to be so by some creature suitably placed in time and space and endowed with appropriate faculties of perception and thought" (465). The realist$_m$, explains Dummett, believes there is something distinct from a true statement in virtue of which it is true. To conceive of a statement as true, then, we must be able to conceive of a state of affairs in virtue of which it is true. But this requires us to conceive of what it would be to recognize that state of affairs as obtaining. If we cannot suppose ourselves capable of recognizing that the state in question obtains, we need a way to conceive of beings with cognitive capacities different than ours who could, under appropriate conditions, recognize it as obtaining. That the world's existence is independent of the existence of knowers cannot imply, therefore, that its nature is independent of what any possible knower could know of it.

Putnam and Rorty offer a similar argument against realism$_m$, although they usually formulate it as an argument against the thing-in-itself. Both believe that the realist$_m$ treats the world as a thing-in-itself, and that we have only a contradictory idea of the latter. This brings their argument into obvious connection with Nietzsche since his attack on the very idea of a thing-in-itself is well known (see Chapters 3–5). However, we can interpret "thing-in-itself" in the same two ways I have interpreted "independence of the knower." If we treat the world as something-in-itself (a thing-in-itself), we contrast its reality with its appearance and regard its real characteristics as independent of those it appears to have. We can, however, contrast its reality with all of its possible appearances, or only with its appearances to a certain kind of knower, for example, the human knower. In the former case, we can show that the idea of a thing-in-itself is incoherent by using the argument attributed to Dummett previously in this section: that we can have no conception, or only a contradictory one, of something that would be independent of all knowers, and therefore of all conceptualization, because to conceive of something is to conceive of it as satisfying some description or other, which is to think of it as being conceptualizable in some way or other.

This is the same argument Nietzsche gives against the thing-in-itself (see Chapter 4), and Putnam and Rorty give against realism$_m$. But it has force only against one who understands truth as independent of all possible knowers or conceptualizations, and it is not clear that anyone does. The metaphysical realist holds only that truth is independent of *human* possibilities for knowledge – that there may be "facts beyond the reach of human concepts," as Rorty puts it, quoting from Nagel (1982, xxiii). But the inconceivability of facts independent of all possible knowledge does not demonstrate the inconceivability of facts independent of possible human knowledge.

To support truth's independence of human capacities, the metaphysical realist can argue that we are, after all, finite beings, limited in many ways. Why, then, should we not be limited in our capacity for truth? We may not be able to prove that we are limited in this way, precisely because we cannot know the truths that limit us. But this is no basis for denying the possibility that we are limited, hence that the truth might differ from what we can know of it, even under ideal circumstances for beings like us. Human beings can surely know more about the world, given our greater linguistic and mathematical capacities, for instance, than can dogs and cats. What basis can we have to deny the possibility of beings with cognitive capacities superior to our own, who thereby possess the ability to verify truths we have no reason to accept and even to determine that some of our best theories are actually false? Even the anti-realist$_m$ Dummett admits the conceivability of truths inaccessible to us, even in principle, as long as they are accessible to beings with perceptual and/or mental capacities other than (though analogous to) our own. Although Dummett argues against such a view of truth, he does not, unlike Putnam and Rorty, consider it absurd.

Nietzsche and other anti-realists$_m$ need an argument, then, against the claim that truth might be inaccessible to the human knower, not to any knower. Putnam and Rorty object, reasonably enough, to the idea of truth as independent of all possible knowers. But they conclude from this that truth cannot be independent of the best human theory, even though they make no attempt to show that truth can be independent of human beings only if it is independent of all knowers. To make their argument against metaphysical realism effective, Putnam and Rorty need to show that those who interpret truth as independent of human knowledge commit themselves to its independence of all possible knowledge.

I believe we can more easily see how to provide the necessary argument when Putnam suggests a slightly different interpretation of metaphysical realism and therefore of his own position than I have so far considered (1978, 125).

> So let T_I be an ideal theory, by our lights. Lifting restrictions on our all-too-finite powers, we can imagine T_I to have every property *except objective truth* – which is left open – that we like. E.g. let T_I be imagined complete, consistent, to predict correctly all observation sentences (as far as we can tell), to meet whatever "operational constraints" there are (if these are "fuzzy", let T_I seem *clearly* to meet them), to be "beautiful", "simple", "plausible", etc. The supposition under consideration is that T_I might be all this *and still be* (in reality) *false*.

Here, Putnam construes realism$_m$ as the thesis that truth is independent not only of our cognitive capacities, but also of what I shall call our "cognitive interests" – that is, of the cognitively relevant properties we want from a theory or set of beliefs *other than truth* (e.g., simplicity, comprehensiveness, etc.). Truth is independent not simply of what we now want, but of what we could ever want, that is, of what we would want even under ideal conditions for inquiry for beings like ourselves. Our standards of rational acceptability express the cognitively relevant properties we want from a theory. Therefore, on the account Putnam suggests here, realism$_m$ holds that a theory might be false even if it would fully satisfy the standards of rational acceptability we would still accept at the ideal limits of inquiry. This differs from the interpretation of metaphysical realism usually suggested by Putnam in that truth is independent not only of what *we* could in principle have reason to accept, but also of what any conceivable intelligence could have reason to accept, given *our* best standards of rational acceptability.

This new version of realism$_m$ gives us a fourth version of anti-realism$_m$. According to the third version (Putnam's usual position), a theory is false only if there would be reason to reject it at the ideal limits of human inquiry. The fourth version admits that a theory might be false even if we could consider it true at the ideal limits of human inquiry. It admits the conceivability of beings with cognitive powers superior to those we possess even in principle (which is surely what is involved in removing the limits on our "all-too-finite powers," as Putnam puts it in the passage quoted above), who would be justified in rejecting the theory we would embrace at the ideal limits of human inquiry. Anti-realism$_m$ opposes metaphysical realism (the new version described previously) by insisting that our best theory would be false only if the cognitively superior beings in question had reason to reject it in accord with *our* own best standards of rational acceptability. Anti-realism$_m$ would thus hold that the ideal theory from "a pragmatic point of view" (Putnam, 1978, 126) – the viewpoint of our cognitive interests – is necessarily true, but (contrary to Putnam's usual position) would imply no guarantee that we have the capacity, even in principle, to acquire the information that would justify accepting the theory.

Rorty clearly interprets Putnam's position in this second way (i.e., as the fourth version of anti-realism$_m$ discussed here) when he endorses it as follows: "the pragmatist has no notion of a truth that would allow him to make sense of the claim that if we achieved all we ever hoped to achieve by making assertions we might still be making *false* assertions, failing to 'correspond' to something" (1982, xxiv). This in no way implies our capacity to achieve all we could ever hope to achieve cognitively. But *if* we did fully satisfy all of our cognitive interests, Rorty claims that our theories would have to be true. We cannot make sense of the idea that they might nevertheless be false.

This fourth version of anti-realism$_m$ is the one I believe Nietzsche has reason to accept. Since it admits that truth is independent of our cognitive capacities (of what we can in principle verify), this version does not make his position vulnerable to the plausible arguments presented earlier. On the other hand, as far as I know, there have been no arguments given to demonstrate truth's independence of our cognitive interests (of our best standards of rational acceptability). Further, if we understand his position in this way, we can see how he could make plausible the argument Putnam and Rorty repeatedly suggest against metaphysical realism: that it requires the objectionable concept of the thing-in-itself (of a thing whose nature is independent of all possible knowers or means of conceptualization).

As I have already argued, the understanding of truth as independent of our cognitive capacities does not require this objectionable concept of the thing-in-itself. However, the understanding of truth as independent of our cognitive interests does require it. To conceive of our best theory as false, I have argued, we must assume that possible beings with cognitive capacities superior to our own could in principle discover its falsity. But how are we to conceive of this cognitive superiority? We seem to have only two choices. Cognitive abilities would certainly be superior to our own if they would give us more of what would satisfy our cognitive interests than our abilities do. To admit this as the only possibility would be to deny that truth is independent of our cognitive interests, to take these interests to be the only standard in terms of which our best theory could be false. The only alternative I can see is to say that abilities are superior to our own if they would allow greater correspondence to things as they are in themselves independently of all possible knowers or conceptualization. Greater correspondence to things as they are in independence of our abilities will not help here, since that is precisely what we are trying to conceptualize. To insist that truth is independent of our cognitive interests, we would therefore need the objectionable concept of the thing-in-itself. This is the argument I believe Nietzsche offers us against metaphysical realism and the metaphysical correspondence theory (see Chapter 4 and 5).

It should not be thought that this version of anti-realism$_m$ concedes everything the realist$_m$ wants. According to the realist$_m$ intuition, the world has a determinate nature quite independently (as far as we can tell from the concept of truth) of anything about our cognitive constitution. Put temporally, the realist$_m$ claims that the world already has its own nature before we come on the scene. Philosophers therefore have the problem of determining whether our cognitive constitution can give access to truth. Given this basic intuition, metaphysical realists should regard truth as independent of both our cognitive capacities and interests (our best standards of rational acceptability). They have no more reason to assume *a priori* that our cognitive interests mesh with the world's constitution than that our abilities do. As I interpret Nietzsche (Chapter 4, section 3), he admits that our best theory might be false, and therefore that truth is independent of our cognitive capacities. But since he denies truth's independence of our cognitive interests, he rejects the basic realist$_m$ intuition that reality has a determinate nature in complete independence of our cognitive constitution.

According to the anti-realism$_m$ I attribute to Nietzsche, truth's independence of human beings amounts to the possibility of a gap between our (cognitive) abilities and desires or interests – to the possibility that we can't always get what we want, even in the cognitive realm. The realist$_m$ tries to explain the possibility of this gap by appealing to the intuition that reality has its own nature in complete independence of us. The anti-realist$_m$ cannot accept this "explanation" because it either 1) appeals to the objectionable concept of the thing-in-itself, or 2) merely repeats that our cognitive aims might be best satisfied by abilities we do not possess and cannot acquire.

I will therefore interpret realism$_m$ as the thesis that truth is completely independent of our cognitive constitution (completely independent of both our capacities and interests, as far as we can tell from our concept of truth), and anti-realism$_m$ as a denial of this thesis. In the next section I will present reasons for interpreting Descartes as a realist$_m$ in this sense and Kant as an anti-realist$_m$. This will support my interpretation of realism$_m$ because Descartes must be considered one of its paradigmatic proponents, whereas its contemporary opponents usually appeal to Kant. This discussion will also show that the conflict between realism$_m$ and anti-realism$_m$, in terms of which I interpret Nietzsche's position on truth, belongs not only to twentieth-century philosophy, but also to the philosophical history from which Nietzsche's philosophy arose.

3. Descartes, Kant, and Nietzsche

That Descartes believes truth to be independent of our cognitive capacities (as far as we can determine from our concept of truth) is evident from his supposition in the first *Meditation* that an evil demon might deceive us even regarding what seems most certainly true, for this means that a belief might be false even if we have the best reasons we can have for accepting it. That Descartes believes truth is also independent of our cognitive interests is less evident, but can be appreciated if we reflect on the kind of answer he proposes to the doubts raised by the evil demon hypothesis.

To establish a secure foundation for our beliefs, Descartes considers it necessary to show that a theory we have the best possible reasons to accept must be true. Since our concept of truth allows that our best theory might be false, he finds it necessary to show that the actual arrangement of the world rules out the possibility. His strategy depends on proving the existence of God. Assuming that God's infinite perfection is incompatible with being a deceiver, Descartes argues that God would be a deceiver if he had given us no way of avoiding error. A proof of God's existence therefore provides a "divine guarantee" of our ability to avoid error. The proof does not guarantee actual avoidance of error, of course, for God has given us free will and thereby the possibility of accepting beliefs on inadequate grounds. But if we do the best we can in deciding what to believe, God would be a deceiver if our belief were nevertheless false. This means that the divine guarantee applies to all, and only, those beliefs that satisfy our best possible criterion of truth, which, according to Descartes, is the test of clear and distinct perception.

What, then, is the divine guarantee supposed to guarantee? Certainly not that any particular belief satisfies the test of clarity and distinctness. Nor that this particular test is the best test for truth (Descartes claims to deduce this from the characteristics of the one indubitable truth, the *Cogito*). The existence and goodness of God guarantees the truth of a belief only if it satisfies what is in fact our best test for truth. The guarantee, therefore, is that our best standard of rational acceptability (=our best criterion of truth) constitutes the correct standard for determining truth. Because this standard expresses our cognitive interests – that is, the cognitive properties, besides truth, we want in a belief or theory – the point of the divine guarantee can only be to show that truth does not in fact diverge from what would satisfy our cognitive interests. Descartes' insistence on the need for this guarantee makes sense only if he believes that, as far as we can determine from our concept of truth, the truth may differ from what would satisfy our cognitive interests, that is, that truth is independent of both our capacities and interests. His position therefore fits, and my interpretation of it supports, the account I have given of metaphysical realism and the metaphysical correspondence theory.

I suggest that this metaphysical realism underlies Descartes' foundationalism, his insistence on the need to locate indubitable or intrinsically credible beliefs that justify our other beliefs by transferring their certainty to them. Many philosophers now reject both the possibility and the need for such foundational beliefs. Insisting that all beliefs are in principle revisable, that no belief can have the privileged status or absolute certainty required by Descartes, they view our belief system as comparable to a boat we must rebuild on the open sea (Quine, 79), and the foundationalist as one who believes it can be repaired only on dry land, that it cannot be used for its normal purposes while being repaired. Anti-foundationalists (Hegel and Nietzsche among them) insist that if this were the case, we could not justify our beliefs at all, because we cannot even inquire into the truth or reliability of a belief except by using other beliefs. The justification of beliefs occurs in a context in which other beliefs must be held unchallengeable for the moment. The anti-foundationalist admits that we must therefore do without guarantees that any particular beliefs are true, but willingly trades in certainty regarding particular beliefs for the bit by bit improvement of our belief system. If we cannot rebuild the whole thing from scratch, we can ultimately replace each plank – that is, subject each part of our belief system to critique. We can thus improve the usability of our belief system while we are using it, that is, while taking some parts for granted.

But this anti-foundationalism adequately responds to Descartes' problem only if it rejects his realism$_m$. Otherwise, no degree of improvement in the usability of our belief system will give us reason to believe we are any closer to the truth. If truth is independent of our cognitive interests, inquiry may be totally futile as far as truth goes, and nothing we find out in the course of inquiry can give us any reason to believe otherwise. This seems to me to be one of the deepest sources of Descartes' desire to secure a foundation for his other beliefs in something indubitable – not a neurotic need for an impossible certainty, but a reasonable need, given the acceptance of metaphysical realism, to believe that what we find out in the course of inquiry, as measured by our standards of rational acceptability, has something to do with the way things are. What makes the anti-foundationalism of Nietzsche and many contemporary philosophers reasonable is therefore the abandonment of the Cartesian assumption that truth is independent of our cognitive interests (Nietzsche implies this connection in BG

16). In the absence of this assumption, we need not fear that we may be completely cut off from the truth, even though we cannot be certain that our best possible theory, much less our present one, is true. We do not need prior assurance because we can find reason in the results of inquiry itself to believe that inquiry is not futile. Insofar as these results give us reason to believe that we have made progress in satisfying our cognitive interests – in giving us what, besides truth, we want from inquiry – they give us reason to believe that we have made progress toward truth, though none to believe we can ever exhaust it.

Before turning to Kant, it is necessary to say something about the beliefs for which Descartes claimed the divine guarantee. Because God has given us an overwhelming inclination to believe in the existence of material bodies (the external world) and no faculty for recognizing something other than these bodies as the real cause of our perceptions, he would be a deceiver, Descartes argued, if the external world did not exist. Yet, this does not mean that everything we believe about the external world must be true, because the divine guarantee applies only to what passes our best test for truth, that of clarity and distinctness. But "sense perception is in many ways obscure and very confused" (191). Therefore, material objects may not be "exactly what our senses perceive them to be." According to Descartes, "light, colors, sounds, odors, tastes, heat, cold and other tactile qualities" are conceived "with so much obscurity and confusion" that we cannot say that they really belong to material bodies (164). Mathematics, in contrast, is a model of clarity and distinctness, and Descartes therefore concluded that the qualities capable of mathematical formulation – size, shape, location, and movement – really do belong to material bodies. Since these are the only qualities we "perceive clearly and distinctly" to belong to bodies (164), only these qualities are protected by the divine guarantee. In other words, sense qualities such as color belong only to the appearance of bodies, to what they are in relation to human perceivers, and these qualities would be "annihilated," as Galileo put it (274), if the "living body" or perceiver were removed. The mathematically formulable properties we have reason to attribute to things, on the other hand, are protected by the divine guarantee of what is perceived clearly and distinctly, and therefore would not be annihilated by removal of the perceiver. To put Descartes' point in another way, mathematical properties belong to things as they are *in themselves*, to what they are in independence of human beings. According to what I have been arguing, this means: to what they are in independence not only of our cognitive abilities, but also of our cognitive interests.

I use Kant's later terminology to formulate Descartes' position because I interpret Kant's denial that we know things-in-themselves as a rejection of Descartes' claim about the kind of truth to which science gives us access. I have argued, in effect, that Descartes and Galileo believed that mathematical science gives us truth satisfying the metaphysical correspondence theory. Both denied that common sense thinking based on sense perception – which seemed to support, for example, the Ptolemaic view – could provide such truth. They argued that sense qualities belong to material objects only because of something about us – our nature as sensuous beings – rather than because of anything about these objects as they are independently of us. Galileo makes this claim more explicit, but it is at least implicit in Descartes' use of the divine guarantee and the test of clarity and distinctness in relation to sense qualities. Agreeing with their view of sense qualities, Kant adds, however, that the mathematically formulable and other structural properties of the material world studied by science (causal properties, e.g.) also belong to the world only in virtue of our constitution: the forms of our intuition – time and space, which must be exemplified by anything that is to be an object of intuition or sense perception for us, and from which Kant believed all of mathematics is derived – and the schematized categories, such as causality, which must be exemplified by anything intelligible to us. At their best, scientific theories correspond to things only as they are relative to our constitution, and not, contrary to Descartes, as they are in themselves. Kant therefore denies that science can give us truth that satisfies the metaphysical correspondence theory.

It is not clear that Kant rejects metaphysical realism completely, however. According to the interpretation of Kant accepted by Nietzsche and many of his nineteenth-century predecessors (see Gram), Kant's denial that we can know things-in-themselves in effect affirms metaphysical realism. It implies that we cannot know the ultimate truth about things because we can know them only as they appear to beings of our cognitive constitution, and therefore that the truth is independent of our constitution. As I will argue below, this implies that truth is independent of our cognitive interests. This interpretation allows Kant, who explicitly defines truth as "agreement with the object" (A58/B82), to grant human beings access to truth if he treats appearances and things-in-themselves as distinct worlds or objects. Understood in this way, his distinction between the phenomenal and noumenal – reality as it is in relation to beings of our constitution, versus reality as it is in itself – gives him two different kinds of truth, correspondence to noumenal reality, of which we are incapable, and correspondence to phenomenal reality, which, contrary to Descartes, is all that either science or common sense can give us. Kant is a metaphysical realist about noumenal reality, but is anti-realist$_m$, and therefore anti-Cartesian, about the only reality accessible to us.

The basis for this interpretation has been attacked recently by several scholars (Prauss, Bird, Allison) who deny that the distinction between appearance and thing-in-itself is between two distinct objects. Kant's distinction, they claim, concerns two different ways of considering the same objects, as appearances or objects of our knowledge, on the one hand, and as they are in themselves, in abstraction from the conditions necessary for them to be objects of human knowledge, on the other. His denial that we can know things-in-themselves does not therefore deny our access to the real nature of things, but only insists on epistemological modesty. Its point is that *if* there is anything that does not satisfy the epistemological conditions under which alone we can have knowledge of it – for example, something without spatio-temporal properties – we can know nothing of it. But it does not imply that there is any such thing.[5]

On this interpretation, Kant's denial of things-in-themselves would not make him an anti-realist of any kind. Given its implication that there may be things of which we can have no knowledge, it makes truth independent of our capacities, and does

5. According to Allison, for instance, when Kant characterizes the cause or ground of the "matter" of human knowledge as non-sensible, and therefore unknowable, his reason is that this cause cannot be represented as in time or space. But, according to Allison, Kant says only that the cause cannot be represented as in space or time, not that it cannot be in space or time. "This prohibition has a strictly transcendental status; it stipulates how an object must be conceived if it is to function in a transcendental account as 'something corresponding to sensibility viewed as receptivity.' As such the prohibition does not bring with it any ontological assumptions about the real nature of things or about a supersensible realm" (Allison, 252).

nothing to deny that truth is also independent of our cognitive interests. In that case, Kant need not deny (though he could not prove) the Cartesian claim that mathematical science gives us truth that satisfies the metaphysical correspondence theory. If we accept this view of Kant, we should reject as misguided the connection drawn by Putnam and Rorty between anti-realists$_m$ and the rejection of the thing-in-itself.

Paul Guyer has recently given us strong arguments (esp. 333–44) against this view of Kant and its implication that Kant's use of the thing-in-itself is innocuous. Guyer argues, convincingly I believe, that Kant claims that things-in-themselves are not spatial or temporal, and that far from an insistence on intellectual modesty, this is "a dogmatic assertion that time and space cannot be properties of the things to which we ultimately intend to refer" (335). If Guyer is correct, Kant means that we can be sure that things-in-themselves are not as we represent them to be (333), thus that the ultimate truth about things is hidden from our knowledge. Even if Guyer's version of Kant is wrong, it seems very close to the one under whose influence Nietzsche wrote (see Chapter 3). I will therefore draw out its implications for the issue of realism$_m$ with which I believe Nietzsche was concerned. If Guyer's type of interpretation is wrong, it will not affect my interpretation of Nietzsche, though it may affect Nietzsche's value as a critic of Kant.

If Guyer is right about Kant's use of the thing-in-itself, I believe that Kant must regard the ultimate truth about things as independent not only of our capacities, but also of our cognitive interests. This is crucial because, if the argument attributed to Nietzsche in the preceding section is correct, it commits Kant to the objectionable concept of the thing-in-itself as independent of all possible knowers. My argument is as follows. In the first place, Kant's distinction between appearances and things-in-themselves (or phenomenal and noumenal reality) must be made in terms of the latter's independence of the human cognitive constitution, because its whole point is to allow us to say that we can know things only as they are relative to our constitution, not as they are in independence of it. Secondly, for reasons I give below, appearances must be regarded as independent of our cognitive capacities. Therefore, appearances cannot be distinguished from things-in-themselves on the basis of the latter's independence of our cognitive capacities. Given that our cognitive interests provide the only alternative for this role, Kant can distinguish things-in-themselves from appearances only if he takes the former to be independent not only of our capacities, but also of our cognitive interests.

We could avoid this conclusion if we identified phenomenal reality with what is knowable by human beings on the grounds that anything else must belong to the noumenal realm. Putnam evidently interprets Kant in this way when he makes him a proponent of the third version of anti-realism$_m$ discussed in the second section of this chapter. According to that version of anti-realism$_m$, rejecting as contradictory the very idea of the thing-in-itself makes phenomenal reality the only reality. A denial that phenomenal reality is independent of our cognitive capacities therefore yields Putnam's usual position (the third version of anti-realism$_m$) that truth cannot differ from what the best human theory would take it to be. But this gives the game away to Putnam's opponent since it makes affirming the thing-in-itself equivalent to insisting that the way things are is independent of human cognitive capacities, and it is difficult to see the contradiction in that. It is therefore in Putnam's interests to recognize that for Kant phenomenal reality is itself independent of our cognitive capacities and to formulate his anti-realism$_m$ (in accord with the fourth version discussed in section 2) as a denial that truth is independent of our cognitive interests.

Kant certainly does not regard phenomenal reality as independent of our *conceptual* capacities, since he regards our basic concepts as the categories in terms of which all rational beings must interpret reality. From this it seems to follow that our best standards of rational acceptability coincide with those of any other beings dependent on sensibility for the matter or data of thought. But Kant gives no basis for ruling out the possibility of beings with observational capacities superior to our own, who would therefore be capable of verifying theories that are superior to ours, in the sense of better able to explain the observations we are capable of making, as judged by our shared standards of rational acceptability. Yet, there would be no basis for insisting that any such theory would have to concern things-in-themselves. For Kant, an intellect could provide knowledge of things-in-themselves only if it were intuitive rather than discursive, that is, capable of providing its possessor with data rather than dependent on sensibility for data that it then handles or organizes. An intellect like ours, one dependent for its data on sensibility, can only know appearance or phenomenal reality, and not things-in-themselves. An intellect better able to handle the data accessible to us in virtue of our sensibility amounts to an intellect with better access to phenomenal reality, not with access to noumenal reality. Therefore, a Kantian need not deny phenomenal reality's independence of our cognitive capacities. The truth about phenomenal reality might differ from what we can even in principle verify.

This interpretation of Kant receives added support from a recent discussion of Kant's Axioms of Intuition (A162/B202–A166/B207). William Harper makes explicit the implications we can draw concerning truth from Charles Parsons's important paper on mathematics and infinity in Kant. The principle of the Axioms is that all appearances are extensive magnitudes to which "pure mathematics, in its complete precision," is applicable (A165/B206). As Harper argues, this means that every object of experience is a determinate extensive magnitude, and therefore that the length along each of its specifiable dimensions has a determinate value, and that at any given time the ratios of such values (the ratios of length along any specified dimensions) determine specific real numbers (151). Yet, we clearly do not have the capacity to determine the exact value of any specific ratio (i.e., with the "complete precision" of mathematics) since we do not have the power to make infinitely fine discriminations. As Harper argues: "certainly our best instruments now fall far short of the precision required, and, though we can expect improvements that allow closer approximations, nothing in the way such improvements have been made in the past makes it plausible to suggest that such approximations could even in principle culminate in exact values" (152). Harper therefore concludes that Kant's principle of extensive magnitude "makes commitments that go beyond the resolving powers of human observation even if these powers are extended by instruments." In other words, Kant believes there is a truth concerning the dimensions of spatial objects, and this truth is obviously beyond what we are capable of verifying, even under ideal conditions for beings like us. The truth about the spatial dimensions of objects is therefore independent of human cognitive capacities. Nevertheless Kant must regard it as a truth concerning only the phenomenal realm, since he denies that we have any basis for considering the Axioms applicable to things-in-themselves (e.g., A 165/B 206). I therefore believe we should conclude from Harper's argument that phenomenal reality and its corresponding truth are independent of our cognitive capacities.

However, we must reject Harper's suggestion that his interpretation points the way to a Kantian foundation for "scientific realism" (152), if he has in mind the metaphysical realism Descartes defended. Harper does nothing to show that phenomenal reality's independence of what we can (even in principle) verify justifies the realist$_m$ intuition that (phenomenal) reality is determinately constituted in complete independence of human beings. In the case Harper considers, Kant's position makes (phenomenal) reality independent of our cognitive capacities. But Kant denies that the reality to which mathematical truth corresponds is determinately constituted in complete independence of anything about us because he believes mathematics applies to things only in virtue of our forms of intuition. In the mathematical case under consideration, there is surely nothing that makes truth independent of our best standards of rational acceptability. Kant would presumably say that *if* we had the ability to satisfy our standards for determining exactly which real number represented the ratio of the lengths along any two dimensions of an object – that is, if we had the power to make infinitely fine discriminations – our best answer could not be false. Descartes could find a basis for doubt here (in the absence of a divine guarantee) precisely because he considers truth independent of our cognitive interests. Kant could not do this without admitting that mathematical truths about material objects correspond to things as they are in themselves – thus abandoning a major component of his project.

These considerations suggest again that contemporary anti-realists$_m$ who want to reject the whole concept of the thing-in-itself as contradictory, but to follow Kant otherwise concerning truth – that is, in denying the Cartesian claim about the kind of truth science can give us – should admit that truth is independent of our cognitive capacities – that our capacities might not be sufficient, even in principle, to determine what the truth is in some cases – and insist only that truth cannot be independent of our cognitive interests, of our best standards of rational acceptability. This neo-Kantian position on truth is the one I shall attribute to Nietzsche.

As I will interpret him, Nietzsche agrees with Kant that we

cannot know things-in-themselves, and thus that, contrary to Descartes, the truth we are capable of discovering does not satisfy the metaphysical correspondence theory. Nietzsche is anti-Kantian, however, in that he denies the very conceivability of the thing-in-itself. It nevertheless seems appropriate to call his position "neo-Kantian" because I believe he arrived at it through his acceptance of, and long reflection upon, Kant's denial of our knowledge of things-in-themselves, and that he was the first of many who criticized the whole idea of the thing-in-itself to draw the correct conclusion concerning our concept of truth from this criticism: that its content does not go beyond what I have called "the minimal correspondence theory," and that it does not allow us to make sense of the possibility that a theory that fully satisfied our cognitive interests could still be false.

My use of the label "neo-Kantian" has led to some misunderstanding – for example, that I think Nietzsche provides a kind of "transcendental standpoint in which putative 'facts' about human needs and human neurophysiology play a role not unlike that of Kant's categories and forms of intuition" (Magnus, 1983, 100, note 4). In fact there is nothing at all transcendental about the position I attribute to Nietzsche. Nothing I attribute to him is out of accord with Rorty's view that "philosophy will have no more to offer than common sense (supplemented by biology, history, etc.) about knowledge and truth" (1979, 176). My interpretation so far commits Nietzsche only to accepting the equivalence principle as governing our use of "true" and to rejecting both subjective idealism (=acceptance of common sense realism) and the Cartesian assumption that we can make sense of the idea that a theory that best satisfies our cognitive interests might still be false. As I shall argue in the next chapter, however, Nietzsche was originally committed to a much stronger thesis concerning truth.

3

LANGUAGE AND TRUTH: NIETZSCHE'S EARLY DENIAL OF TRUTH

Although Nietzsche chose not to publish his early essay "Truth and Lie in the Extra-moral Sense," several factors favor a detailed examination of it here.[1] In the first place, TL exerts considerable influence on the contemporary understanding of Nietzsche's achievements. The common belief that Nietzsche proves the non-existence of truth, at least of any truths accessible to humans, finds its major source in this essay. TL also functions as an important source for the belief that Nietzsche demonstrates the ascetic or life-negating character of the concern with logic and truth, and of philosophical (argumentative, straightforward, nonmetaphorical) style in general (Kofman, 33; trs. 210; Rorty, 1986, 11). Even those with doubts about what Nietzsche proves in TL have high praise for the essay (Danto 38).

TL also forms much of the basis for what I have called the nontraditional or radical interpretation of Nietzsche's position on truth. According to radical interpreters, Nietzsche denies the existence of truth, in the sense of denying that any of our beliefs correspond to reality. TL's extended defense of the claim that truths are illusions provides defenders of the radical interpreta-

---

1. An early and less developed examination of it is found in my paper "On 'Truth and Lie in the Extra-Moral Sense.' "

tion with a major basis for interpreting much sketchier remarks about truth in Nietzsche's published works as denials of truth in this sense.

Further, unlike the notes of the 1880s, TL cannot be dismissed on the grounds that it belongs only to the *Nachlass,* for it possesses, to a relatively high degree, the characteristics that make the published works more reliable than the *Nachlass* for the interpretation of Nietzsche's position. A reworked and polished essay, it is not a mere note that Nietzsche may have thought better of the next day. Although he did not publish it, he does allude to it with approval in a published work, and its length plus its status as an obvious bridge between earlier and later works he did publish (BT and HA) provides the kind of check on interpretation missing for most of the *Nachlass* of the 1880s.

Finally, I do not believe we can plausibly explain away the evidence of Nietzsche's denial of truth in TL. This early essay therefore constitutes an important piece of evidence (the most important, I believe) for the radical interpretation, and against the neo-Kantian interpretation, of Nietzsche's position on truth. I propose to defend the neo-Kantian interpretation by showing that Nietzsche later abandoned the position of TL. In this chapter, I undertake the first part of this defense by analyzing the arguments Nietzsche gives, or has been interpreted as giving, in TL. Sympathizers with Nietzsche's putative denial of truth usually suppose that he derived it from an insight concerning language. I distinguish two different claims about language that might have led Nietzsche to deny truth in TL. In the first two sections of this chapter, I argue that neither of these claims provides a good reason for this denial. Thus, if we accept the interpretation offered by those who embrace TL's argument, the latter seems completely undeserving of the enthusiasm it has recently generated.

I believe we can find a much stronger argument for Nietzsche's position in TL if we deny that he derived it from a claim about language. In the third and fourth sections of this chapter, I argue that Nietzsche derives it instead from a representational theory of perception and the metaphysical correspondence theory. I will need detailed argument for this interpretation since those who sympathize with Nietzsche's early denial of truth have reason to resist it. These defenders of the radical Nietzsche reject both of the doctrines I find at the basis of his denial of truth.

Nietzsche certainly came to reject these doctrines. In Chapter 5, I interpret Nietzsche's perspectivism as a rejection of both representationalism and the metaphysical correspondence theory. In Chapter 6, I argue that Nietzsche later analyzes his early acceptance of the metaphysical correspondence theory as an expression of the ascetic ideal. Far from a precocious statement of Nietzsche's lifelong views, TL belongs, according to my interpretation, to Nietzsche's juvenalia. It stands as a monument not to the ascetic character of (truth-seeking) philosophical style, but to the asceticism of Nietzsche's own early position, including his denial of truth. The latter contradicts the position on truth and the life-affirming (anti-ascetic) ethic he develops in his later works. Detailed analysis of the arguments in TL will allow me to begin defending this interpretation. It will also help me, in the final section of this chapter, to exhibit an internal flaw in the essay's central argument which, I believe, gave Nietzsche reason to move in the direction of a neo-Kantian position on truth.

1. Truths as illusions

In a now familiar passage of TL, Nietzsche makes explicit his denial of truth.

> What then is truth? A movable host of metaphors, metonymies, and anthropomorphisms: in short, a sum of human relations which have been poetically and rhetorically intensified, transferred, and embellished, and which, after long usage, seem to a people to be fixed, canonical, and obligatory. Truths are illusions we have forgotten are illusions (TL 84, WL 880–1).

Nietzsche expresses the same point by saying that to tell the truth is "to lie in accord with a fixed convention" (TL 84, WL 881). He therefore uses "illusions" as equivalent to "lies" – lies "in the extra-moral sense," however, that is, lies told unconsciously or without realizing they are lies. But "lies" in this sense are not lies in our sense at all. To tell what we call "a lie," one must assert what one believes false. Nietzsche's "lies" seem merely false assertions. In that case, "truths are illusions" means that all assertions we call "truths" are actually false.

If this means that any true assertion is also false, Nietzsche's position cannot escape absurdity. If being true and being false aren't mutually exclusive, neither predicate excludes anything.

But then, as Hegel stressed in repeating Spinoza's dictum that all determination is negation, neither has a determinate content. The assertion that truths are false or illusory thus says nothing determinate. To make even minimal sense of Nietzsche's position, we must assume recognition on his part that a belief cannot be both true and false (at the same time, in the same respect, etc). He must mean that we are mistaken concerning the beliefs we call "true," that these beliefs are false rather than true. But this position also faces grave problems. In the first place, it seems to require us to reject basic logic. If "it is not raining" is false, then "it is raining" must be true. To deny this is to reject logic. But if we reject logic, we might as well stop talking or pretending we understand anyone, for we have no basis for interpreting what anyone says. Further, what possible reason could one have to deny that "it is raining" sometimes satisfies "is true": namely, when it is raining in the vicinity of the speaker at the time of the utterance or inscription?

Nietzsche's reason certainly seems to concern language. He uses approximately 40 percent of the essay prior to the claim that truths are illusions arguing for what Derrida (1973, 139), following Saussure, calls the "arbitrariness of signs," the fact that the use of a particular sound or inscription to mean what it does is arbitrary (cf. Davidson, 265). The distinction between truth and lie in the extra-moral sense arises, according to Nietzsche, only with the establishment of "uniformly valid and obligatory designations" for things – that is, with the establishment of linguistic conventions. The truthful person abides by these rules – uses the correct designations for things – whereas the liar violates them, saying "I am rich," for instance, when the correct term for his condition is "poor" (TL 81, WL 877). However, the rules that establish the correct designations for things are completely arbitrary, as Nietzsche proceeds to argue at length. We could just as easily use the word "rich" for the condition we call "poor." Linguistic conventions receive their justification solely from the pragmatic consideration that they facilitate linguistic communication, which is a necessity of human social existence. Contrary to the thesis Socrates discusses in the *Cratylus*, no natural relation of congruence or "adequate expression" connects words to things. "The various languages placed side by side show that with words it is never a question of truth, never a question of adequate expression; otherwise there would not be so many languages" (TL 82, WL 878). Nietzsche evidently concludes that truths are illusions solely on the basis of this argument.

But how does the fact that we might use different words to say the same thing show that what we say is not true? This is a very weak inference, which no major philosopher since Descartes would accept. The sentence or judgment constitutes the smallest truth-valued unit.

To make at all plausible the inference from the arbitrariness thesis to "truths are illusions," I suggest interpreting the latter as a claim that truths and illusions (falsehoods) differ significantly only in their respective relations to linguistic conventions. A statement is true if it conforms to the conventions, false (a lie in the extra-moral sense) if it violates them. On this interpretation, Nietzsche recognizes the distinction between truth and falsity, and accepts some of our beliefs as true. He simply denies that the difference between truth and falsity is as great or important as we tend to believe it is. On this interpretation, he does not deny the existence of truths, but, as Danto claims, only rejects a certain theory of truth. In particular, he rejects the notion of truth as correspondence to reality, since he claims that the difference between truth and falsity can be adequately stated in terms of convention without suggesting that there is anything to which truths correspond. Because Nietzsche thinks that pragmatic considerations establish the conventions we must obey to speak the truth, he may also accept the pragmatic theory of truth Danto attributes to him.

On this interpretation, however, Nietzsche's position is very weak. On his own account, it is either false, or the expression of an arbitrary decision to call "illusions" what we call "truth." Does Nietzsche obey the appointed conventions when he calls truths "illusions"? If he does obey what he claims to be the conventions governing the use of "false" (or "illusion"), "truths are illusions" amounts to the absurd claim that to call a statement "true" always violates the linguistic conventions. To ascribe to Nietzsche an even minimally plausible position, we must assume that he uses "illusion" or "false" in what he considers an unconventional way. But then "truths are illusions" is false, according to his own analysis.

Nietzsche might dismiss as unimportant the falsity of his claim about truth, on the ground that truth-telling is mere obedience to convention. If Nietzsche's usage is arbitrary, so is conventional usage. However, unless Nietzsche has a reason for using "illusion" in a new way, "truths are illusions" amounts to the claim that what we call "truths," he calls "illusions." But we have not been given a reason for caring what he calls them.

Further, Nietzsche fails to show that we can understand truth without suggesting the existence of something to which truths correspond. If, as he claims, the liar uses the "valid designations, the words, to make something which is unreal appear real," for example, to make himself appear rich when he is actually poor, then the truthful person must use the words to make the real appear real, that is, to convey information that corresponds to reality. The following considerations militate against construing such correspondence as merely the use of the conventionally appropriate words.

Suppose that, surprised by what I believe to be a sudden rain shower, I say "it's raining" to a group of Anglophones. My utterance conforms to the conventions accepted by my listeners. It may nevertheless fail to correspond to reality – e.g., if the water I see actually comes from a lawn sprinkler. Nietzsche might respond that this failure of correspondence amounts to no more than a failure to use the conventionally appropriate words for the situation in question. But this defense admits, in effect, that correspondence depends on two different factors: what the conventions are, and what the world is like. We cannot plausibly regard obedience to convention as sufficient for truth-telling unless we build correspondence to reality into the idea of such obedience, which then becomes equivalent to using the correct words for the way the world actually is.

In fact, obedience to the accepted conventions is not even necessary for truth-telling. Change the situation above (I see falling water that is in fact coming from a lawn sprinkler, and I am speaking to Anglophones) so that I start speaking German instead of English (say, because in the excitement of the moment I forget that I am no longer in Hamburg). No matter what I say in German, I fail to abide by the linguistic conventions my listeners expect me to follow. But if I say "es regnet," I say something false. If (having spotted the lawn sprinkler perhaps) I say instead "es regnet nicht," I tell the truth, as my listeners will realize as soon as they 1) realize I am speaking German, and, if they do not know German, get an interpretation of my utterance in their own language, and 2) realize that the falling water we all see is not rain.

Thus, the truth of an utterance does not require obedience to a specific set of conventions. It does depend on which conventions one follows, in the sense that it depends on the meaning of what one says. If, in the situation described above, I had been speaking a dialect in which "es regnet nicht" meant "it is raining," my utterance would have been false. Given that I was speaking standard German (that is, that "es regnet nicht" means "it is not raining") – and that it was not raining – my utterance was true.

Thus the truth of an utterance or inscription depends on two factors: what it means, and what the world is like. Knowledge of the conventions of speakers' languages is, of course, a great practical help for figuring out the meaning of an utterance. But knowledge of these conventions is neither necessary nor sufficient for knowing most of the truths we want to know. The arbitrary character of these conventions is a triviality from which nothing important about truth follows.[2]

2. Language as metaphor

Enthusiasts of "Truth and Lie" will object that Nietzsche derives his argument against truth from the metaphorical (or, more generally, the figural) character of language, and not from its arbitrariness or conventionality. In this case, a fairly straightforward path runs from a belief about language to the denial of truth. If, as Danto suggests, Nietzsche believed that metaphors are never literally true (43), the assumption that all language is metaphorical would give him a reason for denying that we can express literal truth at all.[3] But even if we accept that all metaphors are false, it is difficult to see how Nietzsche could defend the view that all language is metaphorical.

As in the case of "true" and "false," we deprive "metaphor" of determinate meaning if we deny the possibility of its opposite. But a more specific reason exists for denying that all language

2. The arguments of the preceding section are greatly influenced by Davidson's "Communication and Convention," 265–80, and the following section is indebted to his "What Metaphors Mean," 245–64, and to Sue Larson for the extensive conversations I have had with her about Davidson.

3. If Nietzsche did believe that metaphors are never literally true, however, he was surely wrong. As Davidson writes (258): "Patent falsity is the usual case with metaphor, but on occasion patent truth will do as well. 'Business is business' is too obvious in its literal meaning to be taken as having been uttered to convey information, so we look for another use; Ted Cohen reminds us, in the same connection, that no man is an island."

could be metaphorical. Both the creation and the interpretation of metaphors seem dependent on the ability to use language nonmetaphorically. Suppose I say that someone was "cutting through the argument with a rusty razor blade." I have made an assertion, and a quite obviously false one, since arguments do not take up space. Why interpret my statement as a metaphor? Because you know what it means to cut through something with a razor blade (i.e., the conditions under which it would be true to say that someone had done so), you know that my assertion cannot possibly be true, and that I cannot possibly believe it is true (short of insanity, or a quite different interpretation of the assertion). You need not deny that I have made an assertion, that is, have put something forward as true. But you must assume that I have done so for reasons other than the usual ones people have for making assertions: for example, to express their own belief in them or to convince others of their truth. So you assume instead that I have deliberately asserted something blatantly false so that you will look beyond what has been asserted to the point of the utterance: in this case, to think of the analysis of an argument in an imaginative way, as similar in certain ways to trying to cut through a physical object with a rusty razor blade. But I could not use the words in questions to get you to notice or think of these similarities (i.e., could not accomplish the aim of using the words metaphorically) unless both of us knew how to use the words literally: in ordinary assertions intended to express belief in what is asserted. And since I would not know how to use words literally unless I did so at least occasionally, it seems clear that I can use language metaphorically only if I use it literally as well.

Nevertheless many interpreters, especially those influenced by Derrida, believe Nietzsche has demonstrated that all language is metaphorical (or figural). My attempt to show why they might (mistakenly) believe this will focus on Paul de Man because I think he provides the clearest detailed account of TL as a derivation of the illusory character of truth from the alleged insight that all language is figural.[4]

4. The following examination of de Man appears in my article "Language and Deconstruction: Nietzsche, de Man, and Postmodernism." It is reprinted from *Nietzsche as Postmodernist: Essays Pro and Contra,* edited by Clayton Koelb, by permission of the State University of New York Press. Copyright 1990 by the State University of New York Press.

It is not easy to understand how de Man uses "figural" and what I presume to be its opposite, "literal." He claims that for Nietzsche "the paradigmatic structure of language is rhetorical rather than representational or expressive of a referential, proper meaning," and that this marks "a full reversal of the established priorities which traditionally root the authority of language in its adequation to an extralinguistic referent or meaning, rather than in the intralinguistic resources of figure" (106). Thus de Man would classify language as "literal" or "nonfigural" only if it received its "authority" from its adequation to something extralinguistic. But this could mean two quite different things. It could mean, as Socrates speculates in the *Cratylus*, that the literal meaning of a word derives from a natural or nonconventional relation between word and object (e.g., that "bees" is the correct word to use for certain buzzing insects because the sound somehow corresponds to the insects' nature). According to this interpretation, de Man's defense of the figural character of all language would merely restate the arbitrariness thesis. In that case, however, de Man uses "figural" in an idiosyncratic way, and gives us no reason to think that language is figural in the ordinary sense. Further, nothing important about truth would follow from his argument, because, as I have argued, nothing important about truth follows from the arbitrariness thesis.

We can avoid reducing de Man's claim to the arbitrariness thesis if we interpret "literal" as the kind of meaning or use a word has in virtue of an extralinguistic object (physical object, Fregean sense) with which it is matched by the rules or conventions of a particular language. With this interpretation, we do not reduce de Man's position to the arbitrariness thesis. De Man rejects much more than the thesis discussed in the *Cratylus*. He also denies that linguistic rules are like strings that tie words to their proper objects. To deny this "string" picture of how words get their meaning within a language certainly seems the point of his repeated denial of "referential" meaning. The claim that all language is figural (which for de Man is equivalent to taking figure to be the paradigm for language – see p. 105) then affirms a kind of holism with regard to meaning. The meaning (or "authority") of words comes not from a direct (linguistic) tie to objects, but from relations to other words ("the intralinguistic resources of figure").

According to this second interpretation, de Man's claim about the figurality of language is curiously close to certain elements in the philosophy of Donald Davidson, in particular, the inscrutability of reference. Davidson argues that inscrutability follows from Quine's thesis of the indeterminacy of translation. The inscrutability thesis tells us that there is no unique way to pick out what the singular terms of a language refer to or what the predicates are true of. When we interpret another person's speech, there will be different ways of assigning reference or tying words to objects that will prove equally correct, according to the behavioral (including verbal) evidence we have for deciding on a correct interpretation. The behavioral evidence will allow you to interpret my phrase "that rabbit" as referring to a bird, for instance, as long as you presume a suitable permutation upon the predicate I use ("runs fast" might be interpreted as "runs fast or flies," e.g.). The unit of meaning is not the word but the sentence – or, better, the whole language. The meaning of individual words or singular terms is crucially determined by their relations to other words and ultimately by how the whole system functions. Thus, to know the meaning of a word is to know how to use it in sentences. To know the meaning of a sentence is to know the circumstances under which the sentence would be true. Success in interpreting the speech of another person consists not in matching words or phrases to objects, but in being able to match truths with truths and falsehoods with falsehoods. Therefore, as Wallace formulates it: "what good translation preserves is not a word's reference, but the pattern of its acceptable variations of reference relative to acceptable variations in the reference of other words" (152).

I find Davidson's holism quite convincing. Except for the part about truth, I also believe it is close to the point of de Man's interpretation of TL. Like Davidson, de Man wants to deny the existence of an extralinguistic (Fregean) meaning which, for instance, "it is raining" and "es regnet" have in common. But de Man has to admit that they "mean the same thing" in the sense that each correctly translates the other into a different language. His insistence on the "absence of a reliable referent" and the "loss of a primacy of meaning located within the referent" (47) requires only a denial that correct or good translation consists in preserving reference. Although de Man's point in the quoted phrases is made specifically about literature, he believes that literature only makes more explicit the rhetorical structure of all language. His affirmation of the latter amounts to a denial that meaning has a "factual, referential foundation" (111), and a rejection of the "traditional priority" that locates meaning "in a referent conceived as an object." It therefore seems natural to read de Man's position in Davidsonian terms, especially when he defines "the medium or property of language" as "the possibility of substituting binary polarities . . . without regard for the truth-value of the structure" (109). De Man seems to mean that the truth value of sentences, and therefore, the structure as a whole, is independent of the referents assigned to the parts. If he agrees with Davidson on this point, however, de Man nevertheless places himself quite at odds with him when he draws from the denial of referential foundations for meaning (the inscrutability of reference) a denial both of literal meaning and of truth itself.

De Man's view that inscrutability entails a denial of literal meaning seems to arise from a confusion of literal meaning with literal (in the sense of word for word) translation. On the "string picture" of language, the paradigm of translation will be word for word. The translation of a sentence from one language to another will involve discovering the objects to which the words in one language are tied, and then replacing those words with ones tied to the same objects in the second language. The necessary rejection of this understanding of the problem of translation makes it difficult to retain faith in the possibility of literal translation. Retaining the prejudice that sentences have literal meaning only if literal (word for word) translation of them is possible will then seem to make the rejection of the "string picture" entail a concomitant denial of the very possibility of literal meaning. And if, as de Man gives repeated evidence of believing, literal meaning and truth stand or fall together, it will also entail a denial of the possibility of expressing truth linguistically.

Davidson would agree that truth and literal meaning stand or fall together. He would deny, however, that truth requires "referential" meaning (the scrutability of reference). Davidson argues precisely the opposite: that a sentence can have exactly the same truth conditions even if we assume differences in the objects to which the individual words refer. Literal meaning and truth go together because knowing the literal meaning of a sentence consists in knowing the circumstances in which it would be true. But knowing this meaning has nothing to do with the possibility of word for word translation, or with matching words to extra-linguistic objects in unique ways. This, in fact, constitutes Davidson's argument for the inscrutability of reference.

Unlike de Man, Davidson does not sever language from the world. De Man denies the conceivability of "the notion of a language entirely freed of referential constraint" because "any utterance can always be read as semantically motivated" (49). Yet, he usually writes as if meaning depends solely on syntax, and has nothing to do with semantics – as if we have only language, and no connection to the world. He claims that we can and must read sentences as "semantically motivated," that is, as related to the world. But the nature of language subverts or deconstructs this semantic reading, forcing us to read sentences on another level, as related only to other bits of language. I suggest that de Man finds this view of language compelling because he thinks we can accept the inscrutability of reference only "at the expense of literal truth" (112). His view makes perfect sense if we assume that "the correspondence of sentences to reality is the resultant of the more basic relations which terms bear to pieces of reality" (Wallace, 163), and that such correspondence is truth. But a denial of both reference and truth completely severs the connection between language and reality, confusing the human condition with one that exists only at the extreme limits of madness. Perhaps more to the point (if followers of de Man do not admit madness as an objection), the denial of both reference and truth leaves one without a basis for interpreting what anyone says or writes. If we accept the problematic nature of referential meaning – of establishing meaning by matching words to objects – we can preserve the idea of meaningfulness and interpretation only by way of truth. That is, to consider a statement meaningful is to regard it as interpretable. But it makes sense to regard something as interpretable only if we believe that there is a basis for distinguishing between good and bad interpretations, between what counts as an interpretation and what counts as just another, unrelated statement. Without reference to fall back on, only truth can provide this basis. If we cannot translate or interpret by matching words to objects, we must translate or interpret by matching sentences to their truth conditions. Thus, to give a correct interpretation or translation of an entire language is to give the right truth conditions for all of its sentences. The problematic character of reference, which de Man appreciates (and which Derrida, I believe, calls "différance"), does not dictate that there is no truth. It entails only a denial that words are "tied to objects except as these ties are dictated by the truth conditions of statements taken overall" (Wallace, 151). The insistence on truth preserves connection to the world. The rejection of truth that de Man finds in Nietzsche severs the connection between language and the world. It can seem plausible (though I don't see how it can ever seem acceptable) only on the questionable assumption that reference constitutes the only source of semantic content, the only way of connecting language and the world.

Truth even seems to play a role in de Man's interpretation of TL. He presents Nietzsche's denial of truth as based on a claim about language because he accepts the truth of that claim and believes it entails that truths are illusions (i.e., that the latter claim must be true if "language is figural" is true). I have attempted to disarm his interpretation of TL by challenging these beliefs.

An alternative way to connect Nietzsche's denial of truth with his claim about language is to interpret the latter as a claim that the difference between literal and metaphorical usage is not as great as we tend to believe. Nietzsche claims that statements we regard as (literally) true are "metaphors that have become worn out and have been drained of sensuous force" (TL 84, WL 881). We could take this to mean that the only difference between literal and metaphorical usage is that the former is all-too-common usage that lacks metaphor's power to stir the senses or imagination.

One advantage of this interpretation is that there is much to support its claim about metaphor. If we cannot sensibly say that *all* literal usage was once metaphorical, we can say this about much literal usage. According to the interpretation I propose, Nietzsche claims that when a metaphor becomes part of literal usage it simply loses its power to stir the imagination. Imagination is no longer needed to get the point of an expression. To use an example of Davidson's, the American slang expression "he was burned up" is clearly the corpse of a metaphor. When the metaphor was alive, writes Davidson, "we would have pictured fire in the eyes or smoke coming out the ears" (253). When the metaphor becomes part of standard (if slang) usage, it simply conveys the information that the person was angry. The imagination need not be exercised, and similarities between two different things need not be noticed to get the point.

This interpretation also seems to provide a basis for concluding that truths are illusions (that truth-telling is adherence to the approved conventions) since metaphorical usage usually involves making a false utterance, whereas the same utterance would be true if the metaphor had only died and become part of standard usage. If the person referred to is angry, "he is burned up" is true if the metaphor has died and become part of standard usage, whereas it is false if the metaphor is still alive. But it would be mistaken to conclude from this that truth-telling is simply a matter of using the appointed words. The death of a metaphor can change the truth value of an utterance because this death is a change in the meaning of the utterance. When "burned up" dies as a metaphor, it simply comes to include "angry" as one of its meanings. And the truth of what we say depends, of course, on its meaning. But it also depends on the way the world is – the person in question must be angry for "he was burned up" to be true.

If Nietzsche does infer "truths are illusions" from "all language is metaphorical," the latter is most charitably interpreted in the following way.[5] Consider a metaphorical statement, for example, "Henry is an ostrich." This is false, if Henry is a human being, since his properties are not identical with those of an ostrich. One uses the metaphor to call to attention a certain similarity between Henry's behavior and that of an ostrich. However, one states an identity where there is only a similarity, and that is why the statement is false. According to Nietzsche, the concepts necessary for literal usage are formed in the same way. A concept – a word used to fit "countless more or less similar cases" – always arises from "the equation of unequal things" (TL 83, WL 880). "Just as it is certain that one leaf is never totally the same as another, so it is certain that the concept 'leaf' is formed by arbitrarily discarding these individual differences and forgetting the distinguishing aspects." Literal statements thus have the same structure as metaphors: two unequal or non-identical things are stated to be equal or identical. In that case, the difference between literal and metaphorical usage is that the former requires us to forget that there are only similarities between things, to misinterpret similarities as

5. This interpretation was suggested to me by Sidney Morgenbesser.

identities. When we say "that chair is red," we believe that the object shares an identical color with other things we call "red" and has the same essence as other structures we call "chairs." This is why we believe (many) literal claims true, whereas we usually recognize metaphorical claims as false: we recognize the absence of identity in the case of metaphors and forget it in the case of literal usage. But if there is only similarity and no identity, literal claims are as false as metaphorical ones: they are simply "illusions we have forgotten are illusions."

This is the most plausible argument I can find in TL for inferring that truths are illusions from something about language. But this interpretation still leaves Nietzsche with a very weak position. Its basis is nominalism: that only words are universal, whereas reality is purely individual. If he is to be a consistent nominalist, however, Nietzsche should take "x is the same color as y" as positing not an identity, but only a similarity, between x and y. Consider his nominalistic insistence that the same word is used of countless "more or less similar cases." What makes different occurrences of "red" the same word? Surely Nietzsche must admit that what he calls the "same word" is only different occurrences of a similar sound or inscription. But then the same analysis must be applied to things: to say that two different things are both red is to posit not an identity, but only a similarity. But if "x is red" means only that x is relevantly similar to other things we call "red," Nietzsche has no basis for considering it either metaphorical or false.

3. Representationalism and things-in-themselves

I will now argue that Nietzsche does not base his denial of truth in TL on an insight concerning language. Instead, he bases his substantive claim about language (that it is metaphorical) and his denial of truth on the same traditional philosophical doctrines: a representational theory of perception and the metaphysical correspondence theory of truth.

Consider the passage in which Nietzsche explains why he considers language metaphorical.

> The "thing in itself" (which is precisely what the pure truth, apart from consequences [*die reine folgenlose Wahrheit*] would be) is also something quite incomprehensible to the creator of language

and something not in the least worth striving for. He only designates the relations of things to men, and expresses them with the boldest metaphors. A nerve stimulus, transferred into an image: first metaphor. The image is imitated in a sound: second metaphor (TL 82, WL 879).

With language, Nietzsche continues, we resemble a deaf person whose only knowledge of sounds comes from looking at Chlandi's sound figures in the sand:

> We believe we know something about the things themselves [den Dingen selbst] when we speak of trees, colors, snow, and flowers; and yet we possess nothing but metaphors for things, metaphors which in no way correspond to the original essences [die den ursprünglichen Wesenheiten ganz und gar nicht entsprechen]. In the same way that the sound appears as a sand figure, so the mysterious X of the thing in itself [des Dings an sich] first appears as a nerve stimulus, then as an image, and finally as a sound. Thus the genesis of language does not proceed logically in any case, and all the material with which the man of truth, the scientist and the philosopher, later works and builds, if not derived from never-never land, is at least not derived from the essence of things [dem Wesen der Dinge]. (TL 83, WL 879)

Nietzsche's underlying claim in this passage concerns perception rather than language. He insists that perception gives us only metaphors of things. How are we to interpret this strange claim? Since a metaphor is a particular use of language, a percept can't literally be a metaphor. Perhaps, then, Nietzsche uses "metaphor," as it were, metaphorically – to call to our attention certain similarities between perception and the metaphorical use of language. But what are we to notice? Contrary to what we would expect based on the final interpretation discussed in the second section of this chapter, the passage does not suggest that percepts state or present an identity where there is only similarity. Nietzsche calls our utterances "metaphors" because they fail to "correspond to the original essences," that is, to things-in-themselves. To use language metaphorically, he seems to assume, is to say something that fails to correspond to the actual nature of an object, but communicates nevertheless how that object appears given certain workings of the human imagination. Nietzsche apparently views percepts as similar to metaphorical discourse in this regard. Perception gives us only appearance, not things-in-themselves. Nietzsche points to the same similarity between metaphor and other uses of language – the failure to correspond to things-in-themselves – by suggesting that all language is metaphorical. As I shall argue, however, his affirmation of this similarity between metaphor and other uses of language depends on his claim about perception.

George Stack (94 ff.) suggests that Nietzsche's account of perception in this passage shows the influence of F. A. Lange. I will argue instead for the primacy of Schopenhauer's influence. Lange's account of the dependence of perception on our psychophysiological constitution would merely reinforce the representational theory of perception Nietzsche found in Schopenhauer.

At his most extreme, Schopenhauer writes that we do not "know a sun and an earth, but only an eye that sees a sun, and a hand that feels an earth." He means simply that the objects we see and feel are "there only as representation, that is, only in reference to another thing, namely, that which represents" (1819, 1). Schopenhauer believes that the understanding constructs these objects "out of the raw material of a few sensations" (1813, 75). Sensation itself is subjective, a "local specific feeling . . . restricted to the region beneath the skin." As such, sensation "cannot possibly contain anything objective, and so anything resembling intuitive perception."

> One must be forsaken by all the gods to imagine that the world of intuitive perception outside, filling space in its three dimensions, moving on in the inexorably strict course of time, governed at each step by the law of causality that is without exception, but in all these respects merely observing laws that we are able to state prior to all experience thereof – that such a world outside has a real and objective existence without our participation, but then found its way into our heads through mere sensation, where it now has a second existence like the one outside. (1813, 76)

"Subjective sensation becomes objective intuitive perception," according to Schopenhauer, only by means of a "powerful transformation" which occurs "when the understanding applies its sole form, *the law of causality*," to the given sensation. By means of this *a priori* law, the understanding grasps the sensation as an effect for which there must be a cause. It then "summons to its assistance *space*, the form of the *outer* sense also lying predisposed in the intellect."

> This it does in order to place that cause *outside* the organism; for only in this way does there arise for it an outside whose possibility is simply space, so that pure intuition a priori must supply the foundation for empirical perception. In this process . . . the understanding now avails itself of all of the data of the given sensation, even the minutest, in order to construct in space, in conformity therewith, the *cause* of the sensation. . . . [O]nly by this operation and consequently in the understanding and for the understanding does the real, objective, corporeal world, filling space in its three dimensions, present itself (1813, 78).

Nietzsche's classification of the object of perception as a metaphor relies crucially on Schopenhauer's representational theory. That "we believe we know something about the things themselves" when we actually possess "nothing but metaphors for things" means, to begin with, that we believe we perceive extramentally existing things, whereas we actually perceive only representations or images. These representations or metaphors are present to us, Nietzsche makes perfectly clear, only when nerve stimuli are transformed into the perception of external objects. A later passage indicates that Nietzsche accepts Schopenhauer's view as to the crucial role of the *a priori* forms of space and time in this transformation (TL 87–88, WL 885).

> All that we actually know about these laws of nature is what we ourselves bring to them – time and space, and therefore relationships of succession and number. But everything marvelous about the laws of nature, everything that astonishes us therein and seems to demand our explanation, everything that might lead us to distrust idealism: all this is completely and solely contained within the mathematical strictness of our representations of time and space. But we produce these representations in and from ourselves with the same necessity with which the spider spins.

Nietzsche's view of causality's role in the transformation of nerve stimuli is less clear. Breazeale (81) interprets as criticism of Schopenhauer Nietzsche's claim that "the inference from the nerve stimulus to a cause outside of us is already the result of a false and unjustified application of the principle of sufficient reason" (TL 81, WL 878). But Nietzsche's point seems to be in agreement with Schopenhauer's claim that the understanding constructs the external world by applying the principle of causality (one root of the principle of sufficient reason) to sensations, thereby populating our *a priori* representations of space with what we have constructed as the cause of our sensations. When Nietzsche rejects the inference to a cause "outside of us," he merely agrees with Schopenhauer's denial that the principle of causality allows us to infer the existence of anything that exists independently of consciousness. But if Nietzsche agrees with Schopenhauer about our construction of the external world, unlike Schopenhauer, he evidently believes that it involves an illegitimate inference. This makes sense if, in contrast to Schopenhauer, he believes that we take spatially external objects to have existence that is independent of consciousness.

For Schopenhauer, the inference from sensation to an external cause involves a perfectly legitimate application of the principle of causality. We infer the existence of something that exists only within the realm of experience, that is, the realm of representation. The construction of the external world cannot involve an inference to an object that exists independently of consciousness, according to Schopenhauer, for the idea of such an object involves a contradiction in terms. Like Berkeley, Schopenhauer claims to be defending common sense by insisting that the empirical world exists only as representation and not independently of consciousness. Nietzsche, in contrast, apparently thinks that common sense affirms the independent existence of the external world. Nietzsche agrees with Schopenhauer that the world we perceive exists only as representation. But because he thinks "we believe we know something about the things themselves [the extramentally existing things] when we speak of trees, colors, snow, and flowers," he presumably does not reject the whole idea of independently existing objects as contradictory. He simply denies our perceptual access to such objects.

Given his assumption that we perceive only images or appearances rather than the things themselves, Nietzsche reasonably concludes that we can refer only to such appearances, and can say nothing about the things themselves. "Blue" refers only to a sensation we experience in relation to bodies. But even "body" does not refer to anything that exists independently of us, but only to an image the mind constructs out of various sensations. Schopenhauer's representational theory of perception thus allows Nietzsche to infer that we talk and write only about appearances. To draw the conclusion that language is metaphorical and truths illusions, Nietzsche's argument requires one more step: the inference that our linguistic expressions do not correspond to things-in-themselves.

Nietzsche's argument will not seem to require a further step if we conflate things themselves with things-*in*-themselves. But Nietzsche's own words in the passage under consideration mark a distinction between the things themselves [*den Dingen selbst*] and the "mysterious X of the thing in itself [*des Ding an sich*]." The former are simply extramentally existing things in contrast to representations. To speak of "things themselves" is to refer to the world considered as having *existence* independently of perception or representation. The thing-*in*-itself, in contrast, is the world considered *as it is in itself*, that is, considered as possessing a *nature or qualities* apart from human beings. In section 4 below, I will argue that Nietzsche follows the view I attribute to Kant in Chapter 2, which means that "apart from human beings" is equivalent to "independent of human cognitive capacities and interests." To affirm the existence of the Kantian thing-*in*-itself, I have argued, is to insist that, as far as we can determine from our concept of truth, the world's actual nature may be very different from what a theory that would satisfy our best standards of rational acceptability would take it to be. To affirm the existence of things themselves, on the other hand, is merely to reject subjective or Berkeleyan idealism, to insist that the existence of (some) things is independent of (irreducible to) being perceived or represented. These are two quite different affirmations, and the second does not entail the first. To insist that reality consists of independently existing things does not commit one to identifying reality with the Kantian thing-in-itself.

TL appears to reject subjective idealism. Nietzsche assumes the existence of things themselves, objects that exist independently of consciousness. He also identifies these objects with the Kantian thing-in-itself. But his mere affirmation of things themselves does not force him into this Kantian identification of reality with the thing-in-itself. Rather this identification stems from his denial that we have perceptual or linguistic access to things themselves. Nietzsche's representational theory of perception forces him to treat the thing itself (the thing considered as having existence independent of consciousness) as a Kantian thing-in-itself (a thing considered as having qualities independent of human beings). Since the thing itself remains hidden from us (precisely by our representations of it), its nature is also hidden. We can only conceive of this nature as an unknown and unknowable X.

We can sum up Nietzsche's argument for both the metaphorical character of language and the illusory character of truth in the following steps. First, Schopenhauer's representational theory of perception: we do not perceive extramental things, but only representations constructed by the human imagination from nerve stimuli. Second, the inference that we cannot talk about extramental things, but only about our representations of them. Third, the inference that since we cannot therefore say anything about *what* such things are, our linguistic expressions certainly cannot correspond to what they are in themselves. This final step presents a problem to which I shall return in the final section of this chapter.

According to this interpretation, Nietzsche's claims about language play a quite secondary role in his denial of truth. They function only to extend to the realm of theory or science the subjectivity he claims to find in perception. Because the concept is the medium of all theory, and a concept is simply a word insofar as it is used to refer to "countless more or less similar cases" (TL 83, WL 879), it follows that science or theory is constructed on the basis of metaphors, that is, language that reaches only to our representations of things. Contrary to the view that concepts capture a reality inaccessible to perception, Nietzsche considers them twice removed from reality. For we perceive only images, not the things themselves; and we arrive at the concept by overlooking what is "individual and real" in these images. Theory can therefore only pile up "an infinitely complicated dome of concepts upon an unstable foundation, and, as it were, on running water" (TL 85, WL 882).

Far from rejecting the conception of truth as correspondence, Nietzsche's denial of truth evidently presupposes the metaphysical correspondence theory. He concludes that truths are illusions because he assumes both that truth requires correspondence to things-in-themselves and that our truths do not exhibit such correspondence.

This interpretation has the advantage of allowing us to interpret Nietzsche as denying that any of our beliefs are true without requiring him to reject either logic or obvious common sense. I objected earlier to such an interpretation of "truths are illusions" on the grounds that if a statement is false, its contradictory must be true. To reject this claim is to reject logic, leaving us with no basis for interpreting any statement whatsoever. Further, it seems obvious that what we say is often true, for example, when I say "it is raining" and it is raining in my vicinity at the time I say it. But if he believes that truth requires correspondence to things-in-themselves, it is easy to see how Nietzsche could answer such objections. He can claim that both "it is raining" and "it is not raining" concern appearances rather than things themselves, and therefore cannot correspond to things as they are in themselves. It is not that both statements are false; rather they are both illusions. They lack the minimal requisite for truth: saying something about reality as it is in itself.

Recognizing that Nietzsche accepts the metaphysical correspondence theory also allows us to explain his quite obvious emphasis on the arbitrariness of language without forcing us to attribute a simplistic position to him. Given his metaphysical realism, it is hardly surprising that Nietzsche denies that sense perception gives us access to truth (i.e., insists that empirical truths are illusions). Plato and Descartes, among others, agree with him on this point. If we are to possess truth rather than mere appearance, the philosophical tradition tells us that our access to it must be *a priori*, independent of sense experience. In response to the rationalist position that we can win truth by *a priori* means, Nietzsche stresses the conventional character of language.

Nietzsche employs the classical empiricist strategy. He admits the existence of *a priori* truths, but insists that they give no information about reality. Finding truth in the realm of reason (of the *a priori*), Nietzsche writes, is like finding something where one has hidden it (TL 85, WL 883). I interpret this as the Humean position that all *a priori* truths are analytic, that they only state the relation between our ideas, or make explicit what is already contained in our concepts. Given Nietzsche's linguistic view of concepts, this means that *a priori* truths only make explicit the implications of our use of words. If a natural correspondence relation determined the correct words for things, we might discover truths about things-in-themselves by analyzing words. But since arbitrary human conventions determine correctness instead, analytic truths only make clear what our use of words involves – how the use of one is related to the use of others. *A priori* truths give no information about things-in-themselves. This explains why Nietzsche declares that "if one will not be satisfied with truth in the form of 'tautologies' or 'empty husks' " it will always be necessary "to exchange truths for illusions" (TL 81, Wl 878). Because of the conventionality thesis, Nietzsche interprets truth in the realm of reason as mere tautology, and he considers such truth the only alternative to the illusions available in the empirical realm.

4. The metaphysical correspondence theory in "Truth and Lie"

Nietzsche's assumption of the metaphysical correspondence theory seems fairly obvious both when he denies that language can express truth because it is unconcerned with the "thing-in-itself" (TL 82, WL 879), and when he criticizes "anthropomorphic truth" for containing "not a single point that would be 'true in itself' or really and universally valid apart from human beings" (TL 85, WL 883). In both cases, he clearly assumes that reality is independent of human beings and that what fails to correspond to such a reality cannot be true. The question remains as to whether he uses "thing-in-itself" in what I take to be the Kantian sense, and thus whether he interprets truth as independent of human beings in the sense required to make him a metaphysical realist as I have defined that term.

In Chapter 2, I distinguished metaphysical realism from a moderate realism (the third candidate for metaphysical realism) that makes truth independent only of our cognitive capacities. According to moderate realism, as far as we can tell from our concept of truth, the best theory human beings can have reason to accept might still be false. Such realism amounts to no more than an admission of human finitude. It neither relies on nor encourages the intuition that the world is determinately constituted in complete independence of human beings.

Metaphysical realism does rely on that intuition, and therefore holds that truth is independent not only of our capacities, but also of our cognitive interests (best standards of rational acceptability or theory selection). According to the realist$_m$, our concept of truth does not exclude the possibility that a theory that gave us everything else we could want from a theory (e.g., simplicity, coherence, explanatory power, predictive success) might nevertheless fail to be true. I have argued that Descartes accepts the metaphysical form of realism and that Kant accepts it with regard to noumenal reality. On the other hand, Kant rejects metaphysical realism with regard to phenomenal reality. The Kantian thing-in-itself, I have argued, is independent of both our capacities and cognitive interests, whereas phenomenal reality and truth are independent only of our capacities.

According to my interpretation, Nietzsche's mature position is not Kantian, but neo-Kantian. Nietzsche rejects the conceivability of things-in-themselves and therefore rejects metaphysical realism altogether. His view of truth corresponds to Kant's view of truth about phenomenal reality. In TL, on the other hand, Nietzsche accepts the Kantian position that we can conceive of the thing-in-itself and assumes that truth requires correspondence to it. That is, TL accepts metaphysical realism in precisely the sense in which Nietzsche would later reject it. To demonstrate this, I must now show what I have so far assumed: that TL treats things-in-themselves, and therefore truth, following Kant, as independent not only of our cognitive capacities, but also of our cognitive interests.

Consider first what forced Nietzsche to identify reality with the Kantian thing-in-itself. As I have reconstructed the argument, he accepts the existence of independently existing objects. He plausibly identifies these objects with reality (as opposed to what we "make up"). But Nietzsche's acceptance of Schopenhauer's representational account of perception and knowledge makes access to such objects impossible. They remain forever hidden from us precisely by our representations of them. Nietzsche must therefore regard the nature of such objects as the unknowable and "mysterious X of the thing-in-itself." The world therefore possesses a nature that is independent of our capacities. Since it is forever hidden from us, nothing in our concept of truth can guarantee that our best theory might not completely mistake its nature. For the very same reason, truth must be independent of our cognitive interests (or best standards for theory selection). Even if we could remove the limitations on our all-too-finite powers, and could get everything else we wanted cognitively, we would still have no guarantee that our theory would correspond to the hidden object. Therefore, Nietzsche must conceive this object as a Kantian thing-in-itself, a thing whose nature remains independent not only of our capacities, but also of our cognitive interests.

Further, Nietzsche explicitly equates the "thing-in-itself" with the "pure truth apart from consequences" (TL 82, WL 879). Of course, he might mean merely that the truth of a belief is independent of how well it satisfies our practical interests. A concern with practical interests certainly runs throughout TL, and seems to lie at the basis of its denial of truth. The essay's first three paragraphs already make clear that Nietzsche will attempt to expose the deception involved in the human valuation of knowing, at least in part by exposing the connection between knowledge and practical interests (TL 79–80, WL 875–6). We might therefore construe Nietzsche's denial of truth as a deflationary identification of our truths with what satisfies our practical interests, on the assumption that the "pure truth" is independent of these interests. But this interpretation would saddle Nietzsche with the indefensible version of the pragmatic theory of truth discussed in Chapter 2. Further, we can provide a much more charitable interpretation of the pragmatic overtones of TL.

In TL, Nietzsche offers the beginning of the evolutionary theory of cognition he will develop in later works. The theory holds that the human intellect developed as a tool for survival, and that evolutionary considerations (contributions to our ancestors' survival) explain our possession of a particular cognitive constitution – for example, our sense organs and their range, our basic categories and principles of interpretation, including logic. However, this theory does not make the truth of any particular beliefs dependent on its utility for survival. Instead, it uses utility for survival to explain our possession of the framework within which we ask and answer questions, the framework which determines what counts as a good answer. This means that our cognitive interests (standards of rational acceptability) are ultimately rooted in our practical interests. An *a priori* framework of categories and principles that we inherit (either biologically or culturally) because of its survival value determines what counts as a correct answer, and therefore what we have reason to accept as true.

At the beginning of TL, Nietzsche tells us that the intellect originates as a device to maintain us in existence a while longer.

At the essay's end, he contrasts science and art in terms of their relation to practical interests. In science, the intellect acts "like a servant who goes in search of booty and prey for his master" (TL 90, WL 888). The master in question is the "immense framework and planking of concepts to which the needy man clings his whole life long in order to preserve himself." In art, "the intellect is free; it is released from its former slavery" to this framework, which becomes "a scaffolding and toy for the most audacious feats of the liberated intellect." The latter "smashes this framework to pieces, throws it into confusion, and puts it back together in an ironic fashion, pairing the most alien things and separating the closest." None of this implies that any particular scientific doctrine serves our practical interests (and certainly not that it must do so to be considered scientific or true). Rather, scientific doctrines remain subservient to the cognitive framework that our practical interests erect. Nietzsche does not deny that our truths (the ones he calls "illusions") are independent of our practical interests. Rather, he denies that these illusions are independent of our cognitive interests. When he identifies the thing-in-itself with the "pure truth apart from consequences," then, Nietzsche cannot mean that the pure truth (unlike our illusory truths) is independent of our practical interests, but must mean that it is independent of our cognitive interests. In thus making truth independent of both our capacities and cognitive interests, TL accepts metaphysical realism in precisely the sense in which Nietzsche will later reject it.

If this is correct, Nietzsche's insistence that our truths are illusions does not, contrary to Heidegger (see Chapter 1), stem from a deficiency in the understanding of truth as correspondence (or correctness). Nietzsche concludes that truths are illusions not because he understands truth as correspondence to reality, but because he believes the reality to which truths correspond must be completely independent of human beings, of both our capacities and our cognitive interests.

I have so far suggested that Nietzsche's acceptance of this metaphysical correspondence theory can be explained in terms of the representationalism he inherited from Schopenhauer. However, while representationalism does explain why Nietzsche identifies reality with the thing-in-itself, it does not explain his insistence that truth requires correspondence to this reality. Why does he not regard correspondence to phenomenal reality as a plausible candidate for truth? The deeper explanation for his interpretation of truth as correspondence to things-in-themselves is suggested by his claim that *a priori* truths are of "limited value."

Given Nietzsche's interpretation of *a priori* truths as mere tautologies, that he considers them of limited value is hardly surprising. However, his reason is surprising. He minimizes the value of such truths *not* because they provide no information about reality, but rather because they contain "not a single point that would be 'true in itself' or really and universally valid apart from human beings" (TL 85, WL 883). This emphasis on the thoroughly anthropomorphic character of tautologies is certainly gratuitous as proof of their limited value. Here we get a clue as to Nietzsche's underlying reason for accepting the metaphysical correspondence theory. Nietzsche gives the very same reason for calling empirical truths "illusions" as he gives for taking *a priori* truths to be of limited value. He even calls the empirical world the "anthropomorphic world" (TL 88, WL 886). We can therefore interpret Nietzsche's denial of truth as the claim that human truths possess only limited value because they fail to correspond to things-in-themselves. His denial makes sense only if he considers truth to possess unlimited value, that is, unlimited by considerations of happiness or utility (cf. GS 344). Thus, Nietzsche accepts the metaphysical correspondence theory because he believes that only "universal validity apart from human beings" can confer on beliefs the unlimited value he associates with truth.

But Nietzsche certainly does not consider his valuation of truth idiosyncratic. As I have already pointed out, the first paragraphs of TL make clear that it aims to expose the deception involved in the human evaluation of knowing. We should therefore expect the remainder of the essay to substantiate the charge that we are deceived about the value of human knowledge. This gives us reason to interpret "truths are illusions" as Nietzsche's denial that our (empirical) truths have the unlimited value human beings believe they possess.

We can now interpret "truths are illusions" as a claim that the beliefs we recognize as truths do not possess the unlimited value we assume to be possessed by anything deserving of that title. This provides an answer to the objection raised above to the claim that truths are illusions, the objection that it is either false or the expression of an arbitrary decision to call "illusions" what we call "truths." That "truths are illusions" may be an unconventional way of putting Nietzsche's point, but it is not arbitrary since it is based on what Nietzsche takes to be a generally accepted assumption concerning the value of truth. If Nietzsche's position is to be rejected, it will be necessary to reject one of the premises from which it follows: that truth is of unlimited value, that only correspondence to things-in-themselves could give our beliefs unlimited value, and that our beliefs do not correspond to things-in-themselves.

My interpretation in Chapter 6 suggests that the first two premises are vulnerable to Nietzsche's later criticism of the ascetic ideal. In the remainder of this chapter, I argue that there are grounds internal to TL for objecting to the third premise.

5. An internal critique of "Truth and Lie"

We can bring out the difficulty for Nietzsche's denial that our truths correspond to things-in-themselves by comparing TL with the book Nietzsche published a year earlier: *The Birth of Tragedy* (BT). BT also denies that the truths of common sense and science correspond to reality (see Clark, 1987). Regarding truth, BT and TL differ only in relation to BT's claim that Dionysian experience alone gives access to things-in-themselves. TL denies that we have any access whatsoever to things-in-themselves. But how can Nietzsche have a basis for denying that our truths correspond to things-in-themselves when he denies we have any access to these things? In BT, he could claim to have a basis because he claimed to know the transcendent character of reality – contradictory, outside of time and space, beyond individuality and plurality – a character clearly quite different from its empirical character. He could then conclude that the empirical world distorts the true world, assigning responsibility for this distortion to the *a priori* forms (time, space, causality) by means of which the mind structures the world as possible objects of will. But once Nietzsche reverts to Kant with his denial that we can know anything about transcendent reality, how can he know that the empirical world fails to correspond to the transcendent? How can he know that the subservience of will to practical interests distorts the true world or precludes such correspondence?

I have so far written as if the failure to refer to things themselves, as opposed to representations, insures that language cannot say what things are in themselves. But this is not as obvious as it seems. That we refer to representations rather than things does not preclude the possibility that everything we say about our representations is true of the very things hidden by our representations. In that case, reality would be exactly as we believe it is. Our truths would correspond to things as they are in themselves.

Nietzsche appreciates this problem. After asserting that "even our contrast between the individual and species is something anthropomorphic and does not originate in the essence of things," he adds that "we should not presume to claim that this contrast does not correspond to the essence of things: that would of course be a dogmatic assertion and, as such, would be just as undemonstrable as its opposite" (TL 83–4, WL 880). Because such agnosticism regarding transcendent truth seems the more defensible position, some commentators believe that Nietzsche maintained an agnostic position throughout TL, and even throughout his career (e.g., Grimm). This interpretation seems to gain support from Nietzsche's explicit agnosticism regarding the metaphysical world in *Human, All-Too-Human* (HA 9). But, as I argue in Chapter 4, the agnosticism of HA has a different emphasis from that expressed in TL.

Further, Nietzsche does not maintain the agnosticism of TL throughout the essay. Prior to his agnostic statement, Nietzsche unambiguously asserts that our statements "correspond in no way to the original essences" (TL 83, WL 879), an assertion that amounts to atheism rather than agnosticism in regard to transcendent truth. After his agnostic statement, Nietzsche reverts to atheism when he insists on the difficulty of admitting to oneself that (TL 86, WL 884)

> the insect or the bird perceives an entirely different world from the one that human beings do, and that the question as to which one of these perceptions of the world is the more correct is quite meaningless, for this would have to be decided by the standard of *correct perception*, which means by a standard which is *not available*. But in any case it seems to me that "the correct perception" – which means "the adequate expression of an object in the subject" – is a contradictory impossibility [*ein widerspruchsvolles Unding*].

Nietzsche's earlier remarks make clear that he equates "the adequate expression of an object in the subject" with "the pure truth apart from consequences," and that the latter amounts to correspondence to things-in-themselves (TL 81–82, WL 879). We must therefore interpret Nietzsche as claiming that correspondence to things-in-themselves is a "contradictory impossibility." This makes him an atheist regarding transcendent truth. Our statements cannot correspond to transcendent reality if the very idea of such correspondence involves a contradiction.

But if this is Nietzsche's position, he has no need to resort to the agnosticism discussed above. If the very idea of transcendent truth (correspondence to things-in-themselves) is contradictory, it is no more dogmatic to deny that our beliefs possess it than it is to deny that the world contains a square triangle. Why, then, did Nietzsche feel pushed to agnosticism? I suggest that TL contains two incompatible denials of transcendent truth. The first is the Kantian version Nietzsche adopts through most of the essay. Transcendent truth is both conceivable and of overriding value, but unattainable for human beings. The second is neo-Kantian or Nietzschean. Transcendent truth is inconceivable, a contradiction in terms. While the neo-Kantian position escapes vulnerability to the charge of dogmatism, the Kantian position does not. Nietzsche responds to the objection to his Kantian position by adopting agnosticism, the third different position taken in the essay regarding the existence of transcendent truth. But if the neo-Kantian position would not require such qualification, why did Nietzsche adopt the Kantian position in the first place?

The obvious answer is that only the Kantian position provides a basis for considering truths illusions. As I have reconstructed its argument, TL aims to show that science does not possess the value we attribute to it. Nietzsche argues that the beliefs we recognize as truths do not possess the higher value we associate with truth because they do not correspond to things-in-themselves. But if the very idea of such correspondence involves a contradiction in terms, science is hardly limited by its inability to attain it. If this idea does indeed involve a contradiction, then transcendent truth can no more exist than can square triangles. That neither God nor science can acquire the former or construct the latter has no effect on the claim of either to omniscience, or omnipotence. To recognize clearly the contradictory nature of correspondence to things-in-themselves makes it impossible to believe in its higher value, or in the lower value of our truths insofar as they fail to exhibit such correspondence. Nietzsche needed the Kantian belief in the conceivability of transcendent truth to have a basis for devaluing human truths as illusions. But the Kantian position is vulnerable to the charge of dogmatism. Therefore Nietzsche momentarily adopts agnosticism regarding transcendent truth. But this agnosticism did not adequately reflect his basic certainty, to which most of the essay attests, that our beliefs fail to correspond to the thing-in-itself. Nor would agnosticism support Nietzsche's devaluation of human truths. Nietzsche therefore reverts to atheism, but now in its neo-Kantian form. Transcendent truth becomes a "contradictory impossibility." Nietzsche can now explain how he knows that we cannot attain transcendent truth. On the other hand, he loses all basis for his devaluation of *human* truths.

Nietzsche could believe that the argument of TL served its purpose only by failing to distinguish the three mutually inconsistent positions that together constitute the unstable amalgamation that is TL's denial of truth. Clearly distinguishing these positions would have forced Nietzsche to realize that he could maintain his denial of transcendent truth only in its neo-Kantian form. But, as I have been arguing, to accept this neo-Kantian position Nietzsche would have to abandon both his commitment to the value of transcendent truth and therefore to the metaphysical correspondence theory upon which TL's denial of truth depends.

4

THE DEVELOPMENT OF NIETZSCHE'S LATER POSITION ON TRUTH

This chapter provides evidence that Nietzsche's later works overcome TL's denial of truth. In these works, Nietzsche was able to adopt unambiguously the neo-Kantian position of TL – the rejection of transcendent or metaphysical truth as a contradiction in terms – because he rejected as contradictory the very idea of a thing-in-itself. He thereby lost all basis for denying truth, or for its equivalent, the thesis that human knowledge falsifies reality. I will offer this reasoning as the best explanation for the absence of the falsification thesis in Nietzsche's last six books. Although Nietzsche himself initially failed to appreciate this implication of his neo-Kantian position, there is evidence that he later recognized this failure, and my interpretation offers a way of explaining why it occurred.

1. The rejection of the thing-in-itself

Human, All-Too-Human (1878) already differs significantly from TL. The latter's denial of truth shared with BT the aim of devaluing the truths accessible through science and common sense and establishing the cognitive superiority of art. Nietzsche completely repudiates this aim in HA. He now regards it as the mark of a higher culture to value "the little unpretentious truths" won by strict or scientific method more highly than "the beautifying and brilliant errors" of metaphysical and artistic ages (HA 3).

HA may seem to take a position very similar to TL's devaluation of human truths. It explicitly equates the "world as representation" – the world of perception and common sense – with "the world as error" (HA 19). At one point (last line of HA 19), the reason even seems to be TL's reason for denying truth: that the world as representation does not correspond to the thing-in-itself. More often, however, a quite different reason operates. HA considers the world of common sense erroneous because it fails to correspond to the world disclosed by science (HA 10).

In contrast to TL, HA considers the thing-in-itself of little interest. The "strongest interest in the purely theoretical problem of the 'thing-in-itself' and the 'appearance' will cease," predicts Nietzsche, once the origins of religion, art, and morality can be explained without recourse to metaphysics (HA 10). He bases this prediction on the following account of the origin of the distinction in question. The world became "colorful, frightful, profound, and soulful" because human beings projected into it their own "moral, aesthetic, and religious pretensions," as well as their fears, passions, and mistaken conceptions. "That which we now call the world is the result of a host of errors and fantasies which have gradually arisen and grown entwined with one another" and which "are now inherited by us as the accumulated treasure of the entire past." When human beings began to reflect, they were unable to find in the world what they had projected into it. This led to the distinction between two worlds, the thing-in-itself and the world of appearance (HA 16). Unable to find evidence of moral motivation in the world as it appears to us, for instance, they posited moral motivation in the world (or the self) as it is in itself. Nietzsche therefore proposes that naturalistic explanations for the so-called higher human activities would render the thing-in-itself theoretically superfluous. He attempts to provide such explanations by practicing "historical philosophy which is no longer to be thought of as separate from the natural sciences" (HA 1). He argues, for instance, that there are no morally motivated actions, but only egoistic actions mistakenly believed to be unegoistic.[1] Using the same approach to other "higher" activities throughout HA, Nietzsche argues that these activities are not what they seem, but only "human, all-too-human." He also gives a historical account of why they would have seemed more than human. "Strict science is able to liberate us from this world of representation only slightly," Nietzsche writes, because

> it cannot break the force of primitive habits of feeling: but it can gradually elucidate the history of the rise of the world as representation – and, at least for a moment, lift us beyond the whole process. Perhaps we will then recognize that the thing-in-itself is worth a Homeric laugh: that it seemed so much, indeed everything, and is actually empty, namely, empty of meaning (HA 16).

We must conclude therefore that HA represents a change from the position of TL. Nietzsche still believes that most of our beliefs are false. But he can now explain how he knows they are false, namely, that they are incompatible with what we learn through "strict science." Thus, Nietzsche apparently believes that science, especially in its "greatest triumph" – his own "history of the origins of thought" (HA 16) – gives access to truth, even though he does not claim that such truths correspond to the thing-in-itself. This is just what we would expect if he resolved the difficulties in the argument of TL by unambiguously accepting the neo-Kantian position he articulated in that essay: that the whole idea of corespondence to things-in-themselves (i.e., of transcendent truth) is a contradiction in terms.

However, Nietzsche does not reach that point in HA. Instead he adopts TL's agnostic position regarding transcendent truth.

> It is true that there might be a metaphysical world; the absolute possibility of it can hardly be disputed. We view all things through the human head and cannot cut this head off; though the question remains, what of the world would still be there if it had been cut off (HA 9).

1. I argue for this interpretation of HA's critique of morality in the first chapter of my dissertation, "Nietzsche's Attack on Morality." This interpretation is based in large part on a comparison of HA and D. Among the passages from HA that support it are HA 133 and 138, as compared, for instance, to D 9 and 103.

A metaphysical world, on Nietzsche's account, is a *"second real world"* (HA 5), one that differs radically from the empirical world, and therefore, given HA's rejection of metaphysical or *a priori* knowledge, from any world human beings can know. To believe in a metaphysical world is to believe that our best empirical theory is not merely false, but radically false.

I interpret the metaphysical in these terms because Nietzsche claims that the metaphysical conception of the world differs widely from what can be disclosed empirically (HA 10) and that knowledge of the metaphysical world would be "the most useless of all knowledge: more useless even than knowledge of the chemical components of water must be to the sailor in danger of shipwreck" (HA 9). Since HA does not assume that scientific knowledge has direct practical value, the point of this remark is that the metaphysical world does not connect up in any way with the kind of knowledge accessible to human beings. It is not as if we could get to the metaphysical world from where we are by a process of internal criticism, or by developing better theories. Even acquiring information that is in principle inaccessible to human beings would not suffice to give access to a metaphysical world, for such information might be very helpful to us, that is, might help us solve our cognitive problems. HA 9 implies that metaphysics – knowledge of the metaphysical world – would not provide answers that we could find cognitively useful. I formulate this point as the claim that for Nietzsche the metaphysical world differs *radically* from the empirical.

Nietzsche's understanding of a metaphysical world is closely related to the second way of conceptualizing the thing-in-itself discussed in Chapter 2. To believe in the thing-in-itself, on this account, is to believe that truth and reality are independent not only of our capacities, but also of our cognitive interests, in the sense that what would satisfy our best standards of rational acceptability might still be false. As I use the phrase "radically" above, to believe in the thing-in-itself is to believe that our best theory *might* be not only false, but radically false, that the truth *might* differ radically from what can be manifest to us. To believe in a metaphysical world, in contrast, is to believe that our best theory (which would be an empirical theory, given Nietzsche's view in HA) *is* radically false, that truth *does* differ from what would satisfy our cognitive interests.

Belief in a metaphysical world therefore presupposes belief in the existence or conceivability of the thing-in-itself but is not identical to it. There is a metaphysical world only if truth differs radically from what human beings can know (empirically), whereas the world is a thing-in-itself if (as far as we can tell from our concept of truth) its true nature *might* differ radically from the best human theory of it. HA's claim that there *might* be a metaphysical world therefore amounts to the claim that there *is* a thing-in-itself, that is, that the world's true nature is independent of (but not necessarily different from) the best human theory.

This way of construing the difference between the thing-in-itself and the metaphysical world allows for the possibility of a metaphysical realism, an understanding of truth as correspondence to the thing-in-itself, that affirms the ability of empirical science to give us truth. Such realism would insist that the truth could have differed from what satisfies our cognitive interests, but in fact does not, due to the goodness of God (Descartes) or the contingent requirements of the evolutionary process (contemporary scientific realism).

HA's position on the metaphysical world is equivalent to TL's agnosticism regarding truth. We cannot rule out the possibility that the truth differs radically from our best theory, but we cannot know whether or not it does. This means that we cannot know whether or not our truths correspond to things-in-themselves or possess metaphysical truth. HA's position therefore remains incompatible with the neo-Kantian rejection of metaphysical truth. However, the agnosticism of HA shows a marked change of emphasis. In TL, Nietzsche resorted momentarily to agnosticism when he recognized an objection to his much greater temptation to affirm a metaphysical world (to insist that truth does indeed differ from what can be disclosed empirically). In HA, on the other hand, his agnosticism fights what would otherwise be his tendency to discard the whole idea of a metaphysical world. He cannot yet discard it because he has not yet found a way to deny the conceivability of the thing-in-itself.

By the time he writes *Beyond God and Evil* (1886), Nietzsche evidently thinks he has found a way. The following passage explicitly rejects the conceivability of the thing-in-itself.

That "immediate certainty," as well as "absolute knowledge" and the "thing-in-itself," involve a *contradicto in adjecto,* I shall repeat a

hundred times; we really ought to free ourselves from the seduction of words! (B 16)

The remainder of this passage explains Nietzsche's criticism of
the idea of "immediate certainty." It does not make obvious why
the very idea of the thing-in-itself involves a contradiction in
terms. The best explanation I can find in the published works
belongs to *The Gay Science* (1882). In GS 54, Nietzsche repeats the
claim of HA, that the appearance of things to human beings is
determined by what we have inherited from our "human and
animal past, indeed [from] the whole primal age and the past of
all sentient being" (GS 54). However, he no longer stresses the
erroneous character of this apparent world. Instead, he writes:

> What is "appearance" for me now? Certainly not the opposite of
> some essence: what could I say about any essence except to name
> the attributes of its appearance! Certainly not a mask that one
> could place on an unknown X or remove from it! (GS 54)

In TL, Nietzsche wrote of the "mysterious X of the thing-in-
itself" and equated it with "the essence of things" (WL 880, TL
83). The passage above evidently denies that we have any way of
conceiving of such an essence. Nietzsche offers the same argument against the thing-in-itself discussed in Chapter 2, that we
have no way of conceiving of a thing's essence except in terms of
its appearance. If we can conceive of what something is only in
terms of its possible appearances, we have no way of conceiving
of it as it is in itself.

This argument is effective against the thing-in-itself only if we
conceptualize the latter in the first and most obviously objectionable way discussed in Chapter 2, that is, if the thing-in-itself is
independent of (possibly different from) how it could appear to
any possible knower. If we can think of a thing's essence only in
terms of its possible appearances, we cannot think of its essence
as independent of these appearances. But this seems compatible
with understanding its essence as independent of its possible
appearances to human beings, thus insisting on the possibility of
a metaphysical world.

I nevertheless believe that the argument of GS 54 gives Nietzsche all he needs to reject the positions of both TL and HA. TL is
the more obvious case because it explicitly makes the thing-in-

itself into an unknowable essence, forever concealed from view by the thing's appearances. Given TL's representational view of knowledge, this essence must be independent of its appearances not only to human beings, but to any possible knower. Because the object known is always a representation, the thing itself is always hidden by the representation, and its essence may differ from it. This Nietzsche explicitly rejects when he claims that we can think of a thing's essence only in terms of its possible appearances.

HA, on the other hand, does not so clearly commit Nietzsche to an essence that is independent of all possible appearances. In refusing to rule out a metaphysical world, it insists only that truth or essence might differ radically from its possible appearances to human beings. Further, the reason Nietzsche gives for this claim seems convincing:

> We view all these through the human head and cannot cut this head off; though the question remains, what of the world would still be there if it had been cut off (HA 9).

Because we only know things as they appear to us, we obviously cannot know what they would be like if we could remove from their appearance what our way of knowing contributes. How, then, could we possibly know that reality and truth do not differ radically from how things appear to us?

From the viewpoint of GS and later works, the problem with this argument – in particular, with the question as to "what of the world would still be there if [the human head] had been cut off" – is that it presupposes that a thing's essence is independent of all its possible appearances. It suggests that if we could only subtract the contribution our mode of knowing makes to a thing's appearance, we would know what it really is, what it is in itself. But there are two ways to understand "what it really is." The most obvious is "what it is independently of how it appears." In this case, the argument of HA 9 presupposes what GS 54 rejects: the possibility of an essence that differs from all of the thing's appearances. To avoid interpreting HA 9 in these terms, we would have to take its final question to mean that, for all we can know, there might be a better or more adequate way of knowing things than the ways available to human beings. But HA 9 does not seem concerned with other ways of knowing. It suggests a comparison not of human with other ways of knowing, but of a thing's appearance to humans with what it is apart from our way of knowing it. And even if "what it is apart from our way of knowing it" does mean "what it is in relation to a better way of knowing," Nietzsche's argument could not establish the conclusion he wants – that there might be a metaphysical world – unless it presupposes that the thing's essence is independent of its appearances to all knowers. For we must ask what would make the other way of knowing "better." If we say that its results correspond more closely to what the thing really is, we imply that the thing's essence is independent of all of its appearances. To avoid this implication, we would have to say that the other way of knowing is superior because it would, if we could only have it, satisfy our standards of rational acceptability or cognitive interests (other than truth) better than does our own way. In this case, however, we would be talking not about a metaphysical world, but about another world of appearance. As I have argued earlier in this section, HA 9 denies that belief in a metaphysical world would be cognitively useful to us. Its truth or superiority to the empirical world clearly cannot depend on its ability to satisfy our cognitive interests (other than truth).

Therefore, HA's commitment to the thing-in-itself in the apparently innocuous sense – that reality and truth differ radically from their appearance to human beings – actually relies on the more obviously objectionable idea of the thing-in-itself, on the assumption that reality might differ from any of its possible appearances. Nietzsche's argument against the latter in GS 54 is therefore effective against both senses of the thing-in-itself, and therefore against HA's claim that there might be a metaphysical world (see section 4 for more on this issue).

Because he thus repudiates the thing-in-itself as a contradiction in terms, Nietzsche should be able to adopt fully and unambiguously the neo-Kantian position of TL. His position should be that our beliefs do fail to correspond to things-in-themselves, but that, since the whole idea of such things is a contradiction in terms, we cannot consider our knowledge limited or devalued by this "failure." This would leave no basis for understanding truth as correspondence to the thing-in-itself or for judging the truth of our beliefs in terms of such correspondence. Nietzsche would therefore lose the basis for TL's denial of truth and should admit that many of our beliefs are true. The question is whether Nietzsche himself drew this conclusion from his denial of the thing-in-itself. The following sections of this chapter offer evidence that he did.

2. Truth and science in Nietzsche's later works

The most important evidence that Nietzsche drew the correct conclusion from BG's rejection of the thing-in-itself is his remarkably changed view of truth thereafter. In the six books that follow BG, there is no evidence of Nietzsche's earlier denial of truth: no claim that the human world is a falsification, no claim that science, logic, or mathematics falsify reality.

GS and BG do retain TL's claim that truths are illusions. GS insists that only art allows us to bear "the realization of the general untruth and mendaciousness [*Verlogenheit*] that is now given us through science – the realization that delusion and error are conditions of human knowledge and sensation" (GS 107). BG suggests that the human world is a "fiction" (BG 34), and that at its best, science keeps us in a "suitably falsified world" (BG 24). In both works, logic itself appears as a source of error (BG 4; GS 111). In apparent contrast to HA, Nietzsche now counts as falsifications not merely common sense views, but also scientific ones. Although he no longer counts falsity as an objection to a view (BG 4), his conclusion otherwise seems identical to TL's.

In works after BG, we find a completely different view. These works begin with *On the Genealogy of Morals* (1887), the first section of which claims that "such truths do exist" – "plain, harsh, ugly, repellent, unchristian, immoral" truths (GM I, 1). Nowhere does this work qualify its initial claim, suggest that such truths are illusions, or that they are not really true. GM does give powerful expression to Nietzsche's perspectivism, and to his claim that the belief in truth expresses the ascetic ideal. I argue in the next two chapters that these positions affirm rather than deny the existence of truth and actually constitute a critique of Nietzsche's earlier denial of truth. If we prescind for the moment from these two controversial Nietzschean positions, it becomes difficult to find in Nietzsche's final six books any remnant of TL's denial of truth or to avoid the conclusion that his view of truth has changed radically.

Twilight of the Idols and *The Antichrist* make this change most evident. In these books, Nietzsche no longer claims that science falsifies reality. Instead, he celebrates science as "the wisdom of the world" (i.e., of "this" world), which Paul wanted to make something shameful (A 47), and presents science as the great liberator from the falsifications perpetuated by religion and metaphysics, which were invented to exploit and prolong any natural tendency to error that may be found among human beings. In contrast to the suggestion in BG and GS that causality falsifies, he identifies science with "the sound conception of cause and effect," and claims that the concepts of guilt and punishment – *"lies* through and through" – were invented *"against* science, *against* the emancipation of man from the priest to destroy man's causal sense: they are an attempt to assassinate cause and effect" (A 49). An even more striking account of what Christianity destroyed comes ten sections later:

> The whole labor of the ancient world *in vain:* I have no word to express my feelings about something so tremendous. . . . Wherefore Greeks? Wherefore Romans?
>
> All the presuppositions for a scholarly culture, all the scientific methods, were already there; the great, the incomparable art of reading well had already been established – that presupposition for the tradition of culture, for the unity of science, natural science, allied with mathematics and mechanics, was well along on the best way – the *sense for facts*, the last and most valuable sense, had its schools and tradition of centuries (A 59).

The theologian, on the other hand, shows an

> *incapacity for philology.* What is here meant by philology is, in a very broad sense, the art of reading well – of reading facts without falsifying them by interpretation, without losing caution, patience, delicacy, in the desire to understand. Philology as *ephexis* in interpretation . . . The manner in which a theologian, in Berlin as in Rome, interprets a verse of Scripture or an event – for instance, a victory of the armies of the fatherland in the higher light of the Psalms of David – is always so audacious that it makes a philologist climb the walls (A 52).

In contrast to his earlier claims that "delusion and error are conditions of human knowledge and sensation" and that mathematics and logic falsify reality (GS 107–11), Nietzsche takes the following position:

And what magnificent instruments of observation we possess in our senses! . . . Today we possess science precisely to the extent that we have decided to *accept* the testimony of the senses – to the extent to which we sharpen them further, arm them, and have learned to think them through. The rest is miscarriage and not-yet-science – in other words, metaphysics, theology, psychology, epistemology – or formal science, a doctrine of signs, such as logic and that applied logic which is called mathematics. In them reality is not encountered at all, not even as a problem – no more than the value of such a sign-convention as logic (TI III, 3).

Because he treats logic and mathematics as formal sciences that make no claims about reality, Nietzsche must surely abandon his earlier claim that they falsify reality. He also rejects as "miscarriage" doctrines which can get off the ground only on the assumption (shared by Plato, Descartes, Schopenhauer, and the early Nietzsche, among others) that the senses deceive us, that they tell us only about "appearance," and not reality. He evidently calls metaphysics and theology "miscarriage" because they cannot be done on an empirical basis, and psychology and epistemology "not-yet-science" because they are not yet done on such a basis, that is, one that respects the relevance of sense testimony.

These passages from TI and A contain no hint of the view that human truths, science, logic, mathematics, or causality falsify reality. Instead, they exhibit a uniform and unambiguous respect for facts, the senses, and science. I find nothing in Nietzsche's final six works that contradicts them. TI's analysis of how the "True World" became a fable might be presented as a counterexample. Section 3 argues that it supports my interpretation. The only other plausible counterexample – prescinding again from Nietzsche's perspectivism and his claim that truth expresses the ascetic ideal – is TI's claim that "the lie of unity, the lie of thinghood, the lie of substance" involve "falsification of the testimony of the senses" (TI III, 2). Wilcox (1974, 133) includes this passage (the only one he cites from works after BG) in his list of those that give evidence of Nietzsche's belief that concepts falsify reality. I will argue against his interpretation to help show that Nietzsche does not claim that knowledge falsifies in his last six works.

If the quoted line meant that the application of any concept of a thing, and any notion of permanence or unity, involve lies or falsification, it would imply that knowledge inevitably falsifies. In works after BT, Nietzsche denies the existence of nonconceptual knowledge. But concepts always involve unity, and some level of permanence. One cannot know something as a desk, a book, or an electron if one merely apprehends a "chaos of sensation." However, there is no reason to think that Nietzsche regards as inevitable the lies or falsification he discusses in this passage. He explains that " 'reason' is the cause of our falsification of the testimony of the senses" (TI III, 2). Because he places it in quotation marks, Nietzsche evidently does not use "reason" to refer to a faculty he believes human beings possess. He evidently refers instead to the interpretation of our faculty for reasoning by those with whom he disagrees, to the interpretation of reason as a nonnatural faculty (as belonging to human beings only insofar as they participate in a world other than the natural or animal world), and as capable of knowledge of reality uncontaminated by connection to the senses. In that case, "reason" means "pure reason," the faculty of *a priori* knowledge. Nietzsche denies the existence of such a faculty, which is equivalent to rejecting nonnatural interpretations of our reasoning abilities. Chapter 6 will argue that Nietzsche also analyzes such interpretations as expressions of an ideal he rejects, the ascetic ideal. But if only this nonexistent faculty (this wrong and ascetic interpretation of reason) forces us to falsify the testimony of the senses, this falsification is not inevitable. It is forced upon us only by the dispensable assumption that such a faculty exists, by the interpretation of reason as a non-natural faculty.

Nietzsche suggests how this works when he identifies "reason" with "faith in grammar," and "the presuppositions of reason" with "the basic presuppositions of the metaphysics of language" (TI III, 5). This might imply the inevitability of falsification if "faith in grammar" were a matter of following, or believing that one ought to follow, grammatical rules. But it would be completely implausible to equate such faith with "reason" (i.e., a belief in pure reason). Nietzsche's claim is much more plausible if he is suggesting instead (as he seems to be, most obviously in TI III, 5) that philosophers were able to believe in "reason," that is, in their capacity for *a priori* knowledge, because they assumed that grammar reflected the structure of reality. This means that philosophers believed they had nonempirical access to reality and a basis for rejecting the relevance of sense testimony because they were reading (misreading, on Nietzsche's account) the structure of reality off of the structure of language. Whereas the senses show "becoming, passing away, and change" (TI III, 2), the subject-predicate structure of our language(s) led them to assume an underlying substrate for change, something that does not itself change, but which is the subject of properties which do change. The latter is the concept of a thing or substance that Nietzsche holds responsible for "falsifying the testimony of the senses."

We therefore have no reason to suppose that TI presents our ordinary concept of a thing as a "lie." A thing in this ordinary sense remains the "same thing" when we can attribute to it spatio-temporal continuity under the same concept, even though the thing itself will have changed in the process. It seems highly implausible that "everything empirical plainly contradicted" the assumption that this concept of a thing has application. But that is precisely what Nietzsche says about the concepts or categories of reason he calls "lies" and "errors" (TI III, 2–5). To avoid attributing to Nietzsche such an implausible position, we can take the concept of a thing he calls a "lie" to be the metaphysical concept of a substance, the concept of an unchanging substrate that underlies all change.

That Nietzsche understood the metaphysical concept of substance as an unchanging substrate is clear from the following passage of HA.

> *Fundamental Questions of Metaphysics.* – When one day the history of the genesis of thought comes to be written, the following sentence by a distinguished logician will also stand revealed in a new light: "The primary universal law of the knowing subject consists in the inner necessity of recognizing every object in itself as being in its own essence something identical with itself, thus self-existent and at bottom always the same and unchanging, in short as a substance." (HA 18)

HA insists that this belief in "unconditioned substances and identical things is a primary, ancient error committed by everything organic," and that we have inherited it from "the period of the lower organisms" (HA 18). In both HA and GS, Nietzsche considers this belief in self-identical, unchanging things or substances a purely intellectual error, caused by a failure to notice changes in things (HA 18; GS 111). The TI passage offers an alternative explanation of the same belief. Rather than a purely intellectual error, Nietzsche now finds its ultimate source in philosophers' "hatred of the very idea of becoming" (TI III, 1). This fits with Nietzsche's new view, articulated in BG 6, that philosophers have always employed understanding "and misunderstanding" as a "mere instrument" (see Chapters 6 and 7 for more on this). Philosophers' hatred of becoming prejudiced them in favor of being, and inclined them to consider being and becoming mutually exclusive. "Whatever has being does not become; whatever becomes does not have being" (TI III, 1). To defend their prejudice in the face of empirical evidence that everything changes, they claimed that the senses – "which are also so immoral otherwise" (TI III, 1) – deceive us about reality, making it appear to involve becoming. To render this plausible, they had to claim that nonempirical access to reality showed them that reality excludes becoming. They therefore had to interpret reason as "reason," a faculty of *a priori* knowledge. But they also needed something to make this plausible, and they found it, Nietzsche suggests, in "faith in grammar," the tendency to suppose that the structure of language gives us knowledge of the world (cf. HA 11). If the subject-predicate structure of language reflects the nature of the world, it can seem plausible, for instance, that all change involves an underlying substrate, something that does not itself change. Because the senses showed no such thing, philosophers could then seem to have a nonempirical mode of access to reality and a reason to reject the relevance of sense testimony.

If this interpretation is correct, the concepts Nietzsche calls "lies" are quite dispensable. They show up not in common sense beliefs or the sciences, but rather in the *a priori* philosophical disciplines Nietzsche rejects as "miscarriage" (TI II, 3). Of course, nonphilosophers also make use of the concepts in question, particularly in the case of the ego or soul and God, but Nietzsche certainly thinks we can and should dispense with these concepts. (When he denies that we need get rid of the "soul" in BG 12, he specifically rejects the idea of the soul as an unchanging substrate). His final six books do nothing to suggest that these "concepts of reason" need be involved in either the common sense picture of the world of relatively enduring middle-sized objects or the scientific world-view.

Nietzsche's last six books therefore provide no evidence of his commitment to the falsification thesis, no reason to deny his commitment to the possibility of truth in science, nor to the truth of his own theories. Given his earlier works, this seems remarkable and in need of explanation. I find the most plausible explanation to be that Nietzsche abandoned the falsification thesis because he realized that his account of the thing-in-itself as a contradiction in terms deprived him of any basis for it. It constitutes a major objection to this explanation, however – and is probably the main reason other commentators have not seen Nietzsche's development in the way I propose – that Nietzsche maintains his denial of truth in the very works in which he rejects the thing-in-itself. If he abandons his denial of truth because he recognizes its dependence on the thing-in-itself, why does he continue to insist that science, logic, mathematics, and causality falsify reality in GS and BG, the works in which he rejects the thing-in-itself as a contradiction in terms? My next section provides evidence that it took Nietzsche some time to realize that his denial of truth depended on the assumption of a thing-in-itself.

3. The error of the "true world"

Nietzsche includes "How the 'True World' Finally Became a Fable" in *Twilight of the Idols,* one of his last books. If we equate the "true world" with truth, this story provides strong evidence that he continued to regard truths as illusions (fictions, or fables). I will argue that we have reason to interpret it instead as evidence that Nietzsche abandoned his denial of truth in his last works because of its dependence on the thing-in-itself. It also provides evidence of Nietzsche's realization that he initially failed to draw the correct conclusion from his rejection of the thing-in-itself.

Subtitled "The History of an Error," Nietzsche's story contains six stages, six different sets of beliefs concerning the "true" world. In each case, the "true" world is contrasted with "this" world, the merely apparent or illusory world. Nietzsche makes this clear just before he presents his history.

> *First Proposition.* The reasons for which "this" world has been characterized as "apparent" are the very reasons which indicate its reality; any other kind of reality is absolutely indemonstrable.
> *Second Proposition.* The criteria which have been bestowed on the "true being" of things are the criteria of non-being, of *naught;* the

"true world" has been constructed out of contradiction to the actual world (TI III, 6).

To believe in a "true world" is to believe that "true being" belongs to a world other than "this" world, which one therefore regards as merely apparent or illusory (*scheinbar*). But which world is "this" world? Which world has been regarded as illusory? We cannot distinguish it from the "true" world by equating "this" world with the one accessible to human beings, because stage 1 of Nietzsche's history makes the "true world" knowable by at least some humans. "This" world seems instead to be the empirical world, the world to which we grant "true being" if we accept the testimony of the senses instead of insisting that they deceive us. It is therefore appropriate that Nietzsche's history of the "true world" follows the part of TI on " 'Reason' in Philosophy" (TI III 1–5) – discussed in section 2 above – which praises the senses, insists that the senses "do not lie," and claims that we possess knowledge only to the extent that we accept the testimony of the senses (the rest is "miscarriage and not-yet-science").

The "true world" may be knowable, then, but not empirically. The "true world" of TI is equivalent to the metaphysical world of HA. If knowable, it is so only by *a priori* methods. We can therefore interpret Nietzsche's claim that any other reality is "absolutely indemonstrable" as a reiteration of the previous section's rejection of *a priori* knowledge and insistence that all knowledge (except for formal science) is empirically based, that is, based on accepting the relevance of sense testimony. Notice, however, that Nietzsche does not claim that the empirical world is the only world. It is the only *demonstrable* world. Nietzsche therefore leaves open the possibility that reality might differ from our best empirical theory. That he completely denies the existence of a "true" world, as I will discuss, means that this passage gives added support to my earlier interpretation (Chapter 4, section 1) of the "metaphysical world" (now the "true world"). It shows that if in fact truth and reality do differ from what our best empirical theory says they are, Nietzsche would not consider this a reason to say that there is a "true" or metaphysical world. This means that a "true" world must be independent not only of our capacities, but also of our interests or standards of rational acceptability. In accord with my earlier formulation, a metaphysical world must differ *radically* from the empirical world.

Platonism, Christianity, and Kantianism occupy the first three stages of Nietzsche's history. "True being" is ascribed to the world of forms, the Kingdom of God, and the thing-in-itself.[2]

1. The true world – attainable for the sage, the pious, the virtuous. He lives in it; he is it.
(The oldest form of the idea, relatively sensible, simple, and persuasive. Circumlocution for the sentence, "I, Plato, *am* the truth.")

2. The true world – unattainable for now, but promised for the sage, the pious, the virtuous ("for the sinner who repents").
(Progress of the idea: it becomes more subtle, insidious, incomprehensible – *it becomes female*, it becomes Christian.)

3. The true world – unattainable, indemonstrable, unpromisable; but the very thought of it – a consolation, an obligation, an imperative.
(At bottom, the old sun, but seen through mist and skepticism. The idea has become elusive, pale, Nordic, Königsbergian.)

Nietzsche leaves no doubt about the occupants of these three stages. At his most oblique, he calls the third stage "Königsbergian" rather than Kantian. It is otherwise with the final three stages.

4. The true world – unattainable? At any rate, unattained. And being unattained, also unknown. Consequently, not consoling, redeeming, or obligating: how could something unknown obligate us?
(Gray morning. The first yawn of reason. The cockcrow of positivism.)

5. The "true world" – an idea which is no longer good for anything, not even obligating – an idea which has become useless and superfluous – *consequently*, a refuted idea: let us abolish it!
(Bright day; breakfast, return of *bon sens* and cheerfulness; Plato's embarrassed blush; pandemonium of all free spirits.)

6. The true world we have abolished. What world remains? The apparent world perhaps? But no! *With the true world we have also abolished the apparent one.*

2. True being is actually ascribed to the thing-in-itself in all but the sixth stage, as I have construed these terms. The Kantian stage is distinguished from the others not by its commitment to the thing-in-itself, but by the attempt to establish the nature of the thing-in-itself on the basis of practical (moral) reasoning.

(Noon; moment of the briefest shadow; end of the longest error; high point of humanity; INCIPIT ZARATHUSTRA.)

No one denies that Nietzsche places his own philosophy in stage 6. The relationship of his philosophy to the other two stages seems less clear. Magnus (1978, 135–40) finds Nietzsche's philosophy only in stage 6, whereas Heidegger interprets stage 5 as "the beginning of Nietzsche's own way in philosophy" (1961, I, 239) and Wilcox (1974, 123) claims that elements from periods in Nietzsche's own development are found in all three of the final stages.

Wilcox's view seems the most plausible. That each of the final three stages represents a stage of Nietzsche's own thinking fits best with the obvious break between the first and the second half of the list in terms of the explicitness of Nietzsche's allusions (and probably, with his estimate of his own importance). Magnus, who takes Comte as the major representative of stage 4, notes that Nietzsche's reference to positivism here is "uncharacteristically gentle" (136). This is understandable if Nietzsche has in mind not Comte, but his own early work. Stage 4 matches my account of HA, usually regarded as the beginning of Nietzsche's positivistic period: Nietzsche argues that the true or metaphysical world has no function to play, but does not deny its existence (HA 9). The occupant of stage 4 argues that the true world plays no cognitive, and therefore, no practical role, but does not deny its existence. The latter point seems clear from the absence of quotation marks in stage 4; the true world has not yet become the "so-called 'true' world." Stage 4 still considers it possible that "true being" belongs to a world that differs radically from the empirical world.

Stage 5, on the other hand, fits my account of GS and BG. Not content to exhibit its superfluousness, the occupants of stage 5 abolish the "true" world. This means that they deny its existence. Quotation marks around "true world" are now appropriate. The world whose existence stage 5 denies is not one to which it ascribes "true being," and it therefore becomes the "so-called 'true' world," a world to which others have ascribed "true being." This is precisely Nietzsche's position in GS and BG. As I have argued, these works reject HA's claim that there might be a true or metaphysical world on the grounds that we have no way of conceiving of such a world. Even granting its possibility requires us to presuppose that the world is a thing-in-itself in the most obviously objectionable sense, that is, that its essence is independent of its possible appearances. We lack not only knowledge of such a world, but also any noncontradictory way of conceiving of it. That this is Nietzsche's position explains why he claims, on the page before his history of the "true" world, that "to invent fables about a world 'other' than this one has no meaning at all, unless an instinct of slander, detraction, and suspicion against life has gained the upper hand in us; in that case, we avenge ourselves against life with a phantasmagoria of 'another,' a 'better' life" (TI III, 6). Because it is based on a contradictory concept, the belief in a "true world" can have no cognitive basis or significance. Nietzsche therefore looks for some other explanation as to why philosophers have been inclined to believe in such a world and finds it in the need for revenge against life (see Chapters 6 and 7). For Nietzsche and other occupants of stage 5, the "true world" is the nonexistent and inconceivable world others erroneously regard as possessing true being.

Why, then, is not stage 5 the "end of the longest error"? What defines the further stage for which Nietzsche reserves this honor? Stage 6 involves a realization evidently absent from stage 5: that *"with the true world we have abolished the apparent one."* I interpret this as the realization that denying the "true" world destroys all basis for characterizing the remaining world as merely apparent or illusory. The absence of this realization means that stage 5 denies the existence of the "true" world, but continues to regard the empirical world as merely apparent or illusory. The empirical world is regarded as illusory, for instance, if one insists that empirical science cannot give us truth, or that human truths are really illusions. As I have argued, we find such claims in GS and BG coupled with a denial of a metaphysical world. Therefore, Nietzsche would include GS and BG in stage 5. If this is correct, Nietzsche must have overcome the denial of truth found in these works.

Stage 6 brings the realization that we can consider the empirical world illusory only if we ascribe "true being" to another world. Stage 5 does not bring to an end the "longest error" because its devaluation of "this" world makes sense only if it ascribes "true being" to another world. Only stage 6 completely overcomes the "true world." With the complete denial of the "true" world, however, all basis is lost for regarding the empirical world or the results of empirical investigation as illusory. To deny the true world is not to deny truth. Instead, stage 6 overcomes Nietzsche's denial of truth. In TL, GS, and BG, Nietzsche's characterization of truths as illusions or fictions amounts to calling the empirical world, the world accessible through common sense and science, illusory or fictitious. His history of the "true" world indicates that he gives up ascribing reality to any world other than the empirical world (stage 5), *and* that he recognizes that this requires him to relinquish his claim that the empirical world is illusory (stage 6). That he puts the logical consequences of stage 5 in a separate stage gives strong evidence that Nietzsche later recognized his initial failure to appreciate the consequences of denying the thing-in-itself, which means that he himself went through a period in which he denied the thing-in-itself, but continued to characterize the empirical world as mere appearance or illusion. This fits perfectly my description of GS and BG. His "History of an Error" is therefore a major piece of evidence for my account of Nietzsche's development and for my claim that he overcomes his denial of truth, present from TL through BG, in his final works.

In fact, I think he had substantially overcome his denial of truth already in his two previous books, Z and BG. Although I have so far placed BG in stage 5, I think it largely belongs to stage 6 (my discussion of it in Chapter 7 will confirm this), but that it still retains some formulations from stage 5 (e.g., BG 4 and BG 25). As the passage on the "True World" makes clear, because Nietzsche places *Zarathustra* in stage 6, we must presume that he would place all his later works, including BG, in stage 6. My interpretation can explain this in the following way. By the time he wrote *Zarathustra*, Nietzsche had pretty much overcome the ascetic ideal (and certainly recognized the need to overcome it), which had provided the motivation for his earlier view that truths are illusions (see Chapter 6). The spirit of Z and later works therefore belongs to stage 6. But it is hardly surprising that a few of the formulations would be holdovers from stage 5, especially in BG where Nietzsche is in the midst of formulating reasons for the necessity of moving to stage 6 (e.g., BG 15).

Given the importance of my interpretation of stage 6 as evidence for my overall interpretation, I now consider other interpretations. The only alternative to my interpretation of what it means to abolish the "apparent world" – to deny all basis for considering the empirical world merely apparent or illusory – would be that it means to abolish that world itself, the world that has been regarded as illusory. Magnus gives plausibility to this alternative when he interprets stage 6 as reducing this world to "an aimless becoming in which all ultimate distinctions between veridical and delusory disappear" (1978, 137). Magnus believes that for Nietzsche the denial of the "true" world deprives the human world of its highest values (in effect, the distinctions that have made it a world), and therefore brings with it the great danger of passive nihilism. I agree with Magnus that Nietzsche believes something like this (see Chapter 8). However, I find no textual basis for interpreting what he says about stage 6 in these terms.

Nietzsche's history of the "true world" follows a section devoted to denouncing philosophers' devaluation of the senses and empirical knowledge that culminates in the claims that any reality other than that of the empirical world is "absolutely indemonstrable" and that the "true" world is "constructed out of contradiction to the actual world" and has "no meaning at all" (no cognitive significance) except as an expression of revenge (TI III, 6). The issue in this section concerns whether the empirical world or some other is the object of "true" knowledge, and hence possesses "true being." Because we can plausibly interpret stage 6 in terms of these concerns, in such a way that it makes a fairly obvious but important point, there is no textual basis for interpreting it in terms of the otherwise important issues Magnus introduces.

Even if one agrees that abolishing the true world means denying that the empirical world is merely apparent, one might still reject my account of the relation between Nietzsche's final two stages. Heidegger's influential interpretation does just that. Although the apparent world is abolished, he writes, "the sensuous world is the 'apparent world' only according to the interpretation of Platonism" (1961, I, 242). Heidegger thus seems to see in stage 6 a rejection of the Platonic claim that the sensuous or empirical world is merely apparent or illusory. However, Heidegger denies that this leaves the sensuous world as the only one. He takes the addition of a sixth stage as evidence of Nietzsche's belief that he "must advance beyond himself and the simple abolition of the supersensuous [*Übersinnlichen*]" (I, 240).

Stage 5 retains Platonism, Heidegger claims, despite its rejection of the "true" world. I agree with this. It retains Platonism in the sense that it still needs a "true" or metaphysical world, one that differs radically from the empirical world, as a basis for considering the latter illusory. Heidegger gives a different account. He claims that stage 5 retains Platonism because it retains "the vacant niche of the higher world and the blueprint of an above and below." Heidegger takes the addition of stage 6 as evidence of Nietzsche's view that to free ourselves from Platonism we need "neither abolition of the sensuous nor abolition of the nonsensuous [*Nichtsinnlichen*]" (I, 242). We need instead a new "ordering structure" that does not merely reverse the old structural order, "now revering the sensuous and scorning the nonsensuous." Heidegger expresses some doubts, however, concerning whether Nietzsche himself saw his way clear to such a structure (I, 242).

In fact, it seems clear that Nietzsche did not, given his claims on the page that precedes his story of the "true" world. He claims that as far as we can know, the world that has been considered "apparent," the sensuous or empirical world, is the only world: "any other kind of reality is absolutely indemonstrable." He also insists that the "true world" has been "constructed out of contradiction to the actual world" and "has no meaning at all," no cognitive significance, except as an expression of revenge against life. It is therefore difficult to understand how abolishing the "true" world could introduce the danger of retaining Platonism's "blueprint" of a higher and a lower world. To abolish the "true" world is to say that as far as we can know, there is only one world. It is not to say that what we know through nonempirical means has lower ontological reality than what is known empirically; it is to deny that there is any nonempirical, that is, *a priori*, knowledge of the world. It further denies that we have any noncontradictory conception of the thing-in-itself, and therefore any reason to search for *a priori* modes of knowledge that might allow knowledge of the thing-in-itself. Heidegger's interpretation gets much of its plausibility from his failure to make clear exactly what the supersensuous or nonsensuous world is, and his slide from the "supersensuous world" to the "supersensuous world of spirit" (I, 242). If the nonsensuous world is the world accessible to *a priori* or nonsensuous knowledge, Heidegger gives us no reason to doubt that Nietzsche flatly denies its existence.

Of course, Nietzsche is not telling us to revere the senses and renounce spiritual concerns (art and philosophy, for instance). But Heidegger gives us no basis for interpreting his history of the "true" world in terms of this issue. None of the surrounding text suggests that the abolition of the "true" world means scorning spiritual concerns in favor of sensuous ones. The obvious interpretation is that it means denying that we have any conception of a transcendent or metaphysical world, a world that differs radically from the empirical world and would therefore be accessible only to *a priori* knowledge. The addition of stage 6 is fully understandable (and in accord with Nietzsche's claims about the "true" world previously described) as an expression of the realization that one who denies the existence of the "true" world may erroneously continue to regard the remaining world as illusory, the truths about it as "fictions." My next section provides further evidence that Nietzsche did exactly this in GS and BG by explaining how he got caught in stage 5, denying the "true" world but requiring it for his devaluation of the empirical world.

4. Representationalism in Nietzsche's later works

Nietzsche's history of the "true" world, I have argued, indicates that his falsification thesis and denial of truth depended on acceptance of the thing-in-itself. He should therefore have abandoned them in GS and BG when he rejected the thing-in-itself. His continued insistence in these works that knowledge falsifies suggests that his denial of truth had some other basis than his early belief in the thing-in-itself.

Nietzsche himself certainly denied its dependence on the thing-in-itself. Explaining perspectivism in GS as the claim that "all becoming conscious involves a great and thorough corruption, falsification, reduction to superficialities, and generalization," he denies that his falsification thesis has anything to do with "the opposition of 'thing-in-itself' and appearance; for we do not 'know' nearly enough to be entitled to any such distinction" (GS 354).

I will argue that he was wrong about this, that the falsification thesis commits him to a "true" world, which makes sense only on the assumption that reality is something in itself. But his falsification thesis and denial of truth had a deeper source than his commitment to the thing-in-itself, in the representational model of knowledge he inherited from Schopenhauer. I have already argued (in Chapter 3) that TL's denial of truth rests on the assumption that there is a thing-in-itself and that this assumption depends crucially on Nietzsche's representationalism. I will now argue that we find the same view of knowledge in later works. This will help to explain both Nietzsche's continued denial of truth in GS and BG and his failure to recognize that this denial committed him to a "true" world.

Consider, again, GS 54, which rejects the conceivability of the thing-in-itself.

> I have discovered for myself that the human and animal past, indeed the whole primal age and past of all sentient being continues in me to invent, to love, to hate, to infer. I suddenly woke up in the midst of this dream, but only to the consciousness that I am dreaming and that I must go on dreaming lest I perish – as a somnambulist must go on dreaming lest he fall. What is "appearance" for me now? Certainly not the opposite of some essence: what could I say about any essence except to name the attributes of its appearance! Certainly not a mask that one could place on an unknown X or remove from it! (GS 54)

I have interpreted the last three sentences of this passage as a claim that we can conceive of a thing's essence only in terms of its appearance (see section 1). The preceding sentences evidently formulate the conclusion Nietzsche draws from this denial of the thing-in-itself, namely, that life is a dream. This seems a clear expression of subjective idealism. As the dream exists only for the dreamer, the world exists only for the knower. The world has no existence of its own. Why does Nietzsche hold such a position? And why does he think it follows from his denial of the thing-in-itself? Nietzsche's representationalism provides an answer to these questions.

The passage indicates that Nietzsche has not abandoned the representational view of knowledge he assumed in both BT and TL. If life is a dream, the objects of consciousness exists only as representations; they have no existence except in relation to the knower/dreamer. In that case, Nietzsche has only two options: Either there are independently existing things which cannot be direct objects of knowledge or only representations exist. The first option commits him to the thing-in-itself; the second amounts to subjective idealism.

In the former case, the world is always hidden from the knower by the representation. Its essence is therefore independent of what can be known of it. Only an *a priori* argument that the representation corresponds to the object behind it could show it to be knowable. Once Nietzsche denied that there are nonempirical modes of access to the world (i.e., after BT), representationalism left him with a choice between Kant's unknowable thing-in-itself and the Berkeleyan idealism Schopenhauer had adopted with respect to the empirical world. In TL, I have argued, Nietzsche rejected Schopenhauer's view that we have no idea of empirical objects except as representations. Contrary to Schopenhauer, he apparently believed that perception causes us to adopt beliefs about independently existing objects. But his acceptance of Schopenhauer's claim that the object perceived is only a representation forced him to treat any independently existing thing as an unknowable thing-in-itself. Because the thing itself (the independently existing thing) remains hidden from us by our representation of it, we can only conceive of its nature as an unknown and unknowable X, as what would be there if we could only cut our head off. The passage quoted from GS 54 rejects the conceivability of such a hidden essence. This rejection of a thing-in-itself can be made compatible with representationalism only by embracing idealism. If we can only know representations and have no way of conceiving of something hidden by or behind the representation, then we have no conception of anything possessing independent existence. This reasoning explains Nietzsche's conclusion in GS 54, that life is a dream.[3]

It does not yet explain how representationalism could provide a basis for denying truth given Nietzsche's rejection of the thing-

3. It is surprising that Nietzsche would present this essentially Schopenhauerian position as "wonderful and new" (GS 54) at this late date – when he had been fighting Schopenhauer's influence for many years. We can explain this by recognizing that Schopenhauer's position involves an inconsistent affirmation of the thing-in-itself that Nietzsche here discards and that this involves a new way of fighting Schopenhauer. He fought Schopenhauer at first by insisting on the unknowability of the thing-in-itself (e.g., in TL and HA). GS 54 reverses this. It seems to accept the argument for idealism – for the claim that the world is my representation – from the first two pages of Schopenhauer's major work, but, in opposition to Schopenhauer, insists that the argument rules out the conceivability of the thing-in-itself.

in-itself. In conjunction with this rejection, representationalism would seem to work against the falsification thesis. In TL, the thesis made sense because Nietzsche claimed that our representations fail to correspond to the thing-in-itself. But if there are only representations, to what could they fail to correspond? What is left to be falsified? When Nietzsche claims in GS and BG that logic and science falsify reality, what does he believe they falsify?

The most plausible answer (Wilcox 1974, 133; Heidegger 1961, I, 551 ff.) seems to be that knowledge falsifies the "chaos of sensations." Although the most direct evidence for this answer comes from the *Nachlass,* a similar account is found in GS. In GS 354, Nietzsche claims that we think continually without knowing it, but that only the worst and most superficial part of this thinking enters consciousness. Consciousness develops, he claims, "*under the pressure of the need for communication,*" and therefore "the world of which we can become conscious is only a surface- and sign-world, a world that is made common and meaner," and which involves "thorough corruption, falsification, reduction to superficialities and generalization" (GS 354). In WP 569, he makes a similar point: our psychological perspective is determined by the need for communication, which requires something "firm, simplified, capable of precision." Nietzsche concludes from this that "the material of the senses [must be] adapted by the understanding, reduced to rough outlines, made similar, subsumed under related matters. Thus the fuzziness and chaos of sense impressions are, as it were, logicized" (WP 569). He then adds that "the antithesis of this phenomenal world is not 'the true world,' but the formless unformulable world of the chaos of sensations – *another kind* of phenomenal world, a kind of 'unknowable' for us."

In its reference to the "chaos of sensations," Nietzsche's unpublished notes make explicit what is required to make sense of the published passage. The latter asserts the following connection between consciousness and communication (and therefore language): "the emergence of our sense impressions into our own consciousness, the ability to fix them and, as it were, exhibit them externally, increased proportionately with the need to communicate them to *others* by means of signs" (GS 354). When Nietzsche then concludes that consciousness involves corruption and "falsification," the most natural interpretation is that consciousness falsifies precisely sense impressions, which can enter conscious-ness only in communicable, or "logicized" (universal), and there-fore falsified, form.

This interpretation fits nicely with the fact that the specific features of knowledge GS and BG pick out as falsifying reality are ones Kant construed as *a priori:* mathematics, logic, and the concepts of substance and causality. In these works, Nietzsche seems to accept a naturalized version of Kant's theory of knowl-edge. He agrees with Kant's denial that the form or structural features of our representations derive from experience, but ex-plains these features naturalistically, in terms of their contribu-tion to the survival of the species (e.g., BG 4, 11 suggest this). Nietzsche treats the *a priori* features of our representations as the result of an inherited program in terms of which the human brain structures the data of sensation. In this, he follows Scho-penhauer and Lange, but adds from evolutionary theory the idea that the program developed over the very long course of human history in terms of what aided survival. This helps ex-plain why he continued to maintain the falsification thesis in GS and BG. If the data of sensation constitute reality, the *a priori* features the brain's organization imposes on sensations falsify reality, making it appear to have features it does not actually possess.

Given this view, judgments about the desk upon which I am writing involve not only the selection and simplification of sense data, which must be "reduced to rough outlines, made similar, subsumed under related matters" (WP 569), but also the falsifica-tion involved in the assumption of an enduring thing and bearer of properties. That we judge such a thing to be present must result from the organization imposed on sensation, since it is nowhere to be found, as Schopenhauer and Hume both argued, in the sense impressions themselves.

The reasoning just outlined explains why GS treats as a falsifi-cation the common sense idea of an enduring thing or substance. In TI, I have argued, Nietzsche counts as a falsification only the metaphysical notion of a substance, the idea of a thing that does not change (see section 2). I made a large point of this precisely because GS and BG seem to regard as a falsification even the ordinary idea of an enduring thing. In GS 110, for example, Nietzsche counts among "erroneous articles of faith" that "there are enduring things; that there are equal things; that there are things, substances, bodies." Nietzsche's belief that there are no enduring things helps explain why he believes that logic and mathematics falsify reality (BG 4), for he believes that mathematical and logical truths presuppose the existence of substances (GS 111), presumably as possessors of properties, and things to be counted and measured. That logic and math could not have been developed in the absence of a notion of enduring things seems plausible. No such plausibility attaches to the idea that they required the idea of an unchangeable thing. It is not surprising, therefore, that Nietzsche reduces his critique of substance to the critique of an unchanging substrate at the point that he abandons his claim that logic and math falsify reality (see analysis of TI III in section 2).

The most basic assumption underlying Nietzsche's claim that the idea of an enduring thing falsifies reality is his identification of reality with the chaos of sensation. But why would Nietzsche identify reality with the chaos of sensation? His representationalism provides an answer. If only representations exist, it could seem plausible to identify reality with whatever part of the representations we do not "make up." The naturalized Kantian understanding of representations makes sensations the only given aspect, the only thing not made up by our minds. But how could Nietzsche know that reality is constituted by the chaos of sensations, if he claims that the latter is "unknowable by us" (WP 569)? Nietzsche evidently means that it is unknowable by us from a first-person perspective. We can never become aware directly of this chaos of sensations that must be falsified to enter consciousness, but we can nevertheless have knowledge of it on the basis of what Nietzsche considered an empirical theory of knowledge. In GS 354, he explicitly appeals to "physiology and the history of animals" for the theory that leads him to regard consciousness as a corrupter and falsifier. Schopenhauer had already claimed that empirical investigations show that we construct the world by imposing *a priori* forms on the matter of sensation (see Chapter 3 for some relevant passages), and Lange's *History of Materialism* would have added more evidence to this effect. It would therefore seem to Nietzsche that he had the backing of empirical theory for his insistence that the empirical world is illusory or a "fiction."

This explains how he found himself in what he later analyzed as stage 5 of the history of the "true" world, denying the existence of a "true" world, yet insisting on the illusory character of the empirical world. He thought he could regard the empirical world as illusory without belief in a "true" world because he denied that the chaos of sensations is a "true" world (WP 569). It is not a true or metaphysical world because we have knowledge of it by empirical means. If this were the case, no commitment to a thing-in-itself would be involved.

But there is a major problem with this way of justifying Nietzsche's falsification thesis, as he seems to have realized when he writes that "to study physiology with a clear conscience, one must insist that the sense organs are *not* phenomena in the sense of idealistic philosophy; as such they could not be causes" (BG 15). That is, one cannot consistently give an empirical (i.e., physiological) account of the role of sensations in knowledge, and yet reduce to arrangements of sense data the sense organs presupposed by that account.

> What? And others even say that the external world is the work of our organs? But then our body, as a part of this external world would be the work of our organs! But then our organs themselves would be – the work of our organs! It seems to me that this is a complete *reduçtio ad absurdum,* assuming that the concept of a *causa sui* is something fundamentally absurd. Consequently, the external world is *not* the work of our organs – ? (BG 15)

This passage shows Nietzsche's realization that for the purposes of giving an empirical account of human knowledge, he must presuppose the existence of real, independently existing, things: brains, sense organs, the bodies to which they belong, and the bodies with which they interact. It follows that empirical accounts cannot provide a basis for equating reality with the chaos of sensations, since they must presuppose that sense organs and bodies are real.[4] Nietzsche therefore has no empirical basis for his claim that the *a priori* aspects of knowledge falsify reality, nor any basis for denying that the chaos of sensations is just another "true" world insofar as it is equated with reality.

4. I take the final question of the passage to be an invitation to recognize that we need not therefore deny that our interpretations of the world depend on something about us, for example, the type and range of our sense organs. But as my next chapter argues, Nietzsche's mature perspectivism denies that the "subjective" character of such interpretations gives us reason to deny their truth. See Nehamas, 1988, 47–49, for a different reading of this passage.

In TI, Nietzsche clearly links his abolition of a "true" world to a rejection of *a priori* knowledge. To deny the existence of a metaphysical or "true" world, I have argued, is to deny that our best empirical theories can be radically false. In that case, we have no need for *a priori* knowledge, but only for better empirical theories. On the other hand, empirical theories cannot give us knowledge of a "true" world, but only of the empirical one. As I have reconstructed it, Nietzsche did not recognize the chaos of sensations as a "true" world, because he believed he based its identification with reality on an empirical theory. He did not realize (until he formulated the argument BG 15) that his empirical theory presupposed the existence of independently existing things. He therefore believed he could draw from an empirical theory conclusions that would follow only from an *a priori* theory about the thing-in-itself. Only an *a priori* account of the construction of the world from sensations could ground his equation of reality with sensations, and thereby his falsification thesis. But if it is accessible only to an *a priori* account, Nietzsche must count the world of sensations as a "true" world. Contrary to his own claim, then, the account he gives in GS and BG of the empirical world as merely apparent or illusory does presuppose the existence of a "true" or metaphysical world.

Nietzsche's representationalism plays the ultimate culprit in this tale. It is responsible for his continued denial of truth in GS and BG and his failure to recognize that this denial required the positing of a "true" world. As I have argued, representationalism made idealism necessary once Nietzsche rejected the thing-in-itself, and that, in conjunction with his naturalized Kantian theory of knowledge, made the equation of reality with the chaos of sensations seem reasonable. This, in turn, seemed to provide a basis for considering illusory the nonchaotic world of which we have knowledge without committing him to a belief in a "true" world. But this position is vulnerable to the *reductio* Nietzsche himself explained in BG 15.

Nietzsche needed a way out. The way out suggested by both BG 15 and the interpretation I have offered is to reject representationalism. BG 15 implies that Nietzsche cannot "study physiology with a good conscience," that is, base his account of knowledge on an empirical theory, unless he recognizes that the senses are not mere representations. Unless he wants to embrace an independently existing object hidden from knowledge by the representations – and thus be back with the thing-in-itself – he must therefore reject representationalism. This, I shall argue in the next chapter, is accomplished by Nietzsche's mature perspectivism.

5

PERSPECTIVISM

"Perspectivism" is the claim that all knowledge is perspectival. Nietzsche also characterizes values as perspectival, but I shall be concerned here only with his perspectivism regarding knowledge. The latter constitutes his most obvious contribution to the current intellectual scene, the most widely accepted Nietzschean doctrine.

As it is usually interpreted, perspectivism entails that human knowledge distorts or falsifies reality (see section 5). Nietzsche certainly seems to have interpreted it in this way. In TL he appeals to the perspectival character of perception – "that the insect or bird perceives an entirely different world from the one humans do, and that the question as to which of these perceptions of the world is more correct is quite meaningless" (TL 86; WL 884) – to support his claim that truths are illusions. In GS he explicitly identifies perspectivism with the claim that "the world of which we can become conscious is only a surface- and sign-world," from which he concludes that "all becoming conscious involves a great and thorough corruption, falsification, reduction to superficialities and generalization" (GS 354). Interpreted as implying the falsification thesis, however, Nietzsche's perspectivism provides strong evidence against my claim that he overcame his early denial of truth.

Chapter 4's account of Nietzsche's development allows my interpretation to accommodate the passages quoted above since they are not from his last six works. It remains problematic for my interpretation that Nietzsche gives the most important and lengthy statement of his perspectivism in GM. According to my account of his development, GM belongs to stage 6 of Nietzsche's history of the "true" world, the stage in which he completely abolishes the "true" world and recognizes that he thereby loses all basis for the falsification thesis. My interpretation cannot account for Nietzsche's perspectivism, therefore, if the version found in GM and later works entails the falsification thesis. In this chapter, I argue that it does not. GM's statement of perspectivism is a metaphorical expression of Nietzsche's neo-Kantian position on truth that is designed to help us overcome the falsification thesis. After presenting this interpretation, I argue that the important alternatives to it saddle Nietzsche with the falsification thesis, leaving him in an untenable position.

1. A neo-Kantian interpretation of perspectivism

The following passage is the only statement of Nietzsche's perspectivism in the works I have placed in stage 6 of his history of the "true world."

> Henceforth, my dear philosophers, let us be on guard against the dangerous old conceptual fiction that posited a "pure, will-less, painless, timeless knowing subject"; let us guard against the snares of such contradictory concepts as "pure reason," "absolute spirituality," "knowledge in itself": they always demand that we should think of an eye that is completely unthinkable, an eye turned in no particular direction, in which the active and interpreting forces, through which alone seeing becomes seeing *something*, are supposed to be lacking; these always demand of the eye an absurdity and a nonsense. There is *only* a perspective seeing, *only* a perspective "knowing"; and the *more* affects we allow to speak about one thing, the *more* eyes, different eyes, we can use to observe one thing, the more complete will our "concept" of this thing, our "objectivity," be. But to eliminate the will altogether, to suspend each and every affect, supposing we were capable of this – what would that mean but to *castrate* the intellect? (GM III, 12)

A striking characteristic of this passage is its highly metaphorical character. In calling knowledge "perspectival," Nietzsche uses a visual metaphor to say something about knowing. His statement sets up an analogy between seeing and knowing in just the way a metaphor does. Metaphor and simile both induce us to note similarities between things that are dissimilar in other respects. Similes do this in a more straightforward way, by stating that two things are similar. Metaphors merely invite, direct, nudge, or seduce us into noting the similarities, often by saying something that is literally false or nonsensical ("Juliet is the sun"), but sometimes by stating an obvious truth ("No man is an island").[1]

Given the absurdity or triviality of the claim when read on a literal level, we assume that such statements are not intended to convey information in a straightforward way. The metaphorical character of Nietzsche's perspectivist claims becomes especially evident when he claims that the notions of pure reason and "knowledge in itself" always "demand of the eye an absurdity and a nonsense." Read literally, this claim cannot be taken seriously. The concepts in question concern cognition, and demand no particular beliefs about sight, for example, that sight could belong to "an eye turned in no particular direction." As we cannot reasonably suppose that Nietzsche believes something so absurd, we must interpret his (literally false) statement as an attempt to get us to note certain similarities between the cognitive concepts in question and the absurd idea of nonperspectival seeing. A major task for the interpreter of perspectivism is therefore to unpack Nietzsche's metaphor, to explain the analogy it sets up.

In its literal sense, perspective belongs to vision. Seeing is perspectival in the sense that a specific spatial relation – a matter of distance and angle – always obtains between the eye and the object it sees, a relation that affects how the object looks. One takes a different perspective on an object by finding a distance and/or angle from which it looks different than it did from one's original position. A nonperspectival seeing would be a view from nowhere. How the object looks would not be affected by the position of the eye, for the seeing would be accomplished by an eye with no particular spatial relation to its object. This is, of course, impossible. Such an eye would not be in space, and could

---

1. As in Chapter 3, this analysis of metaphor is greatly influenced by Davidson's "What Metaphors Mean," 245–64.

not, therefore, be an eye (or any other physical object). Nonperspectival seeing is therefore "an absurdity and a nonsense."
   But what does this obvious fact have to do with knowing?
Knowing and seeing are two different activities, and the impossibility of nonperspectival seeing proves nothing about knowing. I
propose that Nietzsche's metaphor offers us a model in terms of
which to think about knowing. He uses it to suggest that we think
of knowing as involving a factor analogous to perspective in the
visual realm. To interpret perspectivism, we need to say what this
factor is. We need a nonmetaphorical statement of what a cognitive perspective is.
   To be analogous to the visual case, a cognitive perspective
must be something on the side of the knower that affects the
intellectual "look" of the object, that affects how it is understood
or interpreted. An obvious candidate for this role is our corpus
of beliefs, what we believe at a particular time. Calling knowing
perspectival suggests that how things will look to us intellectually
in any situation – how we are justified in interpreting them –
depends on "where we're at," that is, on what we already believe.
To consider knowledge nonperspectival would be to insist that it
must be grounded in a set of foundational beliefs, beliefs all
rational beings must accept no matter what else they believe,
beliefs that could therefore constitute a neutral corner from
which the justifiability of other beliefs might be assessed. In calling nonperspectival knowledge "an absurdity and a nonsense,"
Nietzsche suggests the impossibility of such self-justifying foundations for knowledge.
   Following this reading, Nietzsche uses the metaphor of perspective to express his rejection of Cartesian foundationalism.
Perspectivism amounts to the claim that we cannot and need not
justify our beliefs by paring them down to a set of unquestion-
able beliefs all rational beings must share. This means that all
justification is contextual, dependent on other beliefs held unchallengeable for the moment, but themselves capable of only a
similarly contextual justification.
   Perspectivism would therefore be equivalent to Nietzsche's
claim that knowledge is interpretation, that "facts do not exist,
only interpretations" (WP 481). I must, of course, deny that Nietzsche rejects the existence of "facts" in the sense of "truths." He
shows the utmost respect for facts in a passage already discussed
in Chapter 4 when he calls the "*sense for facts*" the "last and most

valuable sense" (A 59). Further, he makes perfectly clear that the point of his denial of facts is to deny "facts in themselves" (WP 481), self-justifying facts, facts that impose themselves on us no matter what else we believe. That knowledge is interpretation must therefore amount to anti-foundationalism. Calling knowledge interpretive differs from calling it perspectival, in this view, only in the set of metaphors (textual versus perceptual) one uses to suggest the same anti-foundational point.

Although this anti-foundational account of perspectivism is plausible to a point, it seems far from the whole story. It leaves too much of Nietzsche's perspectivist passage unexplained and leaves perspectivism without obvious relation to truth. Few commentators would deny that perspectivism rejects foundationalism. However, most must think it does something more, for they believe it implies the falsification thesis. Anti-foundationalism does not entail the falsification thesis because it concerns justification and certainty, not truth or falsity. Rejecting foundationalism means accepting the thesis of radical corrigibility or revisability. If we deny that our beliefs possess an absolute or neutral foundation, we must admit that they could be false, or that we may have reason to revise them in the future. But absence of certainty does not entail absence of truth. The fact that our beliefs could be false does not entail that they are false (cf. Nehamas' argument, section 5). If their perspectival character means that our beliefs involve falsification, perspectivism must be something more than anti-foundationalism. Nietzsche's metaphor of perspective must invite us to recognize not only the nonfoundational character of knowledge, but also something about truth.

We can explain how it does this if we interpret perspectivism as a rejection of the metaphysical correspondence theory of truth, the understanding of truth as correspondence to things-in-themselves. I have argued that Nietzsche rejects as contradictory the very idea of a thing-in-itself (Chapter 4), and that the foundationalist position on justification receives its plausibility from the metaphysical conception of truth as correspondence to things-in-themselves (Chapter 2). BG 16 shows that Nietzsche recognized that the two doctrines were connected. This suggests the possibility that he uses the metaphor of perspective to promote recognition of *both* the nonfoundational character of knowledge and of the contradiction involved in the idea of the thing-in-itself.

It seems reasonable to equate nonperspectival knowledge with knowledge of things-in-themselves. Nietzsche begins his perspectivist passage with a plea to "guard against the snares of such contradictory concepts as 'pure reason,' 'absolute spirituality,' 'knowledge in itself.' " "Pure reason" names the putative faculty for knowing things-in-themselves. Reason is "pure" by possessing "absolute spirituality," that is, intelligence or spirituality uninfluenced by merely human capacities, especially the senses, and interests. "Knowledge in itself" could refer to self-justifying beliefs, knowledge that is not mediated by beliefs other than self-justifying ones. In the context of Nietzsche's concern with "pure reason" and "absolute spirituality," it seems at least as plausible to construe it as short for "knowledge of things-in-themselves." I therefore interpret Nietzsche's metaphor of perspective as designed to help us avoid the snares of the idea that we can have knowledge of things as they are in themselves. To call nonperspectival knowing an "absurdity and a nonsense" invites us to think of knowing things-in-themselves as equivalent to the recognizably absurd idea of seeing things from no perspective.

I believe it also invites us to recognize as incoherent the very idea of things-in-themselves. Otherwise, Nietzsche's use of the metaphor of perspective would be compatible with the position of TL, that there is a thing-in-itself that we cannot know. In that early essay, Nietzsche regarded the impossibility of knowing things-in-themselves as a real limitation on our capacity for knowledge. I have argued that his position was internally inconsistent, and that Nietzsche eventually overcame it by insisting on the contradictory character of the very idea of a thing-in-itself. I am now claiming that the metaphor of perspective is useful for articulating this later position because it invites us to think of what things are in themselves as the cognitive equivalent of what they look like "in themselves," what they would look like from nowhere.

There is, of course, no way things look in themselves. A thing's visible characteristics are different aspects of the way it looks from one or more of the possible perspectives on it. Nietzsche uses the metaphor of perspective to make a parallel suggestion about the intelligible character of a thing, namely, that the aspects of its intelligible character are aspects of how it would be interpreted from one or more of the cognitive perspectives on it. The intelligible character it has in itself is equivalent to its visual character when viewed from nowhere. As there is nothing to see of a thing except what it looks like from various visual perspectives, there is nothing to know of it except how it is interpreted from various cognitive perspectives. I do not suggest that this is proven by Nietzsche's use of the metaphor of perspective. Instead, his perspectivism is a metaphorical formulation of the argument he gives for this conclusion in GS 54 (see Chapter 4). Given this reading of the metaphor, we can understand cognitive perspectives as constituted not only by beliefs, but also by those factors on the side of the subject responsible for beliefs, such as cognitive capacities and practical interests. That the latter are of particular interest to Nietzsche in this context is clear from the last line of the quoted passage, which equates divorcing intellect from will with castration.

From his earliest works (perhaps already in BT), Nietzsche saw a strong connection between the human intellect and practical interests. In TL, as I have argued (Chapter 3, section 4), he takes cognitive capacities and interests to be rooted in practical interests, in particular, the interests in control and survival. This was a main factor behind his claim that truths are illusions. They are illusions because they do not correspond to the thing-in-itself, which Nietzsche equates with the "pure truth apart from consequences" (TL 82, WL 879). His argument assumes that the influence of practical interests (however indirect) introduces distortion and keeps human knowledge from obtaining the "pure truth apart from consequences."

As I interpret it, perspectivism is designed to free us from the snares of the idea that knowledge could obtain such "pure truth" – that knowledge is of things-in-themselves. Nietzsche's use of the metaphor of perspective invites us to think of a thing's intellectual appearance as influenced by something about the subject, its cognitive constitution and, ultimately, whatever factors are responsible for that. If we think of the thing-in-itself (and therefore TL's "pure truth apart from consequences") as the cognitive equivalent of the way something looks from nowhere, we must abandon the presumption that subjective factors have a distorting influence. For we are committed to thinking of the truth that we assumed these factors distort as a contradiction in terms.

This analysis of the metaphor explains why perspectivism concerns not only knowledge or justification but also truth. Because it rejects the conceivability of things-in-themselves, it rules out the metaphysical understanding of truth as correspondence to things as they are in themselves. A perspectivist denies that there is any truth in this metaphysical sense.

Understood in this way, perspectivism gives us no reason to deny that many human beliefs are true, however. The perspectival character of knowledge places no limit whatsoever on our cognitive capacities. That seeing is perspectival in the sense I have emphasized – that we cannot see things from no perspective, that the position of the subject therefore influences the way something looks – places no limit on what we can see because there is no look things have from no perspective, no visual characteristics they have "in themselves." The very idea is incoherent or absurd. According to my analysis, Nietzsche uses the metaphor of perspective to encourage us to draw the parallel conclusion about knowledge, namely, that its "subjective" character (the fact that how things are interpreted always reflects something about the constitution, beliefs, and/or interests of the interpreter) places no limit on what we can know. Since things have no "objective" character – no intelligible character that is independent of how they can appear – the perspectival or "subjective" character of knowledge cannot deprive us of anything we could reasonably want or for which we could have any cognitive use.

The crux of the matter is that perspectivism excludes only something contradictory. As creative power is not limited by the inability to make a square triangle, cognitive power is not limited by the inability to have nonperspectival knowledge.

Perspectivism therefore undercuts the basis for TL's commitment to the falsification thesis. Because Nietzsche understood truth as correspondence to things-in-themselves and considered such correspondence unobtainable in principle, he denied that human beliefs could be true. Once he articulates, here with the help of the metaphor of perspective, that the very idea of the thing-in-itself involves a contradiction in terms, he exposes the inaccessible "truth" that TL counted as a limit on our capacity for knowledge as a contradiction in terms, as something for which we could have no cognitive use. That we cannot have it is therefore no loss.

Nietzsche should therefore reject the metaphysical understanding of truth for the minimal correspondence conception discussed in Chapter 2. Although perspectivism denies metaphysical truth, it is perfectly compatible with the minimal correspondence account of truth and therefore with granting that many human beliefs are true. It even seems to require acceptance of this minimal theory since the latter is simply what remains of truth once we reject what perspectivism rejects, namely, the thing-in-itself. Perspectivism therefore amounts to a metaphorical expression of what I have called Nietzsche's neo-Kantian position on truth.

This position need not deny an important sense in which our capacity for truth is limited, namely, that there are always more truths than any human being can know. We are, after all, finite creatures with a limited amount of time to discover truths, whereas there are surely an infinite number of truths to discover. We should therefore expect people with different interests to discover different truths (as well as many common ones). Our interests will determine where we look, and therefore what we see. But perspectivism should not be identified with the claim that our knowledge is always incomplete in this sense. So identifying it would have the advantage of making perspectivism into an obvious and nonproblematic doctrine (as long as we avoid implying that the different truths people discover conflict). That there are many truths I do not know gives me no reason to doubt the truth or reliability of any of my present beliefs. But it would then seem impossible to explain why perspectivism has generated so much interest and why anyone would be tempted to deny it. This interpretation would not even *seem* to make perspectivism entail the falsification thesis.

To show that perspectivism does entail the falsification thesis, critics of my interpretation have two options: to argue that it follows from my own analysis of Nietzsche's use of the perspectivist metaphor that knowledge falsifies, or to offer a different analysis of the metaphor and argue that the falsification thesis follows from it. Both lines of argument can be found in the literature on perspectivism. I explain and attempt to answer them in the following three sections.

2. Perspectivism and representationalism

One way of arguing that I have drawn the wrong conclusion from my analysis of Nietzsche's metaphor is to insist that the metaphor fails of its purpose and actually reinstates the thing-in-itself. After all, to characterize knowledge as perspectival invites us to think of a single thing or object set over against a multiplicity of perspectives. David Hoy (1981) takes this to suggest that there is a thing-in-itself because there is a thing that is independent of the various perspectives. This does capture the reasoning that has led some interpreters to think that Nietzsche ultimately affirms the existence of a thing-in-itself or intelligible world (e.g., Danto, pp. 96–7). But the reasoning is illegitimate, its basis an important conflation of two quite different distinctions: the thing/appearance and the reality/appearance distinctions.

The perspectivist metaphor does invite us to think of a thing that is independent of the perspectives on it. If the same thing can be seen from different perspectives, its existence is not reducible to the existence of representations. It must be an extramentally existing thing, a thing with its own foothold in reality. Such a thing has *existence in itself,* as opposed to having only the kind of existence Berkeley or Schopenhauer would grant it: existence as a representation or appearance, *existence in relation to a mind.* However, this does not make it a thing-in-itself. The possession of extramental existence (*existence in itself*) is neither necessary nor sufficient for being a thing-in-itself. What is required is rather an *essence in itself,* an essence or nature that is independent of what it can appear to be. The affirmation of an independently existing thing (common sense realism) will seem to affirm a thing-in-itself (metaphysical realism) only if one conflates the thing/appearance and the reality/appearance distinctions. Given that conflation, it follows that a thing with extramental existence, that is, a thing that is independent of its appearances, must possess a reality that is independent of how it appears. Kant's first *Critique* (B xxvi) provides an important example of an argument for the conceivability of the thing-in-itself that seems to be based on this conflation.

Without the conflation, we have no basis for assuming that an extramentally existing thing has a reality that is independent of how it can appear (i.e., that it is a thing-in-itself). Nietzsche's use of the metaphor of perspective helps us to see the conflation for what it is. It sets an independently existing thing over against the perspectives on it, but it does not thereby commit him to the existence of a thing-in-itself, for it equates the latter with something completely contradictory (what something looks like from nowhere).

By thus making the object of knowledge an independently existing thing, the metaphor of perspective gives Nietzsche an alternative to a picture of knowledge that had long held him captive, namely, Schopenhauer's representational model, according to which the object of perception and knowledge is only our own representation, and not something that does or could exist independently of us. I have argued that this representational model was a major factor behind Nietzsche's commitment to the falsification thesis (Chapters 3 and 4). Nietzsche's early works do exemplify the reasoning Hoy assumes: Nietzsche assumed that an independently existing object must be something in itself (a thing-in-itself). But this assumption was due to his representationalism, which forced him to consider the nature of any independently existing thing independent of, because hidden behind, its appearances. Retaining the representational model while rejecting the thing-in-itself (in GS and BG) forced him to accept idealism (life as a dream) and, when conjoined with a naturalized Kantian account of knowledge, to identify reality with the flux of sensation that is falsified by conceptualization.

To extricate himself from the falsification thesis, Nietzsche needed precisely the kind of alternative to the representational model that the metaphor of perspective provides. By setting up the object of knowledge as an independently existing thing rather than a representation or appearance, the metaphor of perspective works against Nietzsche's previous basis for affirming the thing-in-itself. Because the thing is no longer hidden behind the representation or appearance, there is no basis for assuming that its true nature is independent of how it can appear. Nietzsche should therefore deny, as he did in GS, that appearance hides an essence or unknown X – "what could I say about any essence except to name the attributes of its appearance!" (GS 54). But with the help of the perspectivist model, he can now do this without turning the object of knowledge into a mere representation, and ultimately into a chaos of sensation falsified by our stabilizing concepts (see Chapter 4).

The perspectivist model therefore fights Nietzsche's earlier and persistent assumption that the *a priori* components of our knowledge falsify reality. To the extent that knowledge is *a priori*, it derives not from contact with the object itself but from something about the subject. How, then – short of a pre-established harmony – can the knowledge or interpretation correspond exactly to the nature of the object? Using the perspectivist model helps here by helping us to deny that the object has a nature that is independent of its interpretation from the various perspectives on it. In that case, the fact that these perspectives involve subjective or *a priori* elements need not introduce falsification or distortion because the object has no hidden nature to be falsified by them, no nature that is independent of how it can appear. Its nature is simply the interpretation of it from one or more of the perspectives on it. Whether this means that the object has multiple natures will be discussed in the next two sections.

3. Perspectivism and incommensurability

Many who would agree that perspectivism effectively fights commitment to the thing-in-itself still insist that it entails the falsification thesis. Although they have not been distinguished, two different ways of making this argument have been suggested by the literature. This section discusses the one that is compatible with my analysis of the metaphor of perspective. The next section deals with a similar sounding argument that actually involves a very different analysis of that metaphor. When the two arguments are separated in this way, it is easier to see that they are not individually sufficient, and cannot be combined, to derive the conclusion that perspectivism entails the falsification thesis.

Danto's influential interpretation of perspectivism seems compatible with my account of Nietzsche's metaphor: that its main function is to reject the thing-in-itself. But Danto rejects my conclusion that perspectivism removes all basis for the falsification thesis. From the rejection of the thing-in-itself, he concludes instead that "we cannot speak of a true perspective, but only of the perspective that prevails," that "we can do little more than insist on our perspective, and try, if we can, to impose it on other people" (77). I reconstruct his argument as follows. Perspectivism leads us to recognize that there are multiple perspectives on a thing. But since it rejects the thing-in-itself, it leaves behind no basis for comparing perspectives, for considering one cognitively superior to another. Given the thing-in-itself, we think of one perspective as cognitively superior to another if we believe that the interpretations it warrants correspond more closely to the thing as it is in itself. If we reject the thing-in-itself, we have no remaining basis for comparing two conflicting perspectives, no common or neutral standard in terms of which to conceive of one as cognitively superior to the other. In other words, perspectives are incommensurable.[2]

If this conclusion is accepted, perspectivism certainly seems to entail the falsification thesis. For it requires us to grant that every belief that can be derived from a consistent set of beliefs is true, or at least as true as any other belief. For each such set of beliefs may count as a perspective, a way in which the world manifests itself. Every belief that can be derived from a consistent set of beliefs is therefore true, relative to some perspective. If perspectives are incommensurable, however, truth can be judged only relative to a perspective. Therefore, every such belief is as true as any other belief. But the concept of truth would be useless to us if accepting certain beliefs as true did not allow us to rule out as false other possible beliefs, including many that can be derived from consistent sets of beliefs. Each perspective, then, will consider false beliefs that perspectivism regards as true relative to some perspective. But if all perspectives are of equal cognitive value, perspectivism then entails that every perspective falsifies – since each perspective induces us to consider beliefs false when they are actually as true as the ones we consider true. That knowledge is perspectival thus means that it provides only a one-sided or distorted view of the truth.[3]

However, this interpretation of Nietzsche's perspectivism trivializes his other claims. It would be a major trivialization of his genealogical claims about morality, for instance, to consider them true only relative to his own perspective. Consider his claim in GM (III, 16) that "man's sinfulness is not a 'fact,' but merely the interpretation of a fact, namely of physiological depression – the latter viewed in a religio-moral perspective that is no longer binding on us." If he remains consistent with his

2. This is, of course, the problem of incommensurability, which has also come into the discussion of Nietzsche through those influenced by T. Kuhn's account of science, for example, Richard Rorty.

3. This argument suggests that, contrary to Hoy (1987), the view that perspectivism entails relativism (which he identifies as the claim that "anything goes" [16] or that any interpretation is as good as any other) need not depend on the assumption that there is a "single, final, complete interpretation." If perspectives are incommensurable, relativism seems to follow whether or not the idea of a "single, final, complete interpretation" is intelligible.

claim that there are no facts, but only interpretations, Nietzsche must admit that the existence of physiological depression is a matter of interpretation, rather than a fact which imposes itself on us no matter what else we believe. Of course, from Nietzsche's own perspective, depression is a fact. Likewise, however, sin is a fact from the religio-moral perspective. Nietzsche's denial of sin becomes trivial unless we interpret him as claiming that his own perspective is cognitively superior to the religio-moral perspective on history.

Apart from his perspectivism, there seems little reason to deny that Nietzsche does consider his own perspective superior. Throughout GM, and even more vehemently in A, he presents the beliefs justified by the religio-moral perspective (the priest's or theologian's perspective) as falsehoods (GM III, 15) and lies (A 26), and claims that they stem from a "faulty Optics" (A 9).[4] On the other hand, he certainly appears to present his own views, which conflict with those of the religio-moral perspective, as truths – the "unchristian, immoral" truths, he insists, "do exist" (GM I, 1). Unless perspectivism implies its impossibility, there is every reason to assume that Nietzsche claims superiority for his own perspective. But even the claim that the religio-moral perspective is "no longer binding on us" implies that it could be binding, and perhaps that it once was, that is, that it was once superior to the other available explanations of suffering. That it is no longer binding would mean that we now have an alternative perspective that is at least its equal. This alternative is Nietzsche's naturalistic, genealogical perspective on history, which substitutes for the principle that suffering is due to sin the principle that it is due to physiological and (perhaps) psychological causes (GM III, 16). But if the religio-moral perspective was once superior to the available alternatives, surely Nietzsche's perspective could be superior now. In that case, Nietzsche's commitment to the genealogical perspective makes it seem ridiculous to deny that he does consider it cognitively superior to the religio-moral perspective.

The issue, therefore, is whether perspectivism denies the possibility that one perspective is superior to another. Given my ac-

4. Kaufmann translates "Optik" as "perspective" here. While that is certainly an appropriate translation, I have refrained from following it to avoid implying that Nietzsche here uses the same word he uses in the discussion of perspectivism I have analyzed.

count of the metaphor, an insistence on the cognitive equality of perspectives must rest on the assumption that only the thing-in-itself could provide the common or neutral standard necessary for comparing perspectives.

But this conclusion seems unnecessary. I have already suggested an alternative in Chapter 2, namely, cognitive interests or standards of rational acceptability. That is, we think of one perspective as superior to another if it gives the occupants of both perspectives more of what they want from a theory – would better satisfy their standards of rational acceptability – than does the other perspective. Of course, people with different perspectives may accept different standards of rational acceptability, which seems to be the case with the two perspectives discussed above. Occupants of the genealogical and the Christian-moral perspective on history may agree on "coherence with other beliefs" as a standard of rational acceptability, but since they have different beliefs, this amounts to having different standards of rational acceptability.

However, those who assume the incommensurability of perspectives do not show that it is impossible for proponents of conflicting perspectives to suspend belief where they disagree, withdrawing to a neutral corner, to a perspective that does not beg any relevant questions. Not that this is always (or even usually) a practical possibility. The point is that we have a basis for conceiving of a theory or perspective as cognitively superior, in the sense that it attains more truth than one it replaces, when the later theory satisfies more fully than the earlier theory the cognitive interests of the perspective constituted by all of the relevant beliefs the two perspectives agree on. This approach does not commit one to foundationalism, for it does not suggest that there is one perspective that is neutral with respect to all other perspectives. It suggests only that for any two conflicting perspectives, there may be a third perspective that is neutral in regard to what is at issue between the two. Where such a third perspective exists, the two perspectives are commensurable.

Some would agree to the possibility of a neutral perspective in regard to our cognitive interests, but not in regard to truth (e.g., Kuhn, 205–6). However, an uncommitted observer should have no more trouble comparing two perspectives in regard to truth than in regard to our cognitive interests. These interests just are our standards of rational acceptability, standards by which we decide what to accept as the truth. The uncommitted observer cannot compare problem-solving ability any better than he can compare truth – that is, without assuming a perspective that is uncommitted where the two theories disagree. Therefore, unless it is shown that the occupants of conflicting perspectives cannot withdraw to a perspective that is neutral between them, it has not been shown that Nietzsche's use of the metaphor of perspective commits him to the cognitive equality of perspectives. As I have interpreted it, perspectivism denies that we can compare perspectives either in terms of the way things are in themselves, or in terms of a single set of beliefs that is neutral with respect to all perspectives. In this section I have been arguing that these denials do not rule out the possibility of a neutral perspective for any two conflicting perspectives, and therefore do not entail incommensurability. In that case, we have no basis for denying that Nietzsche did regard his own perspective as superior to its competitors.

In fact, perspectivism does not even seem to rule out the *possibility* that one perspective is superior to all others – that there is one perspective that would give the occupants of all other perspectives more of what they want cognitively than do the perspectives they now occupy. This would require that for every other perspective, there is a perspective that is neutral between itself and the highest perspective and from which the superiority of the latter is evident, but the neutral perspective need not be the same in each case.[5]

My claim here seems to run counter to the common view that perspectivism excludes the possibility of a "privileged perspective" (e.g., Nehamas, 1985, 49). But this phrase has two different meanings that have not been sufficiently distinguished. As we might call "privileged" a person who has more than others, a "privileged perspective" might be one that is cognitively better than another, or all other, perspectives. Danto apparently understands it in this way when he presents as one of the "logical features of the concept of perspective itself" that "there is no one perspective which is privileged over any other" (77). His reason is the same one he gives for denying the possibility of one perspective being cognitively higher than another – that we cannot say

---

5. I owe this distinction and the implied response to Kuhn above to Isaac Levi, especially to *The Enterprise of Knowledge*.

what a thing is "except from one or another perspective, and we cannot speak about it as it is in itself " (77). His claim that perspectivism rules out a privileged perspective thus depends on the erroneousassumptionagainstwhichIhavebeenarguing,thattherejection of the thing-in-itself entails perspectival incommensurability.

But we might reserve "privileged" for those persons who do not merely have more, but are granted this higher status quite apart from their contributions to the common good, or to the interests of those who have less. A perspective is privileged in this sense if we grant it cognitive superiority quite apart from its greater ability to satisfy the cognitive interests of lesser perspectives. As I interpret it, perspectivism does rule out the possibility of a privileged perspective in this sense. It insists that the claim of one perspective to be better than another can only be made in terms of what it could do for the occupants of the lesser perspective.

It should be clear that I am not attributing to Nietzsche's perspectivism the claim that there is a highest perspective, or that all perspectives are commensurable. There may well be incommensurable perspectives. Science and common sense seem to be good candidates for incommensurable perspectives. Perspectivism offers us the possibility of treating them as noncompetitors, as offering answers to different questions, in accord with different standards of acceptability, rather than competing visions of the whole truth. In this case, perspectival incommensurability does not encounter the problems that afflict the claim that all perspectives are incommensurable. In the latter case, sets of beliefs must be regarded as both incommensurable and in competition. Otherwise, every belief would be compatible with every other, and would therefore have no content. But if there are a limited number of incommensurable human perspectives, we could have both truth and pluralism. Truth would be relative to one or the other of these incommensurable perspectives, and would not be threatened by the fact that there are different truths to be had from other, incommensurable perspectives.

As I have interpreted it, however, perspectivism is also compatible with the following possibility: that all human perspectives are commensurable, that science and common sense do offer competing accounts, one of which is superior. That knowledge is perspectival cannot decide this issue, the resolution of which depends on what else the perspectivist believes. I do not find in Nietzsche's published writings much indication of his view on this issue. In some of his works (HA, e.g.), it seems clear that he regarded the perspective of common sense as inferior to that of science (see Chapter 4). However, that was at a time when he accepted the conceivability of the thing-in-itself. In the books in which he finally overcomes his attachment to the thing-in-itself, I find little evidence of his view on this issue, (though in section 2 of Chapter 4, I interpreted a passage [TI III, 2] that seems to suggest that common sense falsified the truth disclosed by science so that it is compatible with the incommensurability of science and common sense). Nietzsche may not have been very interested in the question once he gave up the "true" world and with it the attempt to reduce the empirical world to the status of mere appearance.

Perspectivism does, of course, rule out the assumption that there *must* be a highest perspective. So if all arguments for the superiority of science are based on this assumption, then perspectivism would lead to the conclusion that the perspective of common sense is either superior to or incommensurable with that of science. But Nietzsche has certainly provided no such argument, and I have not found one offered by his interpreters.

I conclude that one who accepts my reading of the metaphor of perspective has strong reason to deny that perspectivism entails the falsification thesis. It would entail the falsification thesis if it implied that all perspectives are incommensurable. In this section, I have argued that it does not. Because perspectivism is compatible with some (or one) perspective being cognitively superior to others, we have no reason to deny what otherwise seems obvious: that Nietzsche considers his own perspective(s) cognitively superior to competing ones. And if it should turn out that there are a number of incommensurable human perspectives, they would not be in competition, and would therefore not threaten the truth of beliefs from other perspectives. A plausible argument that perspectivism does entail the falsification thesis would have to be based on a different account of how Nietzsche's metaphor works.

4. An alternative account of the metaphor of perspective

Those who believe that perspectivism entails the falsification thesis often rely on a different analysis of the metaphor of perspective than I have offered. Bernd Magnus makes this analysis explicit when he presents the metaphor as an invitation to imagine a camera taking pictures while circling a physical object "360 degrees about it in equi-distant orbits, orbits which eventually traverse the object as if it were encased in an invisible globe" (1988, 152).[6] In his analysis, nonperspectival vision would amount to having simultaneous pictures of the object from all of the orbital points traversed by the camera. According to Magnus, Nietzsche urges us to consider impossible the cognitive equivalent of this, namely, knowledge of the totality of interpretations that can be given of a thing, its interpretation from all of the different cognitive perspectives on it.

Whereas I interpret Nietzsche's metaphor as an invitation to focus on the fact that seeing is always from a particular perspective, thus that the position of the viewer always affects the look of the thing seen, Magnus takes it instead as an invitation to focus on the fact that there are always other perspectives than the one any perceiver occupies. For Magnus we are to notice that there is no omniperspectival seeing, whereas I suggest we are to notice that there is no nonperspectival seeing.

Two quite different interpretations of perspectivism follow from these different readings of the metaphor. As an invitation to focus on the fact that seeing is always from somewhere, that there is no view from nowhere, the metaphor rules out only a contradictory conception of knowledge and of the object of knowledge. My conclusion, that perspectivism places no real limits on what we can accomplish cognitively, follows from this reading of the metaphor. But if, as Magnus implies, the metaphor invites us to focus on the fact that there are always other visual perspectives to occupy, it suggests that we are limited cognitively by our inability to occupy all of the different cognitive perspectives. From this second reading of the metaphor, the route to the falsification thesis is fairly short.

There are only two ways of explaining why Nietzsche would want to focus our attention on the impossibility of omniperspectival seeing. Either he thinks that philosophers have traditionally

6. Magnus suggests (correctly I believe) that Danto, Wilcox, Nehamas, Magnus, and Schacht all assume the analysis of the metaphor he presents in this paper, and contrasts it with the one I offer in "Nietzsche's Perspectivist Rhetoric." I am very grateful for his distinction, which has helped me to clarify my objections to other interpretations of perspectivism.

(and mistakenly) identified true knowledge (and therefore truth) with the cognitive equivalent of omniperspectival seeing, or he himself accepts such an identification. Because the former option seems to lack plausibility, Magnus must suppose that Nietzsche himself equates truth with the way things are from all perspectives. In that case, however, the perspectival character of knowledge must introduce distortion or falsification. If the truth about anything is equivalent to an omniperspectival view of it, and our views are always only perspectival, our views can only be partial or one-sided. This means not merely that we cannot know all there is to know, but that what we know is only partially true, that it would be completely true only if we supplemented it by the way things appear from other perspectives (see the account of Nehamas in section 5 for a concrete case of how this works). Evidence that Nietzsche did equate true knowledge with an omniperspectival view can be found in *The Will to Power* (556).

> The question "what is that?" is an imposition of meaning from some other viewpoint. "Essence," the "essential nature," is something perspectival and already presupposes a multiplicity. At the bottom of it there always lies "what is it for *me*?" (for us, for all that lives, etc.)
>
> A thing would be defined once all creatures had asked "what is that?" and had answered their question. Supposing one single creature, with its own relationships and perspectives on all things, were missing, then the thing would not yet be "defined."

Because this passage is from the *Nachlass*, it does not constitute evidence against my interpretation of the published works. However, Nietzsche might be interpreted as making a similar point in the main passage under consideration in this chapter. When he writes that "the *more* eyes, different eyes, we can use to observe one thing, the more complete will our 'concept' of the thing, our 'objectivity,' be," he certainly could mean that the truth about anything is the cognitive equivalent of an omniperspectival view. But in that case, contrary to my interpretation, perspectivism entails the falsification thesis.

The question, then, is whether one of these interpretations of perspectivism is superior to the other. Magnus finds it appropriate that perspectivism can be interpreted in two different ways, that there are two different, but equally legitimate, perspectives on perspectivism. I am less sanguine about this situation. If we accept both interpretations, Nietzsche's use of the metaphor has two opposed and contradictory, therefore self-canceling, points. I will argue that my reading of the metaphor makes more sense of the passage from GM in which it appears and of Nietzsche's perspectivism. That is, it makes it easier to explain how the metaphor can serve the apparent intent of the passage and to defend perspectivism.

The passage begins with a plea to avoid the snares of such "contradictory concepts as 'pure reason,' 'absolute spirituality,' 'knowledge in itself.' " The metaphor of perspective is apparently designed to promote the avoidance of these concepts. My interpretation makes it easy to see how the metaphor could serve this purpose. As I argued above, the concepts in question all involve the idea of the thing-in-itself. "Knowledge in itself" is short for "knowledge of things-in-themselves," "pure reason" the faculty for such knowledge, "absolute spirituality" the state of such a faculty or knower. If the point of Nietzsche's metaphor is to rule out nonperspectival knowing, it invites us to think of the object of this pure knowing as the equivalent of the way things look from nowhere. If we accept the invitation, we have a way of defending ourselves against the snares of the concepts in question, a way out of Wittgenstein's fly bottle. If the metaphor does not prove the contradictory character of these ensnaring concepts, it does give us a concrete way of appreciating Nietzsche's independent argument for the contradictory character of their central component, the thing-in-itself.

On the other hand, there is no intuitive connection between pure reason and omniperspectival knowledge. Magnus' interpretation makes it difficult to see therefore how the metaphor could serve Nietzsche's purpose. Pure reason is a capacity for knowledge that is independent of senses and interests, whereas the cognitive equivalent of omniperspectival seeing would seem to be a knowledge of how things appear in relation to every cognitive constitution, and therefore to every different set of senses and interests. Even if the latter is impossible, that tells us nothing about the possibility of pure reason.

Magnus might respond by granting that Nietzsche stigmatizes pure reason by connecting it to the idea of nonperspectival seeing, but adding that the metaphor also calls our attention to the impossibility of omniperspectival seeing/knowing. However, this impossibility should be of no interest to us unless we identify truth with an omniperspectival view. Magnus seems to think that this identification follows from a denial of nonperspectival knowing, as when he argues that once we rule out an "absolute standpoint" (which I take to be a nonperspectival view), an "unconditionally true perspective" would require "a God's-eye-view, a view from no point whatsoever save from all the possible perspectives seen simultaneously" (1988, 153). My argument in section 3 shows that this does not follow because the denial of nonperspectival knowledge (knowledge of things-in-themselves) is compatible with the claim that a particular perspective is superior to some or all other perspectives. But if one perspective is cognitively superior to another, why should the truth it makes manifest need supplementation by the interpretations of things from an inferior perspective? A complete account of the whole world would, of course, include facts about inferior perspectives. But that is because such perspectives belong to the world, not because a completely true account of anything must include all of the perspectives on it. A denial of nonperspectival knowledge does not, therefore, entail that truth is omniperspectival.

Magnus' interpretation does have the advantage of providing a more natural seeming interpretation of the claim in the main passage under consideration, that the more different eyes we use to observe one thing, the more complete our concept and objectivity will be. I will attempt to explain away Nietzsche's apparent suggestion that truth is omniperspectival – and therefore that human knowledge is radically limited – in terms of three different factors.

The first factor is that when Nietzsche writes about seeing things with different eyes, he has switched topics from knowledge to objectivity. I interpret him as saying that once we get rid of the thing-in-itself, we lose all basis for regarding objectivity as the transcendence of subjective factors. If we recognize the perspectival character of knowledge, our only alternative is to think of objectivity as an openness to perspectives other than our own. Such openness need not imply that one's own perspective distorts matters. It might distort, of course, and being "objective" involves admitting that, thereby considering seriously the possibility that some other perspective is superior to one's own. Objectivity would thus involve the ability and practice of stepping back from one's original perspective, to see how things look without some of its assumptions, without the beliefs that put it in conflict with another perspective. The objective person does not thereby transcend the perspectival character of knowledge, but only assumes for the moment a different perspective, one that does not take a stand on the points at issue between her usual perspective and a competing one. But such objectivity is perfectly compatible with deciding that one's original perspective is superior to its competitors. We can thus take Nietzsche's praise of seeing things from other perspectives as a claim that objectivity requires the ability to take seriously other perspectives without committing him to characterizing truth as omniperspectival or to accepting the falsification thesis.

A second factor is that his emphasis on different perspectives is useful for making the point that if there is something wrong with our perspective, it is not because it is a perspective, but because it is the wrong perspective, because some other perspective would satisfy our cognitive aims better than our present one if we would give it a chance.

A third factor influencing Nietzsche's formulation may be his earlier use of the metaphor of perspective to challenge the adequacy of human knowledge. In GS 354, for instance, he equates perspectivism with the claim that knowledge falsifies and with phenomenalism, the reduction of physical objects to actual and possible sensations. I have argued in Chapter 4 (section 4) that Nietzsche's commitment to the falsification thesis in GS and BG was made possible by his retention of Schopenhauer's representationalism, which prevented him from realizing that the thesis made sense only if he assumed the existence of a "true" world and therefore a thing-in-itself. I believe that his discussion of perspectivism in GM is designed to answer the earlier passage. Nietzsche now insists that we (and he himself) must guard against the snares of the whole idea of nonperspectival knowledge, knowledge of things-in-themselves. If we do, we cannot devalue human knowledge in the way he did in GS 354. For, as I have argued (Chapter 4), he could legitimately draw the conclusion of GS 354 only from an *a priori* theory that told him what reality is in itself, that is, only if he had nonperspectival knowledge. But Nietzsche had used the metaphor in the old way for a while, and it may well have had a life of its own. I suspect that when he used the metaphor to combat the effects of his old use of it, the old use crept in. As a result, his formulation came dangerously close to claiming that the addition of different perspectives always increases truth, which implies that truth is omniperspectival and knowledge falsifies.

Nietzsche's discussion of perspectivism would have been less confusing if instead of saying that we need more different eyes, he had explained objectivity in terms of the ability to take seriously (and hence to learn from, where appropriate) perspectives that compete with one's own, and had said: "If there is something inadequate about your perspective, do not attack the perspectival character of human knowledge. Rather, find a better perspective." The hold of his earlier, discredited use of the metaphor of perspective on his imagination led him, I believe, to formulate these points in a way that sounds too much like the suggestion that truth is omniperspectival.

The ultimate argument for understanding Nietzsche's claim about the importance of multiple perspectives without committing him to the omniperspectival nature of truth is that it leaves him with a much more defensible position than would the alternative. In the final section of this chapter, I argue that recent interpretations have been unable to rescue perspectivism from the difficulties with which it is plagued by its association with the falsification thesis.

5. Other interpretations of perspectivism

It is hardly surprising that radical interpreters – those who believe that Nietzsche denies that any of our beliefs correspond to reality – believe that perspectivism implies the falsification thesis. They would largely agree with Danto. He equates the idea that common sense is only our perspective with the claim that it is "a fiction [albeit] a useful and necessary one" (78) and interprets perspectivism as another expression of TL's claim that truths are illusions. So interpreted, perspectivism is one of the major supports for the radical interpretation. It is the major evidence that Nietzsche continued to maintain his early denial of truth in his later works.

Interpreted as implying the falsification thesis, however, perspectivism shares the faults of the radical interpretation discussed in previous chapters. It becomes vulnerable to the objections already raised against Nietzsche's early claim that truths are illusions. We cannot make sense of a position that denies that any of our beliefs are true, in a sense that precludes their being false (see Chapter 3). Nor can we plausibly evade this problem by interpreting Nietzsche's rejection of truth as his acceptance of some alternative to the correspondence theory of truth (see Chapter 2).

In addition to the general problem regarding truth, the problem of self-reference plagues the radical interpretation of perspectivism. As Danto (80) asks: Is perspectivism itself only a perspective? If not, then apparently some knowledge is not after all perspectival. If so, then there are apparently other perspectives from which knowledge is not perspectival. If the latter alternative is chosen, we would want to know what reason there is to accept Nietzsche's perspective. Some radical interpreters insist that the reason to accept Nietzsche's perspective is not cognitive superiority – its greater truth – but its superiority in serving a noncognitive end, for example, that it is more life-affirming (Kofman) or that it reflects the active rather than the reactive position (Deleuze). But this only pushes the self-reference problem back one step. The question naturally arises as to whether it is only a perspectival truth that Nietzsche's position is more life-affirming than the Christian position. If so, there is apparently an equally legitimate perspective from which Nietzsche's position is not more life-affirming. If not, then all knowledge is not after all perspectival.

In view of these problems, it is surprising to find substantial agreement with the radical construal of perspectivism among thinkers who occupy quite different positions on the spectrum of Nietzsche interpretation. I use as my examples here the two most important books on this topic recently published by American philosophers. Although they disagree with each other and would accept the above criticisms of the radical interpretation, both Richard Schacht and Alexander Nehamas interpret perspectivism so that it implies the falsification thesis. They give us evidence of the prevalence of this interpretation and of the difficulty of extricating Nietzsche from an untenable position if one accepts it.

It is especially puzzling to find Schacht agreeing with radical interpreters about the falsifying character of perspectives. Although he also attempts to incorporate some elements of the "new Nietzsche," he offers an essentially conservative picture of Nietzsche as engaged in the traditional philosophical enterprise of lay-ing out basic truths about the world. But this enterprise must fail if all knowledge is perspectival and perspectives always distort or falsify. Schacht attempts to render the position consistent by limiting the truths Nietzsche considers illusory to those of common sense and science. Such truths, Schacht claims, correspond to things only as they are relative to a general human perspective established by our practical interests and concerns (or drives and affects). And "at least as a rule, the kinds of interpretations to which [such drives and affects] give rise are strongly colored by them, and so have a more or less distortedly perspectival character" (9–10). But Nietzsche believes that his own philosophical positions escape such distortion, according to Schacht.

Such escape seems impossible. Given the assumption that the perspectival character of knowledge introduces distortion, only nonperspectival knowledge can escape, but Nietzsche denies this possibility. Schacht attempts to face this problem in two ways. First, he argues that Nietzsche would have no basis for calling human truths illusory or *"erroneous* rather than merely extra-systemically *meaningless"* (63–4) unless he believed he had attained a perspective from which the inadequacy of interpretations from normal human perspectives could be discerned (8). To make sense of Nietzsche's claim that other perspectives distort, we must attribute to him the belief that he has a more adequate perspective. As further evidence that Nietzsche claims a higher status for his own perspective, Schacht appeals to his definition of "objectivity" as the ability to employ a variety of perspectives in the service of knowledge (GM III, 12). To make sense of this claim, Schacht believes we must suppose Nietzsche distinguishes " 'knowledge' [from] 'perspectives and affective interpretations' merely as such" (9). Nietzsche can present his own views as knowledge rather than perspectival distortion, Schacht suggests, because he plays a variety of perspectives off against each other, refusing to be locked into any one of them. He can thereby achieve a "meta-level perspective" (10) that overcomes the distortion introduced by perspectives "merely as such."

But Schacht's problem remains. If the perspectival character of an interpretation "merely as such" (i.e., the mere fact that a belief reflects one among a number of possible perspectives) introduces falsification, consideration of a few more perspectives cannot remove it. Nietzsche's "meta-perspective" is still a particular perspective. If distortion attaches to perspective "as such," we cannot escape it unless we can achieve either a nonperspectival or an omniperspectival knowledge. Further, given that Schacht holds the human character of our perspectives responsible for distorting the truth, only the introduction of nonhuman perspectives will keep us from error. But Nietzsche explicitly rejects that possibility (e.g. GS 374).

Why does Schacht find it plausible that the perspectival as such falsifies? In explaining Nietzsche's claim that truths are illusions, he claims that while the truths of common sense and science are true relative to a particular domain of discourse – that is, correspond to the way things are for us, or from a particular human perspective – they "acquire negative truth value . . . if [they are] elevated from [their] place within some domain of discourse and human experience, and [are] advanced to candidacy for inclusion in an account of the way the world is" (112). Schacht clearly means that these perspectival truths fail to correspond to the way the world is, for he insists that these truths are "the issue of our long-term collective interaction with an underlying reality with which [they are] far from agreeing" (112). But how could Nietzsche know that such truths fail to correspond to an underlying reality, apart from knowing the latter's nature?

Schacht seems to answer that we know that the truths of common sense and science reflect our perspective, in the sense that the latter determines, for instance, what counts as an object and as a difference between objects (112). We can therefore know that "the terms in which such propositions are cast cannot appropriately be applied to the way the world is apart from our schematization of it; and so, however things may actually stand with the world, in relation to its nature such 'truths' turn out to be 'errors' " (63). In other words, our perspective influences how the world appears to us. To the extent that beliefs are perspectival, we see the world, at least in part, in terms of something that comes from our perspective rather than from the nature of the object. But, Schacht might argue, it seems highly implausible that the "way the world is apart from our schematization of it" should just happen to correspond exactly to the way it is given that schematization. Therefore, we can know that our perspectival truths fail to correspond to the world's actual nature and that if we are to avoid misinterpreting the latter, we must pull out again what we have merely projected into it (206), what depends on our perspective.

I believe that this answer presupposes the very model of knowledge Nietzsche uses perspectivism to combat. It presupposes the existence of a thing-in-itself whose nature is distorted by the subjective factors that influence its appearance from the various perspectives on it. Schacht would certainly deny the involvement of the thing-in-itself, for he recognizes that Nietzsche rejects its conceivability. But there are only two ways to interpret his idea of "the way the world is apart from our schematization of it." Either it means "the way the world is in itself, that is, apart from, or independently of, any of its interpretations," or it means "the way the world is from some superior perspective." Schacht cannot opt for the latter without circularity because he wants to base the superiority of Nietzsche's perspective on the inadequacy of the perspectives of common sense and science. Therefore, his interpretation commits Nietzsche to the existence of the thing-in-itself.

Nehamas' interpretation promises to make Nietzsche more consistent. Arguing against Schacht's interpretation (1984, 643), he insists that Nietzsche's own views are perspectival in the same sense as common sense and scientific beliefs, and he interprets the multiplicity of Nietzsche's styles as an attempt to "make his presence as an individual author unforgettable to his reader" (1985, 4–5), to remind us that his views are interpretations, reflections of one among many possible perspectives. On the other hand, he explicitly sets out to save perspectivism from the objections to the radical interpretation discussed above: the problems of truth and self-reference.

Nehamas attempts to preserve a place for truth within perspectivism by rejecting the radical claim that for any interpretation, there is always a cognitively equal alternative. Perspectivism commits us, he thinks, to the thesis that for any interpretation, "an alternative *could*, in principle, always be devised" (1985, 63). But he denies that this gives a basis for dismissing theories as "mere interpretations" (i.e., as false), unless we actually have a better interpretation to offer, an interpretation whose truth can then be called into doubt only by a still better interpretation. Perspectivism commits us to the claim that any view may be false, not that it is false.

Nehamas uses the same strategy to dissolve the problem of self-reference. Interpreting perspectivism as the thesis (P) that every view is an interpretation, he draws from it the conclusion that P itself is an interpretation. But if P is only an interpretation, it is possible that some views are not interpretations, which seems to mean that P is false. Nehamas denies this inference on the grounds that the interpretive character of P shows only the *possibility* that some views are not interpretations, and therefore the possibility that P is false. But this cannot show that P *is* false.

These arguments effectively defend perspectivism against the objections discussed above, if perspectivism amounts only to anti-foundationalism (the claim that any view might be false). They show that anti-foundationalism does not give rise to self-reference problems and that it is perfectly compatible with claiming that one's own beliefs are true. But if perspectivism is nothing more than anti-foundationalism, it is difficult to see how Nehamas can use it to fulfill a major aim of his interpretation, namely, to account for Nietzsche's claim that knowledge falsifies.

Nehamas very explicitly sets out to explain the falsification thesis in terms of perspectivism when he titles his chapter on perspectivism "Untruth as a Condition of Life." But how can perspectivism entail the falsification thesis without entailing that every interpretation is false (or at least as false as any other)? Nehamas argues that knowledge necessarily involves selection and simplification, but that we cannot believe we are simplifying while we are doing it. In other words, our beliefs may be true, but they nevertheless involve falsification since we are unable to recognize them as the simplifications they are while we are engaged in our cognitive practices. I believe that this ingenious solution fails. There are actually three different kinds of simplification that might be involved in our cognitive practices, only one of which could account for the claim that untruth is a condition of life. But if perspectivism implies that kind of simplification, I will argue, it is much more than anti-foundationalism, and it is vulnerable to the very objections against which Nehamas sets out to defend it.

One kind of simplification Nehamas identifies with perspectivism is that we form our beliefs on the basis of only part of the relevant data (1985, 49). Beliefs about human beings are based on acquaintance with relatively few human beings. From this would follow that our beliefs could be wrong and might have to be revised if we were able to take more of the relevant data into account. But this is just the revisability thesis, which, as Nehamas has shown, introduces not falsification, but only the possibility of falsification. I see no reason to think we must remain ignorant of the possibility of error – or of the fact that we can't take all data into account – while we are engaged in forming our beliefs.

At other times, Nehamas identifies perspectivism with a different kind of simplification, which he does not distinguish from the first, namely that no complete or final theory of anything is possible (1985, 51). Knowledge involves selectivity or simplification in the sense that we always "leave something out." No matter how many truths we formulate about a particular subject, there are always other truths that could be formulated. I believe that this is true, but deny that it introduces falsification into our beliefs. I am presently attempting to articulate truths about Nietzsche's philosophy. Why can I not at the same time believe that no matter how many I manage to articulate, there will always be other truths about Nietzsche's philosophy to discover and formulate? My project in no way depends on articulating all of the truths about Nietzsche's philosophy. I have not set out to do so, and the fact that I cannot do so gives me no reason to suspect the truth of anything I claim to have discovered. As long as the truths I have not formulated do not compete with the ones I have formulated (i.e., as long as they can be true at the same time), there is no logical or psychological basis for supposing that I must deny or ignore that the former exist while I am engaged in formulating the latter.

Given the first kind of simplification, for any set of beliefs, there is always a competing set that *might* be true. Given the second kind of simplification there is always a noncompeting set that is true. Neither kind of simplification must be ignored in order to get on with our cognitive practices. However, if we conflate these two kinds of simplification, it will appear that our beliefs simplify in the sense that for any set of beliefs, there is a competing set that is true. If this kind of selectivity were involved in knowing, we would certainly need to suppress knowledge of it while engaged in our cognitive projects. I could not honestly argue for the truth of my interpretation while believing that a competing interpretation (one which I must reject if I accept the interpretation for which I am arguing) was true.

That Nehamas associates perspectivism with this third kind of simplification becomes clear when he attempts to illuminate its nature by quoting the following (attributed to Nietzsche, but no source cited): "They say: the world is only thought, or will, or war, or love, or hate . . . separately, all this is false: added up, it is true" (1985, 50). On the model suggested by this quote, perspectivism holds that every set of beliefs simplifies in the sense of denying or leaving out of consideration competing, but equally legitimate views. That the world is *only* war competes or is logically incompatible with the claim that it is *only* love; and we must therefore deny the one if we believe the other. If our cognitive projects require us to engage in this kind of simplification, they clearly require falsification; we cannot admit that we are engaged in this kind of simplification while we are doing it. However, this kind of simplification also makes the beliefs themselves false. It makes beliefs perspectival or partial not merely in the sense that they leave out other (logically compatible) truths, but in the sense that they leave out logically incompatible, but equally true views. This can only mean, as the quote itself makes clear, that the beliefs are themselves false. We have here the Hegelian view that truth is the whole, in which beliefs lose their pa.tiality by abandoning their claim to be the whole truth.

However, we have no reason to believe that all beliefs simplify in the third sense distinguished here, that they leave out equally true, but competing views. Nehamas gives no argument for this, and I can find in what he says no basis he could think he has for this except an illegitimate conflation of the other two kinds of simplification. His interpretation would be plausible if our beliefs all took the form of "reality is only x." But we have no reason to accept this characterization of them, nor to suppose that we could or should subsume all competing views in some higher view in which their partiality is overcome. Suffering is due to physiology and suffering is due to guilt are certainly compatible in that way – if one's physiology reflects one's guilt. But we have no reason to accept that as the truth.

For Nehamas, then, perspectivism is much more than antifoundationalism. It claims not merely that there may be other perspectives that are cognitively better than our own, but that there are other, competing perspectives that are cognitively as good as our own. But this is precisely the radical interpretation to which he wanted to provide an alternative. With this interpretation, the perspectivist cannot handle the problems of self-reference and truth in the way Nehamas suggests. If there are always competing perspectives that are as good as our own, then it is not merely the case that perspectivism itself could be false. Rather, from some equally legitimate perspective, it is false. Further, in making all beliefs equally true, his interpretation makes them all false. Only the whole that incorporates them all is true. Thus, if we accept Nehamas' account of how our beliefs falsify, we make perspectivism vulnerable to the very objections against which he wanted to defend it. Nehamas can defend perspectivism against these objections by reducing it to anti-foundationalism. In that case, however, perspectivism will not explain Nietzsche's claim that knowledge falsifies or any other claim about truth.

My solution to these problems has been to demote the falsification thesis to Nietzsche's earlier works and to interpret the metaphor of perspective as a rhetorical device designed to help us overcome the devaluation of human knowledge involved in the falsification thesis. According to my interpretation, the perspectival character of knowledge is perfectly compatible with some interpretations being true, and it introduces no paradoxes of self-reference. Perspectivism is, of course, a perspectival truth, but this does not imply that any competing claim is also true.

6

THE ASCETIC IDEAL

The most important remaining objection to my interpretation of Nietzsche's mature view of truth concerns its compatibility with his account of the ascetic ideal, in particular, with GM III's extended analysis of the faith in truth as the latest expression of the ascetic ideal. Walter Kaufmann defends Nietzsche as one who believed in truth by portraying him as a proponent of the ascetic ideal (1974, 245, 359–61; 1968a, esp. 584 ff.) Because I argue (in sections 1 and 2 of this chapter) that Nietzsche opposed all versions of the ascetic ideal, I must find some other way of reconciling his analysis of the faith in truth with my claim that he accepts the existence of truth.

Quite apart from the defense it provides of the interpretation I have already given, my account of Nietzsche's analysis of the ascetic ideal plays a central role in this study. It takes us beyond the arguments I have already given to Nietzsche's ultimate reason for rejecting the metaphysical correspondence theory – not simply that it involves an internal contradiction (which I have argued he thinks it does), but that it reflects and is used to support an ideal he opposes and considers dangerous. It thereby gives Nietzsche's explanation for how it is that so many brilliant philosophers have found themselves bewitched by what he considers nonsense (section 3). I will argue (Chapters 7 and 8) that this analysis of the ascetic ideal also allows us to understand Nietzsche's doctrines of the will to power and eternal recurrence as constituting the "fundamentally opposite doctrine and valuation of life" he claimed to discover for himself (BT P, 5).

1. Nietzsche's opposition to the ascetic ideal

The ascetic ideal is the idealization of asceticism, the belief that the best human life is one of self-denial. The third essay of *On the Genealogy of Morals,* Nietzsche's analysis of this ideal, leaves little doubt that he opposes it. However, the essay also seems designed to confuse readers concerning how many ascetic ideals there are and which ones he opposes.

Nietzsche initially responds to his title question – "What is the meaning of ascetic ideals?" – by distinguishing different ascetic ideals (or different versions of the ascetic ideal), most importantly, the philosophers' and the priests'. Yet, all talk of "ascetic ideals" soon drops out and he refers only to "the ascetic ideal." The conclusions formulated in the essays's final paragraph concern *the* ascetic ideal. This ideal, Nietzsche claims, saved the will from suicidal nihilism at a time when human beings did not know how "to justify, to account for, to affirm" themselves. The ascetic ideal gave their lives meaning, making it possible for them to will something. However, Nietzsche concludes

> We can no longer conceal from ourselves *what* is expressed by all of the willing that has taken its direction from the ascetic ideal: this hatred of the human, and even more of the animal, and more still of the material, this horror of the senses, of reason itself, this fear of happiness and beauty, this longing to get away from all appearance, change, becoming, death, wishing, from longing itself – all this means, let us dare to grasp it – a will to nothingness, a willing directed against life [*einen Widerwillen gegen das Leben*], a rebellion against the most fundamental presuppositions of life; but it is and remains a *will!* . . . And to repeat in conclusion what I said in the beginning, human beings would rather will *nothingness* than *not* will (GM III, 28).

If this passage leaves any doubt that Nietzsche opposes the ascetic ideal, his later comments on GM III erase it.

GM III explains, he writes in EH, "whence the ascetic ideal, the priests' ideal, derives its tremendous power although it is the

harmful ideal *par excellence,* a will to the end, an ideal of deca-
dence": "because it was the only ideal so far, because it had no
rival. . . . Above all, a *counterideal* was lacking – *until Zarathustra*"
(EH III, GM). Nietzsche clearly sees his own task as that of
providing an alternative to the ascetic ideal. (See Chapter 8 for a
discussion of his counterideal.)

That Nietzsche equates the ascetic ideal with the priests' ideal
helps to explain why he opposes it. The problem is not its requirement of self-denial – the self-restraint and self-denial it fos-
ters is its saving grace (GM III, 16; cf. BG 188) – but its valuation
of human life.

> The idea at issue here is the *valuation* the ascetic priest places on
> our life: he juxtaposes it (along with what pertains to it: "nature,"
> "world," the whole sphere of becoming and transitoriness) with a
> quite different mode of existence which it opposes and excludes,
> *unless* it turn against itself, *deny itself:* in that case, the case of the
> ascetic life, life counts as a bridge to that other mode of existence.
> The ascetic treats life as a wrong road on which one must finally
> walk back to the point where it begins, or as a mistake that is put
> right by deeds – that we *ought* to put right: for he *demands* that one
> go along with him; where he can he compels acceptance of *his*
> evaluation of existence.
>
> What does this mean? So monstrous a mode of valuation stands
> inscribed in the history of mankind not as an exception and curios-
> ity, but as one of the most widespread and enduring of all phe-
> nomena. Read from a distant star, the majuscule script of our
> earthly existence would perhaps lead to the conclusion that the
> earth was the distinctly *ascetic planet,* a nook of disgruntled, arro-
> gant, and offensive creatures filled with a profound disgust at
> themselves, at the earth, at all of life, who inflict as much pain on
> themselves as they possibly can out of pleasure at inflicting pain –
> which is probably their only pleasure (GM III, 11).

This description of the ascetic ideal emphasizes a valuation of
human life Nietzsche calls "monstrous." I take his point to be
that the priest's idealization of self-denial – denial of one's natural or animal self – implies a negative valuation of natural human existence, which is granted positive value only insofar as it
becomes a means to its own negation (nirvana or heaven, for
example). One might, Nietzsche implies in his discussion of philosophers (see section 2), praise poverty or chastity as a means of
avoiding distraction from one's tasks, without thus devaluing

human existence. Interpreting them as valuable because they involve self-denial, on the other hand, surely implies that natural, earthly, or material existence is devoid of value and in need of redemption. The idealization of self-denial makes sense only on the basis of such a devaluation of human life.

If the ascetic ideal involves such a devaluation of human life, it seems clear that Nietzsche opposes it, for he identifies himself with a quite opposed valuation of life. His first book, he tells us, already revealed an instinct that turned against Christian morality and its devaluation of human life: "it was an instinct that aligned itself with life and discovered for itself a fundamentally opposite doctrine and valuation of life" – one he baptized "Dionysian" (BT P, 5). He also claims to be the first to turn the Dionysian yes-saying into a philosophical pathos (EH III, BT 3). He clearly opposes the valuation of natural human existence he identifies with the ascetic ideal.

Nehamas would reject this interpretation on the basis of Nietzsche's insistence that "judgments of value concerning life, for it or against it, can in the end never be true" (TI II, 2). Nietzsche evidently denies all value to statements that life has or does not have value. He gives as his reason *"that the value of life cannot be estimated."*

> Not by the living, for they are an interested party, a bone of contention, and not judges; not by the dead, for a different reason (TI II, 2).

Judgments of the value of life therefore have value, he claims, only as symptoms, expressions of one's fundamental attitude toward life. Nehamas thinks it follows that "Nietzsche cannot take any general attitude towards life and the world seriously," and that he cannot offer an opposed valuation of life to replace the ascetic one (1985, 135). Nietzsche's opposition to the ascetic valuation of life, on Nehamas' interpretation, is merely his objection to "any general valuation of this sort, positive or negative."

I agree that Nietzsche cannot object to the ascetic ideal on the grounds that life really is valuable. It follows from the passage in question that Nietzsche cannot take seriously general attitudes towards life insofar as they masquerade as judgments possessing a truth value. It also follows that he cannot criticize or promote a general attitude towards life on the grounds of its truth. But it does not follow that he cannot adopt and promote a general attitude towards life. Nor need he confine his objection to the meta-level claim that no such valuations can be true. Nehamas' assumption to the contrary would follow only if truth provided Nietzsche's only basis for opposing the ascetic devaluation of life. However, Nietzsche's objection to the ascetic ideal centers around its harmfulness – he calls it "the harmful ideal par excellence" (EH III, GM). Although Nehamas recognizes his concern with the ideal's harm, he apparently thinks Nietzsche could not have found it generally harmful since so much of GM is devoted to explaining its benefits (saving the will from suicidal nihilism, e.g.). Nehamas supposes that GM attempts to show that the ideal was beneficial to some but harmful to others, and that Nietzsche therefore opposes not the ideal itself, but only its demand for universal acceptance.

But giving up "the very idea of trying to determine in general terms the value of life" (Nehamas, 1985, 136) does not require Nietzsche to give up trying to determine in general terms the value of the ascetic ideal – for life. Nietzsche indicates in BG that he adopts as his measure of value what benefits life in general (I take this to mean "human life in general") – what is "life-promoting, life-preserving, species-preserving, perhaps even species-cultivating" (BG 4). And GM III certainly seems concerned with life in general. Of the ascetic priest, this "*life-inimical* species," Nietzsche insists that "it must be in the *interest of life itself* that such a self-contradictory type does not die out" (GM III, 11). The ascetic ideal, he concludes, is "an artifice for the preservation of life," and the ascetic priest is "among the greatest conserving and yes-creating forces of life" who creates "more favorable conditions for being here and being human" (GM III, 13). Although GM III certainly stresses differences in how the ascetic ideal served different groups – for example, priests and their followers – its conclusion points to a general benefit: it saved the will from suicidal nihilism. That is, it saved the human species, at a time when its "existence on earth contained no goal; . . . the *will* for human beings and earth was lacking" (GM III, 28). It gave these beings ways of affirming their lives, of finding them worth living, when no alternative was available. While it may have done this in different ways for different groups, I see no evidence that Nietzsche thinks some groups could have done without it.

True, the life-affirming nobles of GM's first essay do not seem to need it. But they "compensate themselves in the wilderness" for the restraint necessary within the walls of society by going back "to the innocent conscience of the beast of prey, as triumphant monsters who perhaps emerge from a disgusting procession of murder, arson, rape, and torture, exhilarated and undisturbed of soul" (GM I, 11). We should not ignore Nietzsche's suggestion at the end of the same section that the instincts of resentment that helped to overthrow "the noble races and their ideals" are *actual instruments of culture.*" Nietzsche's quickness to deny that the bearers of such instincts represent culture (or perhaps better, civilization) draws attention away from his important suggestion that the overthrow of the noble ideals promoted the spread of civilization. GM II's discussion of the bad conscience helps explain why.

Nietzsche presents the bad conscience as a necessary development when the walls of society are built high and wide enough to eliminate any area where hostile impulses can be freely expressed against other human beings. The absence of external enemies makes necessary the internalization of aggression, hostility, and cruelty in the form of guilt – self-castigation, and various forms of self-punishment. Given the impossibility of external expression of hostile impulses, Nietzsche makes clear in both GM II and III, the absence of such internalization leads to depression, a sickness of the will. In GM II, Nietzsche writes as if the saving internalization occurs automatically when the threat of depression becomes serious enough. But this cannot be right. An ideal of some kind must be present to provide a basis for self-castigation and self-punishment. Nietzsche clearly thinks the ascetic priest provided (eg. GM III, 17, 20; cf. II, 16) the means for avoiding depression with his ideal of self-denial (see Chapter 7 for the psychology involved in this claim).

In GM II, Nietzsche discusses only the oppressed as originators of the bad conscience. But the contemplatives he discusses in GM I, the priests, reached the relevant state he ascribes to the oppressed – inability to express hostile impulses against others – at an earlier stage, and the nobles would reach it later when their wilderness became part of civilization. Nietzsche seems to be saying that it is in everyone's interests to have an ideal on the basis of which to internalize impulses, and the ascetic ideal is the only ideal offered so far. He also seems to believe it is in the general interest to have the ideal widely accepted, an ideal that *"alters the direction of resentment"* – directing it back against the self in the form of "self-discipline, self-surveillance, self-overcoming" (III, 16) – thus preventing the explosive *ressentiment* from leading to an anarchy that would "blow up herd and herdsmen" (III, 15). At the same time, it rules out the barbaric behavior of the nobles described in GM I.

If he thinks it has so many benefits, how can Nietzsche oppose the ascetic ideal? If what benefits life constitutes his measure of value (BG 4), surely he must support an ideal that brings the benefits he describes – unless he has an alternative way of gaining these benefits. Given such an alternative, his positive attitude towards life might require him to oppose an ideal that helps life only at the cost of slandering it, and Nietzsche clearly does have an alternative in mind. I have already quoted the passage in which he implies that Zarathustra supplies a counterideal (EH III, GM). Further, he offers what seems like a recipe for this counterideal at the end of GM II. Although millennia of "conscience vivisection and self-torture of our animal natures [*Selbsttierquaelerie*]" have made the "evil eye" for our natural inclinations inseparable from our "bad conscience," Nietzsche insists that

> an attempt at the reverse would *in itself* be possible – but who is strong enough for it? – that is, to wed the bad conscience to all the *unnatural* inclinations, all those aspirations to the beyond, to that which runs counter to sense, instinct, nature, animal, in short all ideals hitherto, which are one and all hostile to life and ideals that slander the world. To whom should one turn today with *such* hopes and demands? (GM II, 24)

I interpret this to mean that while human beings need the bad conscience, that is, a demand for the internalization of aggression, this demand could be made in the name of an ideal that condemns what condemns life, instead of the ascetic ideal which condemns life itself. The continuation of this passage implies that this "attempt at the reverse" constitutes our only chance for redemption from "the hitherto reigning ideal but also from what was bound to grow out of it, the great nausea, the will to nothingness, nihilism," our only hope of something that "liberates the will again and restores its goal to earth and hope to human beings." Nietzsche then tells us that he has no right to speak further about this project, that we must turn to Zarathustra with our hopes (GM III, 25). Because, as I shall argue in Chapter 8, Nietzsche's suggestion for reversing the bad conscience constitutes a recipe for Zarathustra's Übermensch ideal, this seems entirely appropriate.[1]

This passage helps our understanding of Nietzsche's opposition to the ascetic ideal. If the ascetic ideal were doing its job of saving the will from suicidal nihilism, Nietzsche's proposal for an alternative ideal would seem an insufficient reason for opposing it. One could argue that the effectiveness of the old ideal has been confirmed for millennia, whereas we have no experience to confirm the workability of the counterideal. However, the above passage makes clear Nietzsche's belief that the ascetic ideal is no longer accomplishing much that is positive. He seems to view the ascetic ideal's strategy for saving the will from suicidal nihilism as ultimately self-defeating. Even though the ascetic priest is "an incarnate wish to be different, to be in a different place" and his ideal deprives life of positive value, the ideal helped, in the short run, to "create more favorable conditions for being here and being human" (GM III, 13). It did so by giving human beings a way of affirming life, of finding it valuable or worth living, namely, as a means to the world beyond. But the self-denial promoted by the ascetic ideal, Nietzsche argues at the end of GM III (see section 4), ultimately called into question the ideal's metaphysical supports, in particular, the existence of God, freedom, and immorality. At this point, the ascetic ideal offers little that is life-enhancing. It no longer encourages widespread self-discipline or restraint. And it no longer provides much help with the affirmation of life – except among those who, like the old saint in *Zarathustra*, have not yet heard that God is dead – since it now deprives life of its value as a means to another world after having previously stripped life of any intrinsic value.

But if the ascetic ideal is now so ineffective, why does Nietzsche care enough about it to analyze it at length and style himself its opponent? I believe he thinks it is still very effective today in

---

1. I will argue, however, that the Übermensch ideal is still an expression of the ascetic ideal, that it is therefore unsuccessful in providing a counterideal, and that part of the point of Nietzsche's presentation is to allow us to see this. But I will also argue that *Zarathustra* does finally present us with an ideal that takes us beyond the ascetic ideal.

philosophy, where it works against the development of ideals, in particular, counterideals to the ascetic ideal. This is what I shall argue in the remainder of this chapter.

2. Philosophers and the ascetic ideal

Nietzsche devotes several sections of GM III to developing what appears to be a distinction between the philosopher's ascetic ideal and the priest's. I inferred his rejection of the ascetic ideal from his rejection of the priest's ideal and his reference to the latter as "the ascetic ideal." His distinction between two versions of the ascetic ideal would allow one to infer instead that he rejects the priestly version while accepting the philosopher's. This inference seems to underlie Kaufmann's interpretation of Nietzsche as a proponent of both the ascetic ideal and of the belief in truth Nietzsche calls its latest expression. Even those who think Nietzsche finds the belief in truth problematic often interpret him as supporting the philosopher's ascetic ideal.[2] I will argue that the distinction Nietzsche draws is largely apparent, that GM III presents the philosopher as an instance of the ascetic priest.

Nietzsche's initial description certainly seems designed to differentiate the philosopher's ascetic ideal from the priestly version. Although he begins by noting the "peculiar philosopher's irritation at and rancor against sensuality" (GM III, 7), he apparently denies that there is anything moral or life-denying about philosophers' asceticism. Like every other animal, the philosopher "instinctively strives for an optimum of favorable conditions under which it can expend all its strength and achieve its maximal feeling of power." To this end, philosophers avoid the entrapments of family life, love of luxury and refinement, and "unrestrained and irritable pride" (GM III, 8). For them, asceticism constitutes "so many bridges to *independence*" and establishes the most favorable conditions for the development of a higher spirituality. There is nothing of virtue in their asceticism, Nietzsche insists, meaning not to deny its value, but to insist that it does not fit the priest's understanding of virtue. Rather than denying themselves or exis-

2. Nehamas, for instance, uses this interpretation to support his view that Nietzsche opposes not the ascetic ideal but only its demand for universal acceptance. Nehamas treats the absence of that demand as the major factor that differentiates the philosopher's version of the ascetic ideal from the priest's.

tence, Nietzsche claims, philosophers simply follow the lead of their dominating instinct, and avoid what interferes with it. Here speaks prudence and self-affirmation, not morality or the devaluation of life.

Why, then, does Nietzsche consider philosophers friends of the ascetic ideal? The attitude he attributes to them – their chastity is not "from any kind of ascetic scruple or hatred of the senses, just as it is not chastity when an athlete or jockey abstains from women" (GM III, 8) – is no more ascetic than the one attributed to the early Wagner, who Nietzsche says did not pay homage to chastity "in an ascetic sense" until the very end (GM III, 2). I propose that Nietzsche's account of philosophers has been deliberately misleading and that he actually believes that they accept the priest's ascetic ideal.

Nietzsche himself describes GM as "perhaps uncannier than anything written so far" regarding "expression, intention, and the art of surprise," and tells us that each essay has "a beginning *calculated* to mislead" (EH III, GM). It is also noteworthy that he prefixed to GM III an aphorism from the section of *Zarathustra* "On Reading and Writing," which informs us that "another century of readers – and the spirit itself will stink" (Z I, 7). Nietzsche seems to have constructed this essay as a test for readers. He finally makes explicit in GM III itself that an examination of history reveals a stronger bond between philosophy and the ascetic ideal than he previously suggested. "It was only on the leading-strings of this ideal that philosophy learned to take its first small steps on earth" (GM III, 9). It becomes clear that "this ideal" refers to the priest's ascetic ideal when Nietzsche explains that

> the philosophic spirit always had to use as a mask and cocoon the *previously established* types of the contemplative man – priest, sorcerer, soothsayer, in any case a religious type – in order to be able *to exist at all: the ascetic ideal* for a long time served the philosopher as a form in which to appear, as a precondition of existence – he had to *represent* it so as to be able to be a philosopher; he had to *believe* in it in order to be able to represent it. The peculiar, withdrawn attitude of the philosopher, world-denying, hostile to life, suspicious of the senses, freed from sensuality, which has been maintained down to the most modern times and become virtually the *philosopher's pose par excellence;* for the longest time philosophy would not have been *possible at all* on earth without ascetic wraps and cloak, without an ascetic self-misunderstanding (GM III, 10).

Here Nietzsche claims that philosophers have both represented and believed in the priestly version of the ascetic ideal. There has been no independent philosopher's ascetic ideal. "Only now that we behold the ascetic priest do we seriously come to grips with our problem: what is the meaning of the ascetic ideal?" (GM III, 11). This means: We will understand philosophers' commitment to the ascetic ideal only by understanding the philosopher as an ascetic priest, that is, as sharing the latter's valuation of human existence.

As evidence for this interpretation, consider Nietzsche's assertion that philosophy has involved an "ascetic self-misunderstanding." The self-misunderstanding in question is surely not the belief that philosophy involves the denial of some desires. It would be absurd for Nietzsche to suggest that practicing philosophy is compatible with satisfying all of one's original desires. Nor could he plausibly claim that philosophers have misinterpreted the necessity of self-restraint as self-denial instead of self-fulfillment. Even in the *Phaedo,* his great panegyric to the ascetic ideal, Plato presents philosophy as the highest pleasure and self-fulfillment. Why Nietzsche would nevertheless find an ascetic misinterpretation of philosophy in this dialogue – which he knew well and taught repeatedly at Basel – becomes apparent if we consider its connection to the ascetic priests' valuation of natural human existence.

In the *Phaedo,* the dying Socrates interprets philosophy as a turning away from life or natural human existence, as, in effect, a "being towards death." Philosophers should not be afraid of death, he argues, since they have actually "been looking forward to death all their lives" (64 a). Philosophy requires one to achieve a state that fits the definition of death, namely, the separation of mind from body, because its aims can be realized only by a mind freed from the contaminating influences of the senses and bodily pleasure, the contaminating influence of our animal nature. Plato has Socrates argue that philosophy aims at knowledge and truth, whereas the senses can provide only opinion and illusion. The philosopher must avoid sensuous pleasure, because it ties us to the empirical world, encouraging us to mistake what the senses perceive for reality (83 d).

Plato's interpretation of philosophy counts as ascetic, I suggest, not simply because it takes philosophy to require abstinence, but because its promotion of abstinence embodies a negative valuation of human life. The message behind Plato's understanding of, and praise for, philosophy seems clear: Human life has value (one possesses virtue) only by turning against the natural human condition. As Nehamas suggests, Nietzsche cannot give as a reason for considering this ascetic view of philosophy a misinterpretation that life is really valuable. But he can – and does, I suggest – consider it a misinterpretation on the grounds that philosophy is actually on a continuum with other human activities, whereas Plato posits a radical discontinuity (cf. section 3).

According to my interpretation, GM III's initial distinction between philosophers and priests is misleading because it suggests that philosophers have accepted a naturalistic account of philosophy when Nietzsche actually believes they have accepted instead an "other-worldly" account that reflects the ascetic priest's devaluation of human existence. It is not that Nietzsche lies when he claims that philosophers have found the rejection of sensual pleasures necessary for the development of a higher spirituality (GM III, 9) and to remove obstacles to their engagement in the activity that gives them their highest feeling of power (GM III, 7). But this gives a deliberately incomplete and misleading statement of what he actually believes, namely, that the philosopher's understanding of higher spirituality (as excluding sensuality) derives from the priest's ascetic ideal, and that the obstacles asceticism removes are less the distractions of ordinary human existence than the philosopher's irritation at, or resentment of, this natural existence.

But Nietzsche is obviously making some kind of distinction between philosopher and priest. Once we recognize that he is deliberately misleading us, it becomes tempting to suppose that the distinction he wants us to grasp is between his ideal philosopher and the ascetic priest (including philosophers as they have actually existed). This seems at least partially true (see section 5 for the truth involved). Nietzsche ends this part of his discussion by suggesting that philosophy as he envisions it will be possible only when philosophers discard the "repulsive and gloomy caterpillar form" they have borrowed from the ascetic priest (GM III, 10). On the other hand, BG suggests that current "free spirits" and "philosophers of the future" are "full of malice against the lures of dependence that lie hidden in honors, or money, or offices, or enthusiasms of the senses" (BG 44). Taken together, the two passages suggest that Nietzsche's ideal philosopher will avoid much of what the priest avoids, but will not misinterpret this avoidance ascetically, that is, in a way that devalues natural human existence. These philosophers of the future will not interpret the avoidance in question as self-denial, but as necessary in order to satisfy "the will of their dominating instinct" (GM III, 8), the will with which they most identify themselves.

The danger of this interpretation lies in thinking that the main things Nietzsche's ideal philosopher avoids are what the priest avoids, that is, different forms of sensual enjoyment. Nietzsche does, of course, recognize that the philosopher's concern with worldly goods and pleasures must have limits, limits which others might perceive as self-denying, and that independence as well as time and energy is at issue here. But as much as Nietzsche recognized that concern for worldly possessions could distract a philosopher from important tasks, his own biography suggests that he recognized a decent income as a better solution than poverty. GM III gives us no basis for denying that this was Nietzsche's view, nor that he had a comparable view of chastity. Whatever self-restraint Nietzsche's ideal philosopher did find necessary for the philosophical life would, of course, be interpreted as an expression of the will to power and not as self-denial. It will, in fact, turn out that Nietzsche's ideal philosopher has a great deal of such self-mastery, but it is not the mastery of sensuous impulses that is particularly at issue (see section 5).

I therefore conclude that Nietzsche writes of a philosopher's ascetic ideal not because his ideal philosopher would advocate it, but because he thinks most actual philosophers have interpreted philosophy under the influence of the ascetic priest's devaluation of human life. GM III endeavors not to distinguish a good from a bad version of the ascetic ideal but to point to the previously unrecognized scope and influence of the priests' ascetic ideal.

3. Metaphysics and the ascetic ideal

The most important aspect of the ascetic ideal's influence on philosophy comes into view when Nietzsche asks what will happen if the ascetic priest, this "incarnate will to contradiction and anti-naturalness, is induced to *philosophize:* upon what will it vent its innermost contrariness?"

Upon what is felt most certainly to be real and actual: it will look for error precisely where the instinct of life most unconditionally posits truth. It will, for example, like the ascetics of the Vedanta philosophy, downgrade physicality to an illusion; likewise pain, multiplicity, the entire conceptual apparatus "subject" and "object" – errors, nothing but errors! To renounce the belief in one's own ego, to deny one's own "reality" – what a triumph! not merely over the senses, over appearance, but a much higher kind of triumph, a violation and cruelty against *reason* – a voluptuous pleasure that reaches its height when the ascetic self-contempt and mockery of reason declares: "*there is* a realm of truth and being, but reason is *excluded* from it!" (GM III, 12)

Nietzsche thus claims that philosophical doctrines themselves reflect the influence of the ascetic priest. He includes especially those that reduce the empirical world to the status of "appearance" or "illusion," which result from looking for "error precisely where the instinct of life most unconditionally posits truth." This suggests that we are naturally inclined to accept as true beliefs supported by the testimony of the senses and that the acceptance of doctrines that demote sense testimony to illusion requires self-denial, a denial of satisfaction to our natural impulses. To renounce belief in one's own ego presumably requires even more self-denial. In other words, philosophical doctrines can require the same internalization of cruelty that priests have fostered in the name of the ascetic ideal. Instead of forcing an enemy to accept something against his will, one forces oneself to accept the truth or untruth of certain beliefs when this acceptance is very difficult and goes against one's natural inclinations.

But the difficulty and self-denial involved in accepting them are not sufficient to make philosophical doctrines expressions of the ascetic ideal. As I have discussed, Nietzsche suggests that such internalization of cruelty could be fostered instead by an ideal quite opposed to the ascetic ideal, one expressing an opposite attitude towards life. He counts philosophical doctrines expressions of the ascetic ideal only insofar as they demand self-denial in the service of an interpretation that devalues natural human life. Nietzsche's best account of how philosophical doctrines express the ascetic devaluation of life comes from a passage that explains metaphysics as an expression of the ascetic ideal, although it does not mention the ideal explicitly.

Nietzsche introduces his analysis of metaphysics at the beginning of *Beyond Good and Evil* by raising the "problem of the value of truth" (BG 1). Elsewhere he claims that human purposes are served by both truth and untruth (GS 344, BG 230). Here he asks: "*What* in us really wants truth? . . . why not rather untruth?" In other words, if both are useful, why do we praise truth so extravagantly over untruth? The next section of BG explains why metaphysicians have done so.

"How *could* anything originate out of its opposite? for example, truth out of error? or the will to truth out of the will to deception? or selfless deeds out of selfishness? or the pure sunlike gaze of the sage out of lust? Such origins are impossible; whoever dreams of them is a fool, indeed worse; the things of the highest value must have another *peculiar* origin – they cannot be derived from this transitory, seductive, deceptive, paltry world, from this turmoil of delusion and lust. Rather from the lap of Being, the intransitory, the hidden god, the "thing-in-itself" – there must be their basis, and nowhere else."

This way of judging constitutes the typical prejudgment and prejudice which gives away the metaphysicians of all ages; this kind of valuation looms in the background of their logical procedures; it is on account of this "faith" that they trouble themselves about "knowledge," about something that is finally baptized solemnly as "the truth." The fundamental faith of metaphysicians is *the faith in opposite values* (B 2).

Nietzsche evidently counts as metaphysicians those who believe in a metaphysical or "true" world, for his main claim is that such a world is required by the metaphysician's faith in opposite values (*die Gegensätze der Werte*). In accord with my discussion in Chapter 4, this means that a metaphysician believes that truth differs from what is empirically accessible and therefore understands truth as correspondence to things-in-themselves and true knowledge as *a priori*. The passage also purports to explain this understanding of knowledge and truth – why metaphysicians have wanted what they call "knowledge" and "truth" – in terms of the faith in opposite values. It is less evident what this faith amounts to.

In some sense, all valuation involves opposite values. "Good" and "bad," "beautiful" and "ugly," "intelligent" and "stupid," "courageous" and "cowardly" are terms used of items placed at opposite ends of a value scale, and in that sense name opposite values. But every value term seems to have a place on a scale with such opposite ends. However, the "faith in opposite values" clearly refers to a commitment to a particular kind of value or value system. We can understand this commitment as a faith that things at opposite ends of the value scale are themselves opposites, that is, negations of, and therefore unconnected to, each other. This is how Nietzsche explains the motivation for belief in a "true" or metaphysical world: Such a world is needed as a source for things of the highest value given the belief that these have no connection to things of lower value.

HA already connects metaphysics to a belief in opposites. In its first section, Nietzsche claims that philosophical problems still take the same form they did two thousand years ago, namely, "how can something originate from its opposite, for example, the rational from the irrational, the sentient from the dead, logic from illogic, disinterested contemplation from covetous desire, living for others from egoism, truth from error?" He claims that metaphysical philosophy answered this question by denying that "the one originates from the other" and assuming "for the more highly valued thing a miraculous source in the very kernel and essence of the thing-in-itself" (HA 1). This sounds very similar to BG's later account. In both works, Nietzsche claims that the thing-in-itself (in its role as metaphysical or "true" world) functions to explain the origin of highly valued things without connecting them to their opposites. But there are important differences between these two accounts of metaphysics.

In HA, the problem that gives rise to metaphysics is a purely cognitive one of explaining the origin of certain things that happen to be highly valued. Nietzsche attempts to undermine metaphysics by showing it to be cognitively superfluous. He does this by providing naturalistic interpretations of things of the highest value, explanations which connect these things to their apparent opposites, thus showing them to be "human, alas, all-too-human" (EH III, HA).

> Historical philosophy, which is no longer to be thought of as separate from the natural sciences, has discovered in individual cases (and this will probably be the result in all others) that there are no opposites, except in the customary exaggeration of popular or metaphysical interpretations, and that a mistake in reasoning lies at the base of this antithesis. According to its explanation, there

exists, strictly speaking, neither an unegoistic action nor a completely disinterested contemplation; both are only sublimations, in which the underlying element appears almost evaporated and shows itself to be still present only under the most acute observation (HA 1).

Nietzsche thus agrees with metaphysicians that a thing cannot come from its opposite (based, I assume, on the definition of "opposites" as qualities that negate each other or have no aspect in common). He rejects the inference to a metaphysical world by arguing that there are no opposites, that things come from their apparent opposites by a process of sublimation (*Sublimirung*). He thereby provides an alternative solution to the metaphysicians' original problem and views metaphysics as based on a "mistake in reasoning," a belief that something that is only the sublimation of another thing is really its opposite or negation.

HA thus considers metaphysics to be based on an innocent mistake. The metaphysician fails to solve his purely cognitive problem concerning the origin of opposites due to mistaken observations. BG rejects this view; Nietzsche now turns from the business of solving philosophical problems to that of diagnosis. No longer content to expose the metaphysical world as cognitively superfluous, he sets out to abolish it. He denies its existence, I have argued, by exposing as a contradiction in terms the thing-in-itself presupposed by the "true" world. To combat metaphysics, then, he no longer has any need to argue that there are no opposites, or that all apparent opposites are interconnected. Why, then, does his account of metaphysics in BG sound so similar?

His critique of metaphysics would have been less convincing if he had merely pointed out the contradiction on which he claims it depends. For this leaves a major question: How could it have happened that some of the greatest minds (which Nietzsche surely thinks the great metaphysicians were) got confused in this way? If the idea of truth, as metaphysicians understand it, involves a contradiction in terms, why did they want it? The answer Nietzsche offers here is that they did not after all want such a truth. What they wanted was to keep the things they valued unsullied by connection to things they did not value.

Gradually it has become clear to me what every great philosophy has been: namely, the personal confession of its author and a kind of involuntary memoir; also that the moral (or immoral) intentions in every philosophy constituted the real germ of life from which the whole plant has grown. Indeed, if one would explain how the most abstruse metaphysical claims of a philosopher really came about, it is always well (and wise) to ask first: at what morality does all this (does *he*) aim? Accordingly, I do not believe that a "drive to knowledge" is the father of philosophy; but rather another drive has, here as elsewhere, employed understanding (and misunderstanding) as a mere instrument (BG 6).

This passage denies that the bottom line of a (great) philosophy is ever an innocent mistake or a purely cognitive problem. Nietzsche does not deny that philosophers address such problems or that they (sometimes) achieve knowledge or truth. His point is that they do so (as they make important mistakes) in the service of what they consider more important purposes. Nietzsche makes clearer what these (moral, or, sometimes, immoral) purposes are a few sections later when he claims that the Stoics, who pretended to find the canon of their moral law written into nature, actually constructed nature in the image of their morality, "as an immense, eternal glorification and generalization of Stoicism." In other words, Stoics arrived at their idea of natural law, which they used to defend their ethical ideal, by projecting that ideal of self-tyranny onto nature. Nietzsche adds that this "is an ancient, eternal story: what formerly happened with the Stoics happens today, too, as soon as any philosophy begins to believe in itself. It always creates the world in its own image" (BG 9).

Nietzsche thus claims that, at least in the case of the great philosophies, knowledge, mistakes, and cognitive problems are always employed in the service of constructing the world (i.e., a picture of the world) so that it reflects the philosopher's values or ideal. It is not surprising, therefore, that BG's account of metaphysics brings values to the fore. Values entered into HA's account only peripherally, insofar as the "true" world was needed as a source for things that happened to be highly valued. In BG, Nietzsche insists that philosophers' basic concern was not to explain where these highly valued things came from, but to keep them unsullied by connection to things of a lower value. The metaphysicians' belief that there are opposites, that is, their denial that things at opposite ends of the value scale are connected, is no longer an innocent or purely intellectual mistake based on insufficient observation, but an attempt to express, defend, and reinforce certain value judgments. Metaphysics is based on a faith in opposite values in the sense that metaphysicians' value judgments forced them to insist that things of the highest value have no connection with things of a lower value, thus giving them a need for a metaphysical world to account for the existence of the former.

These value judgments correspond to those of the ascetic ideal. This is implied by the reasoning Nietzsche attributes to metaphysicians at the end of the first paragraph quoted above from BG 2. Metaphysicians deny any connection between the things they value and the things they do not in order to save the former from any contamination by nature, by the things of "this" world. The point is that a connection to nature would deprive the highly valued things of their value. Metaphysicians' faith in opposite values turns out to be the belief that things of the highest value must be negations of things of this world. This is precisely the ascetic ideal. Natural human existence is deprived of value, which is taken to reside only in what turns against or negates "this" world. The "true" world, Nietzsche implies, was needed to promote the values of the ascetic ideal, to insure that highly valued things did not reveal any connection to nature.

I return now to the explanation of the metaphysical understanding of knowledge and truth offered by BG 2. It is because of their faith in opposite values, Nietzsche claims, that metaphysicians "trouble themselves about 'knowledge,' about something that they finally baptize solemnly as 'the truth.' " He insists, further, that "this kind of valuation looms in the background of their logical procedures." That is, we can explain why metaphysicians rely on logical procedures rather than empirical knowledge and why they want what they call "knowledge" and "the truth" – knowledge of, and correspondence to, things as they are in themselves – in terms of the valuation Nietzsche calls "the faith in opposite values," but which he might have called instead "the ascetic ideal." Since they accord truth and knowledge the highest value, metaphysicians cannot allow them to be intimately connected to what belongs to us as natural creatures. Knowledge cannot, therefore, depend on the senses; it must be *a priori*. Its object, truth, must be completely independent of human beings, independent of both our merely human capacities and our interests. The ascetic ideal's devaluation of natural human existence underlies these positions.

Nietzsche makes this same point explicit when he claims (in the passage from GM III quoted at the beginning of this section) that the ascetic priest, when induced to philosophize, will vent his "innermost contrariness" upon what is felt to be most real, and therefore "will look for error precisely where the instinct of life most unconditionally posits truth" (GM III, 12). The latter is precisely what metaphysicians do, when they insist that knowledge is of a "true" world, that the empirical world is illusory. Nietzsche's statement thus makes clear his view that such metaphysical doctrines concerning knowledge and truth are themselves expressions of the ascetic ideal.

But his description of the ascetic priest's philosophical views also fits Nietzsche's own position in TL (see Chapter 3). That "truths are illusions" certainly posits error where the instinct of life posits truth. That TL does not claim knowledge of a "true" world only makes its position more ascetic, more demanding of self-denial. Traditional metaphysics offers to satisfy the desire for truth, after all, if we will overcome our impulse to accept the reliability of the senses. TL demands the same self-denial, but without the compensation.

Further, the demand for self-denial in TL (the relinquishing of any claim to possess truth) was based on the same life-devaluing conception of truth that Nietzsche later finds among metaphysicians. As I have argued, TL based its claim that truths are illusions on the assumption that only something independent of human beings, and nothing merely "anthropomorphic," has sufficient value to deserve the unqualified status of "truth." That this assumption was inspired, at least in part, by the realization that knowledge is itself a product of nature (that cognitive interests ultimately reflect practical interests) gives further reason to conclude that TL reflects the values of the ascetic ideal.[3] Having

3. This is not to deny that TL already opposed the ascetic ideal insofar as it denied that the statements or beliefs we call "truths" possess a higher source of value than nature or life can provide. But I believe it also accepted the ascetic ideal's devaluation of life, as revealed by its refusal to use the value-laden term "truth" for anything without a higher source of value. While Nietzsche opposed the ascetic ideal in TL, he also retained that ideal's valuation of human life. It was this ambivalence in relation to the ascetic ideal that ultimately forced him to reject the existence of truth. I argue that this ambivalence is already quite apparent in BT in Clark, 1987.

discovered the connection denied by metaphysicians between knowledge (and truth) and nature, Nietzsche devalues our knowledge and truths. This explains why Nietzsche places his major statement of perspectivism, the passage analyzed in Chapter 5, immediately after his passage on the ascetic priest who is induced to philosophize (GM III, 12). After presenting metaphysics as a reinterpretation of knowledge and truth designed to separate them from what the ascetic ideal devalues, Nietzsche presents perspectivism as his alternative to the metaphysician's ascetic understanding of knowledge and truth. By getting rid of the thing-in-itself, perspectivism reconnects knowledge and truth to nature – knowledge to the senses and truth to our cognitive interests which Nietzsche still sees as rooted in our practical interests, our interests as natural beings. It removes any excuse for demoting the empirical world to illusion, for insisting that knowledge must be *a priori*, and for regarding truth as independent of our cognitive interests.

When perspectivism is interpreted as limiting our capacity for knowledge, it is difficult to explain why Nietzsche would consider it unascetic. In fact, when he uses it to insist on the limits of human knowledge – in the works before GM, works belonging to the penultimate stage of his history of the "true" world – perspectivism does serve the ascetic ideal (e.g., GS 354). For it devalues the knowledge and truth of which we are capable. The underlying point of Nietzsche's earlier perspectivism is the same as TL's denial of truth: If knowledge and truth are so intimately connected to nature, they cannot have the value we accord them. This is why BG is a turning point. Nietzsche sees the technical problem involved in combining perspectivism with representationalism (BG 15) – a combination which is necessary, as the discussion of Chapter 4 (section 4) implies, if perspectivism is to be tied to the falsification thesis. But he also makes the crucial claim that "the falsity of a judgment is for us not yet an objection to a judgment" (BG 4). Once falsity does not devalue a judgment, Nietzsche's point in calling truths illusions is lost, and it is not surprising, therefore, that he no longer puts forward any version of this claim in the books he published after BG.[4]

4. He does put forward a version of this claim in GS V, which first appeared in the second edition of GS published slightly after BG. However, it is still the case that Nietzsche makes no such claim in any new book published after BG.

As I shall argue in the following two sections, however, even his new version of perspectivism (the one I present in Chapter 5) does not suffice, according to Nietzsche's account, to overcome the ascetic ideal's influence on philosophy.

4. Truth and the ascetic ideal

Nietzsche's account does not confine the influence of the ascetic ideal on philosophy to metaphysics. That the ideal has greatly influenced the development of antimetaphysical philosophy is a major implication of his famous claim in GM III that the faith in truth is the latest expression of the ascetic ideal.

The extended discussion of the will to truth at the end of GM III, Nietzsche warns, will bring us to "the ultimate and most terrifying aspect" of his question concerning the ascetic ideal: that it has no match, – that we have had no alternative to it. He begins by considering science as a match for the ascetic ideal's "closed system of will, goal, and interpretation" (GM III, 23; cf. EH III, GM). Modern science seems to provide a counterideal, he claims, because

> it has not merely waged a long and successful fight against this ideal, it has already conquered this ideal in all important respects: all of modern *science* is supposed to bear witness to that – modern science which, as a genuine philosophy of reality clearly believes in itself alone, clearly possesses the courage for itself and the will to itself, and has up to now survived well enough without God, the beyond, and the virtues of denial (GM III, 23).

But Nietzsche denies this:

> The truth is precisely the opposite of what is asserted here: science today has absolutely *no* belief in itself, let alone an ideal above it – and where it still inspires passion, love, ardor, and *suffering* at all, it is not the opposite of the ascetic ideal but rather *the latest and noblest form of it.*
>   . . . these last idealists of knowledge in whom alone the intellectual conscience dwells and is incarnate today – they certainly be-

The transitional nature of GS V – some sections point forward to GM (e.g., 344 and 357, quoted in GM III), others (e.g., 354) clearly belong to the fifth stage of Nietzsche's history of the "true" world – makes its publication as part of GS appropriate.

lieve that they are as completely liberated from the ascetic ideal as possible, these "free, *very* free spirits"; and yet to disclose to them what they themselves cannot see – for they are too close to themselves: this ideal is precisely *their* ideal, too; they themselves are its most spiritualized product, its most advanced front-line troops and scouts, its most captious, tender, intangible form of seduction – if I have guessed any riddles, I wish that *this* proposition might show it! – They are far from being *free* spirits: for *they still have faith in truth.* (GM III, 23–4).

Nietzsche thus claims to have uncovered the faith in truth as the latest expression of the ascetic ideal. The interpretation of his discovery must be able to explain why he considers it so important and difficult – that is, why he claims to be discussing here the "ultimate and most terrifying aspect" of the ascetic ideal and why he is willing to have his reputation as riddle-guesser depend on it.

Radical interpreters assume that "the faith in truth" Nietzsche considers ascetic is the belief that truth exists (that some beliefs are true rather than false or illusory). Given Nietzsche's opposition to the ascetic ideal, GM III then appears to be a challenge to the belief that truth exists, or that science gives us truth. As this interpretation would provide a strong basis for rejecting my account of Nietzsche's development, I will present several reasons to reject its initial assumption.

If Nietzsche's analysis of the faith in truth shows that we must give up the belief that anything is true, it might well seem both terrifying and important. However, it is the fact that the belief in truth is *ascetic* that Nietzsche seems to find both terrifying and difficult to recognize. It is difficult to see how Nietzsche could consider a belief in the existence of truth ascetic. Earlier in GM III, he labels ascetic the desire to find "error precisely where the instinct of life most unconditionally posits truth" (GM III, 12), that is, the desire to deny the truth of claims supported by the evidence of sense testimony. Because this implies that, when uninfluenced by the ascetic ideal, human beings are naturally inclined to accept the truth of claims supported by the evidence of the senses, belief in the existence of truth seems more self-indulgent (accepting of our natural impulse to believe in truth) than self-denying.

Nehamas attempts to connect the belief in truth to the ascetic ideal with the suggestion that the former does not overcome the dogmatism on which the latter depends. According to his account, Nietzsche objects to the ascetic ideal because it conceals that it is an interpretation. However, his demonstration that it is an interpretation is still offered "in the name of truth" since "an interpretation, simply by virtue of being offered, is inevitably offered in the conviction that it is true" (1985, 131). Therefore, Nehamas concludes, "the dogmatism on which asceticism depends has not yet been eliminated" even in attacks on the ascetic ideal.

But, as Nehamas interprets it, dogmatism also seems self-indulgent rather than ascetic. The ascetic ideal is distinguished from other ideals not by its dogmatism, which evidently afflicts every interpretation according to Nehamas, but by its demand for self-denial and its devaluation of life. Nietzsche's claim is that the belief in truth is the latest, the most spiritual, elusive, and therefore, the most terrifying form of this life-devaluing ideal (GM III, 25). It is difficult to see how its dogmatic character could make any ideal a candidate for this description.

Danto seems to suggest the right kind of connection between the ascetic ideal and faith in truth by arguing that the latter devalues life. To believe in truth, he claims, is to believe in "something outside of man to which he must attune himself and from which he derives his meaning extrinsically, as it were, and derivatively." Danto's Nietzsche infers from this that science "shows us that we are meaningless" (193). This would explain how faith in truth is ascetic. It demands self-denial; it demands that we subordinate ourselves to something outside us, thus denying satisfaction to our desire for power or autonomy, and it does so in the name of an interpretation that devalues human life by making it seem worthless. However, the view Danto attributes to Nietzsche seems utterly implausible. That there are facts or truths to which we must attune ourselves (if we are to fulfill any of our purposes) shows that we are not omnipotent. To infer meaninglessness from lack of omnipotence, however, would seem to betray a form of megalomania we have no other reason to think Nietzsche exhibits here.

When truth is understood as correspondence to things-in-themselves, Danto is right that Nietzsche believes human life is assigned only derivative value. But not because truth requires attunement to something outside ourselves. His reason is rather that the value judgment underlying the metaphysical interpretation of truth is that only what is completely independent of human beings can be truly valuable. Human life must then derive its value from its link to a transcendent world. Nietzsche's perspectivist understanding of truth, I have argued, denies that truth is independent of human interests. But this in no way denies that truth is something we discover rather than make, or that we must attune ourselves to things outside of us.

An even more important reason against taking the faith in truth as a belief in the existence of truth is that it makes nonsense of the conclusion Nietzsche draws from his whole analysis of its ascetic character. This conclusion is that "science itself henceforth requires justification (which is not to say that there is any such justification)," and that "the will to truth requires a critique . . . the value of truth must for once be *experimentally* called into question" (GM III, 24). That is, we can no longer take for granted the value of truth, nor therefore the value of science, but must instead determine by experiment how important truth (and therefore science) is. This would be an absolutely incoherent conclusion to draw from an attack on the existence of truth. Only if we assume that some beliefs are true can we possibly perform experiments to see how valuable truth is, that is, how valuable it is to have true beliefs. I take this point to be the most decisive kind of evidence one could have against this interpretation, unless there is no plausible alternative way to understand what Nietzsche means by "the faith in truth" (in which case, his analysis is incoherent and cannot be taken seriously).

There is, however, a quite plausible alternative, namely, to understand faith in truth as faith in the overriding value of truth. Not the least advantage of this interpretation is that Nietzsche's own words make it fully explicit, for example, in the following part of his account of those who believe in truth:

> That which *constrains* these men, however, this unconditional will to truth, is *faith in the ascetic ideal itself*, if only as an unconscious imperative – don't be deceived about that – it is faith in a *metaphysical* value, the absolute value of *truth*, sanctioned and guaranteed by this ideal alone (it stands or falls with this ideal). (GM III, 24)

The faith here said to depend on the ascetic ideal is quite obviously faith in truth's absolute value, which cannot plausibly be thought to follow from a belief in its mere existence. "Absolute value" seems to mean "overriding value" (GS 344 gives the strongest evidence for this). The faith in truth is an unquestioning commitment to truth, an unquestioning acceptance that truth is more important than anything else, for example, happiness, life, love, power. It now becomes easy to explain the conclusion Nietzsche draws from his analysis. Because faith in the overriding value of truth has rested on the ascetic ideal, rejection of the latter deprives us of our previous basis for valuing truth. Nietzsche's analysis therefore has the effect of calling that value into question. This means not that we must reject the value of truth, but that we will be able to judge its value only on the basis of the experimental evidence, which we will be positioned to gather only after we stop taking its value for granted. Again, this would be utterly incoherent if the existence of truth were not presupposed.

A somewhat longer discussion is necessary to show that this interpretation also explains why Nietzsche considers faith in truth ascetic, and why this is "terrifying." To begin with, commitment to the overriding value of truth requires self-denial, according to Nietzsche, as "much ascetic virtue as any denial of sensuality" (GM III, 24). The committed seekers of truth who have destroyed the religious and metaphysical underpinnings of the ascetic ideal had to sacrifice for the sake of truth "whatever is comforting, holy, healing; all hope, all faith in hidden harmony, in future blisses and justices" (B 55). For the sake of truth, they gave up the comforting ideas that had given human life meaning: that we are children of God and possessors of a supernatural destiny; that we live in the center of the universe, which was created for our use; that we are free and masters in our own house, the realms of mental activity and voluntary action. These doctrines were destroyed, Nietzsche thinks, by the acceptance of the basic doctrines of modern science: Copernicus, Darwin, and the Freudian-like theories found in Nietzsche's writings.[5] Danto rightly saw that Nietzsche considered the acceptance of these theories ascetic. However, the self-denial they require is not that of submission to a power outside ourselves, but the willingness to

5. The destruction of these beliefs may be apparent only in the case of a relatively small group of intellectuals. But, as GS 125 shows, Nietzsche believes that the wider cultural event has already taken place, though, as when distant stars are destroyed, it is not yet evident to us.

give up the comforting illusions that have made us happy and our lives meaningful.

It may seem problematic to claim that accepting the truths of modern science requires self-denial given Nietzsche's claim that the rejection of truth is ascetic. If we have a natural inclination to accept beliefs supported by empirical evidence, how can accepting just such beliefs be ascetic? Nietzsche's anwer, according to GS 344, parts of which he quotes in GM III, is that both "truth and untruth [have] constantly proved to be useful." It is certainly often best to know the truth, to avoid deception. We could not carry out any of our purposes unless we did so much of the time. But sometimes, surely, people are better off – even in the long run – if they do not know certain truths. The frequency of self-deception among human beings certainly suggests that this is what we are naturally prone to believe and act on. To commit oneself to truth "at any price" is therefore to take a stand against one's natural inclinations.

But this does not suffice to make faith in truth ascetic. As the *Phaedo* (69 a) argues, in effect, giving up one pleasure for another does not make one ascetic. Difficult tasks that require the denial of natural impulses express the ascetic ideal, I have argued, only if they involve an interpretation that devalues natural human existence. That Nietzsche considers the belief in truth ascetic in this sense should be clear from the part of GS 344 cited in GM III: "The truthful man, in the audacious and ultimate sense presupposed by the faith in science, *thereby affirms another world* than that of life, nature, and history; and insofar as he affirms this 'other world' does this not mean that he has to deny its antithesis, this world, *our* world?" This suggests that faith in truth expresses the ascetic ideal in the same way metaphysics does: that value is located in a transcendent world and therefore denied to its opposite, our world, the empirical world.

Although Nietzsche's argument for this conclusion has proved frustrating to interpreters,[6] it is actually one of the easiest things he ever wrote (if we ignore for the moment its initial claim about science) to put into premise/conclusion form. His first premise, admittedly obscured by a distinction between the will not to be deceived and the will not to deceive, is that the unconditional will

6. Nehamas suggests that Nietzsche should have gone "against his nature" in this one case and spelled out its premises (1985, 131).

to truth (the commitment to truth "at any price") is based on either prudential or moral considerations. One can value truth on the grounds that one's other needs and interests are best served by knowing as much truth as possible. Or one can consider it important for moral reasons to avoid deception, to be truthful, regardless of whether it serves one's other interests. To deny Nietzsche's first premise, one needs another kind of consideration that could underwrite the overriding value of truth. I do not know of one.

His second premise is that the will to truth cannot be based on prudential considerations. Now this might seem obvious on analytic grounds. If the will to truth is unconditional, how could the value of truth be conditioned by, dependent upon, its service to our other interests? However, Nietzsche bases his premise on empirical considerations, on the fact that "both truth and untruth" constantly prove to be useful. If possible, we should therefore avoid including a belief that the value of truth is unconditioned by anything else as part of the meaning of "the will to truth." We can interpret it instead as a commitment to choosing truth over deception in each and every case and recognize that such a commitment might follow from a belief that it is required by some other commitment. The view rejected by Nietzsche's second premise is that the commitment to always choosing truth stems from a prudential calculation, from a belief that our (long-term) interests (in happiness e.g.) are best served by always preferring truth to deception, no matter how much it hurts in the short run. In arguing against this view, Nietzsche assumes that a prudential calculation would be based on empirical considerations. Because experience constantly shows us the value of both deception and ignorance, he argues, no one could have reasonably inferred from experience that long-term happiness is best served by knowing the truth at any (short-term) price. Therefore, Nietzsche concludes, the will to truth could not reasonably have arisen from prudential considerations

> but must have originated *in spite of* the fact that the disutility and dangerousness of "the will to truth," of "truth at any price," is proved to it constantly. "At any price": how well we understand these words once we have offered and slaughtered one belief after another at the altar of this faith (GS 344).

The will to truth is therefore a moral commitment to truthfulness regardless of its long-term utility. But whence does truthfulness derive this overriding value? As the second premise of Nietzsche's argument for the above conclusion rules out deriving its value from its connection to the natural world, that is, from its suitability for fulfilling interests or purposes we have as natural beings, he concludes that the value of truthfulness must be derived from its presumed connection to another world. This is how we can interpret his claim that "the truthful man, in the audacious and ultimate sense presupposed by the faith in science, *thereby affirms another world.*" Not that those who possess the will to truth believe that its value is derived from such a metaphysical world – for they are all "godless anti-metaphysicians" – but that their commitment to truth makes sense only as a holdover from the belief in a metaphysical world, from Plato's faith that "truth is divine."

But why can one not accept the moral value of truthfulness while denying that there is any other world? This is precisely what Nietzsche's godless anti-metaphysicians and believers in truth attempt. Does Nietzsche claim that their position is incoherent? GS 344 seems to imply this, but Nietzsche is not committed to that view in GM III, which mentions (only by quoting GS 344), but no longer emphasizes, the will to truth's affirmation of another world. GM III strengthens the point of GS 344 – "that even we seekers after knowledge today, we godless anti-metaphysicians, still take our fire, too, from a flame lit by a faith that is thousands of years old, that Christian faith, which was also the faith of Plato, that God is truth, that truth is divine" (GS 344) – by reformulating it as a claim that the belief in truth "is a faith in a *metaphysical* value, the absolute value of *truth,* sanctioned and guaranteed by [the ascetic] ideal alone" (GM III, 24). Nietzsche can now admit that commitment to the absolute value of truth (of facing up to the truth in all things) can cohere with the denial of another world, but insist that it makes sense only if one holds that self-denial itself has value, quite apart from any contribution it makes to the satisfaction of our other desires. Thus, faith in truth rests on an acceptance of the ascetic ideal – "if only as an unconscious imperative" (GM III, 24) – for it takes natural human existence to be without value, except on condition of self-denial.

Although this interpretation makes sense of Nietzsche's analysis of faith in truth as an expression of the ascetic ideal, it leaves us with the question as to where he actually finds this belief in truth. There is a tendency to suppose he finds it in science and that GM III and GS 344 therefore argue in some sense against science. GS 344 does seem to claim that the belief is presupposed by all science. Nietzsche declares that "there simply is no science 'without presuppositions,' " and that science itself rests on the faith that "*nothing* is needed *more* than truth, and in relation to it everything else has only second-rate value." But it is difficult to see how science can be said to presuppose this faith. I see two different ways of interpreting the claim that it does, neither of which make it plausible. Nietzsche might mean that the *truth* of scientific doctrines presupposes (is logically dependent on) the belief that truth has overriding value. Nietzsche's attack on the faith in truth would then be directed against the truth of scientific doctrines. But it does not seem remotely plausible that the truth of Darwin's theory of evolution, for instance, depends on whether or not truth has absolute value. I can see no reason for attributing such an implausible view to Nietzsche.

Perhaps, then, Nietzsche means that the *practice* of science presupposes the belief in truth, in the sense that one would have no reason (or perhaps, no motivation) to undertake scientific inquiry if one did not accept truth as of overriding value. But one can engage in all sorts of scientific inquiry for prudential reasons, including self-enjoyment, and Nietzsche clearly knows this. In an earlier section of GS, he makes that explicit: "Without this new passion – I mean the passion to know – science would still be promoted; after all, science has grown and matured without it until now" (GS 123). Nietzsche goes on to mention various other interests that science has served (and could continue to serve): interests in pleasure, honor, sustenance, the avoidance of boredom, salvation, and virtue. Further, GM III explicitly distinguishes those who have faith in truth, "those rarer cases . . . the last idealists left among philosophers and scholars . . . in whom alone the intellectual conscience dwells and is incarnate today" (GM III, 24) from the majority of scientists and scholars who may "work rigorously in the sciences" yet have no ideals at all (III, 23).

Therefore, neither the truth nor the practice of science presupposes a belief in truth's absolute value, and we have little reason to think Nietzsche believes they do. We need to look for an alternative interpretation of Nietzsche's claim that science presupposes faith in truth. Nietzsche helps us when he formulates the second premise of his argument in GS 344 (analyzed above) as a denial that "faith in science" could owe its existence to a utilitarian calculus. To be parallel to what Nietzsche means by "faith in truth," faith in science would be a faith or unquestioning acceptance of the overriding importance of being scientific in the formation of one's beliefs. It therefore seems reasonable to conclude that "the latest expression of the ascetic ideal" is not the practice of science, nor the belief in its capacity for informing us of the truth, but faith in the absolute value of truth, which Nietzsche equates with faith in the overriding importance of being scientific.

This faith, which Nietzsche claims "undeniably exists," is an ideal shared by most contemporary intellectuals (the *Erkennenden* Nietzsche begins GM by discussing) and, to some extent, by modern Western culture. GS 344 begins with an account of what it is to be scientific: to give up one's convictions, that is, to treat one's beliefs as hypotheses open to rejection in light of current and future evidence. We need not interpret this in an unsophisticated way, as claiming, for example, that being scientific requires us to abandon a belief if one experimental conclusion is inconsistent with it. It is quite compatible with (and perhaps demanded by) Nietzsche's treatment of our beliefs as an interconnected web, in which a specific belief may always be retained in light of the evidence if we make enough adjustments in other beliefs. However, if we commit ourselves in advance to maintaining a particular belief no matter what the evidence, no matter what else we have to give up, we are certainly not being "scientific" about it. One might perhaps hold onto the title of "scientist" while insisting that there is insufficient empirical evidence to accept evolutionary theory. But a biologist who rejects evolution for explicitly religious reasons and is committed to its denial whatever the evidence should show would certainly be accused of failing to act as a scientist. *Qua* scientist, a person must be without commitments, that is open to revising her beliefs in light of current and future evidence.

Nietzsche seems to be claiming that this requirement for being a scientist has now become a wider cultural ideal. A nonscientist who rejects evolution on religious grounds is also criticized by many people as "unscientific" – and this is a criticism of him as a person, not as a scientist. What Nietzsche calls the "scientific spirit" (GS 344) – openness to revising one's beliefs in light of current and future evidence – constitutes an ideal for the human person that is accepted by an important segment of the Western world, and that acts as an important opposing force to the ideal of submission to religious authority. Nietzsche is claiming that this ideal involves a commitment to the absolute value of truth, which rests on the ascetic ideal. This would be incoherent if Nietzsche were denying that science gives us truth. Nietzsche treats as interchangeable the ideal of being scientific and commitment to the overriding value of truth only because he thinks science (inquiry which accepts the relevance of sense testimony) gives us whatever truth we have.

Professing the ideal and living up to it are different matters, of course. Though professed by many, on Nietzsche's account the faith in truth is possessed only by a few rare and noble exceptions (GM III, 23), those "hard, severe, abstinent spirits who constitute the honor of our age" (GM III, 24). Nietzsche's admiration of, and identification with, the believers in truth seems obvious, especially since he also calls them "atheists, anti-Christians, immoralists" (III, 24). In fact, Nietzsche may consider himself alone in possessing the faith in truth fully since one cannot be open to revising all of one's beliefs in light of the evidence unless one is willing to question the value of truth, and Nietzsche evidently thinks he is the first of those who pursue truth to do so. There are, then, degrees of faith in truth. Those who possess the faith to a lesser degree than the Nietzsche of GM III are the thinkers – atheists and anti-metaphysicians – who were all heirs of the Enlightenment, for example, Voltaire, Hume, and the Nietzsche of HA (originally dedicated to Voltaire), but perhaps also such scientists as Newton and Darwin. These thinkers helped destroy the metaphysical and cosmological underpinnings of the ascetic ideal by finding naturalistic explanations that either conflict with religious accounts or make them cognitively superfluous. To a lesser degree, the "whole of modern philosophy" since Descartes belongs here. "At bottom," Nietzsche claims, it seeks

> to assassinate the old soul concept . . . which means an attempt on the life of the basic presuppositions of the Christian doctrine. Modern philosophy, being an epistemological skepticism, is, covertly or overtly, *anti-Christian* – although, to say this for the benefit of more refined ears, by no means anti-religious (BG 54).

Nietzsche denies that modern philosophy is anti-religious precisely because it labors under the influence of the ascetic ideal. In
the preceding section of BG (53), he answers his own question
"Why atheism today?" with an insistence that "the religious instinct is in the process of growing powerfully – but the theistic
satisfaction it refuses with deep suspicion," which is precisely
what he then goes on to suggest about modern philosophy. The
concluding section of GM's analysis of the belief in truth tells us
that the refusal of "theistic satisfaction" is due to the ascetic ideal.

> Everywhere else that the spirit is strong, mighty, and at work
> without counterfeit today, it does without ideals of any kind – the
> popular expression for this abstinence is "atheism" – *except for its*
> *will to truth*. But this will, this *remnant* of an ideal, is, if you will
> believe me, this ideal itself in its strictest, most spiritual formula-
> tion, esoteric through and through, with all external additions
> abolished, and thus not so much its remnant as its *kernel*. Uncondi-
> tional honest atheism (and *its* is the only air we breathe, we more
> spiritual men of this age!) is therefore not the antithesis of that
> ideal, as it appears to be; it is rather only one of the later phases of
> its evolution, one of its terminal forms and inner consequences –
> it is the awe-inspiring *catastrophe* of two thousand years in truthful-
> ness that finally forbids itself the *lie involved in belief in God* (GM
> III, 27).

This is the solution on which Nietzsche stakes his reputation as
puzzle solver: that atheism itself (which should be understood to
include the rejection of all metaphysical worlds), brought about
by taking "the concept of truthfulness . . . more and more
strictly" (III, 27), is an ultimate product of the religious tradition's ascetic ideal. The ultimate product of the theistic tradition
is to deny oneself the comfort and satisfaction of belief in God.
This has nothing to do with rejecting the existence of truth.
Because Nietzsche explicitly calls the latter a "lie," he must accept
as the truth what the will to truth has wrought.

Then why does he have a problem with it? His problem is that
the "ultimate and most terrifying aspect of the question concerning the meaning of this ideal" (GM III, 23) is revealed by the fact
that the will to truth is its latest expression. It is terrifying, to
begin with, because it attests to the incredible power of the ascetic ideal and the lack of any alternative. If the whole Enlightenment attack on God, metaphysics, and asceticism, is itself in-

spired by the ascetic ideal, what hope do we have of escaping its influence? And what if we cannot?

Nietzsche's answer is suggested by BG 55, the passage immediately following the one on modern philosophy cited above. He writes that there is "a great ladder of religious cruelty, with many rungs," three of which he then discusses. First, one sacrificed human beings, for example, the first born, to one's god.

> Then, during the moral epoch of mankind, one sacrificed to one's god one's own strongest instincts, one's "nature": *this* festive joy lights up the cruel eyes of the ascetic, the "anti-natural" enthusiast.
>
> Finally – what remained to be sacrificed? At long last, did one not have to sacrifice for once whatever is comforting, holy, healing; all hope, all faith in hidden harmony, in future blisses and justices? didn't one have to sacrifice God himself and, from cruelty against oneself, worship the stone, stupidity, gravity, fate, the nothing? To sacrifice God for the nothing – this paradoxical mystery of the final cruelty was reserved for the generation that is now coming: all of us know something of this (BG 55).

In the first two stages, sacrifice is not "for nothing" since one receives in return hope of fortune and favors, "future blisses and justices." The ascetic ideal saved the will from suicidal nihilism – helped human beings to find life worth living – even though it denied intrinsic value to that life, because it gave them something to will, something to hope for and work towards (a disguised negation of this life, such as heaven or nirvana). When the will to truth gives up God "for the nothing," the ascetic ideal no longer performs this life-enhancing function. The most spiritual human beings now offer only one ideal that still inspires passion, love, and striving, according to Nietzsche, that of facing up to the truth. But this ideal of truthfulness destroys everything that was life-enhancing in the ascetic ideal – all hopes and goals and redeeming visions – and puts nothing in its place, neither a new way of affirming life's value, nor (what is necessary for that) an ideal that distinguishes the valuable from the not so valuable in this life. Instead of saving the will from suicidal nihilism, it now encourages nihilism, "the great nausea, the will to nothingness," which Nietzsche claims was bound to grow out of the "hitherto reigning ideal" (GM II, 24).

This is why the will to truth brings us to the "ultimate and most terrifying aspect" of the ascetic ideal and why Nietzsche considers it not so much the remnant of that ideal as its kernel (GM III, 27). The core of the ascetic ideal, according to the concluding section of GM, is a will directed against life. This will is acted out initially by devaluing life, by denying its intrinsic value and making it a mere means to its own negation. In this phase, the will expressed by the ascetic ideal actually serves a life-enhancing function. But when this will directed against life becomes the will to truth, it destroys "what is exoteric in this ideal" (III, 25), not the life-devaluing ideal of self-denial, but only the aspects of it that conflicted with this core, its satisfying, comforting, and therefore life-enhancing exteriors. Nietzsche therefore sees in the will to truth "at any price" the purest form of the will to nothingness, the will directed against life, against everything that makes human life seem worth living, stripped of that which allowed it to serve life.

5. Overcoming the ascetic ideal

Having exposed it as the very kernel of the ascetic ideal, Nietzsche ends his discussion of the will to truth by predicting that it will overcome the ideal.

> All great things bring about their own destruction through an act of self-overcoming [Selbstaufhebung]: thus the law of life will have it, the law of the necessity of "self-overcoming" [Selbstüberwindung] in the nature of life – the lawgiver himself eventually receives the call: "patere legem, quam ipse tulisti." In this way Christianity as a dogma was destroyed by its own morality; in the same way Christianity as morality must now perish, too: we stand on the threshold of this event. After Christian truthfulness has drawn one inference after another, it must end by drawing its most striking inference, its inference against itself; this will happen, however, when it poses the question "what is the meaning of all will to truth?" (GM III, 27)

This means that the ascetic ideal (Christian morality) will overcome itself when its latest and noblest adherents, those most fully committed to truth, ask why they want truth, that is, what justifies and motivates their pursuit of truth "at any price." Nietzsche's answer to this question – that commitment to the ascetic ideal underlies their will to truth – must initiate this self-overcoming. In discovering the truth about itself – that it expresses the ascetic ideal – the will to truth overcomes the ascetic ideal. My concern in this section is to understand what this overcoming involves and why it is necessitated by Nietzsche's analysis of the will to truth. I am especially concerned with whether Nietzsche believes that the will to truth must overcome itself to overcome the ascetic ideal.

If the will to truth does overcome itself, we know at least that this does not involve a denial or watering down of the common sense assumption that some beliefs are true and others false. As I have argued at length, the existence of truth is not at issue here but is presupposed from beginning to end of Nietzsche's argument. Nor is the nature of truth Nietzsche's concern. Those who exemplify the will to truth are the "godless anti-metaphysicians" who have already rejected the metaphysical correspondence theory. GM III gives us no reason to believe that they must go on to recognize that truth is incomplete, partial, revisable, or anything else along these lines. The will to truth is a commitment to the overriding value of truth, to truth at any price. Overcoming the will to truth would mean overcoming this commitment to truth. However, it is far from clear what this would involve or how the truth about the will to truth could overcome either the will to truth or the ascetic ideal.

One possibility is that Nietzsche's analysis of the will to truth leads to the realization that human beings do not in fact value truth for its own sake. A passage I have already quoted from GS claims it is something new that knowledge wants to be regarded as "more than a mere means" (GS 123). In the past, Nietzsche claims, science (which is clearly interchangeable with "knowledge" in this passage) was valued only as a means to happiness, virtue, salvation, or more mundane ends. This is still largely why knowledge is wanted, GM implies, namely, that gaining the truth serves one or more other interest, such as pleasure, survival, wealth, worldy power, or escape from boredom (GM III, 23; cf. BG 6). Of course, in these cases, truth will be pursued only to the extent that seems conducive to the satisfaction of these other interests. One gives up short-range happiness for the sake of the truth only to the extent that doing so contributes to one's long-range power, wealth, or salvation, or whatever. This does not yet give us what Nietzsche calls the "will to truth."

With the triumphs of modern science, on the other hand, we find cases where people seem willing to sacrifice everything for the truth, and therefore do not seem to be pursuing it for the sake of something else. Knowledge comes to be regarded as an autonomous or unconditioned value, that is, as having a value that is independent of its service to our other interests. A major point of Nietzsche's analysis of the will to truth (equivalent to "the passion to know" mentioned in GS 123) is to deny precisely that. Nietzsche claims that knowledge is not an autonomous value. Although human beings may appear to seek it solely for its own sake, they actually do so out of their prior commitment to the ascetic ideal. The upshot is that, according to Nietzsche, the passion for knowledge or truth is always subordinate to our other passions.

This interpretation seems correct, but it does not explain why the will to truth – the commitment to truth "at any price" – must overcome either itself or the ascetic ideal. If we accept Nietzsche's account, we must admit that truth is not an autonomous value, that it is always wanted for the sake of something else. But this is compatible with accepting the overriding value of truth. It does not override what the ascetic ideal demands, of course, but according to Nietzsche, the demands of that ideal are best served by the commitment to truth at any price. When it understands the truth about itself, why cannot the will to truth affirm its dependence on the ascetic ideal and reaffirm both itself and that ideal? After all, those with faith in truth have fought only the externals of the ascetic ideal, not its inner core, its basic valuation (GM III, 27). Once they recognize their basic value commitment to the virtue of self-denial, why is not the affirmation of this valuation a possibility? The passage on the self-overcoming of the ascetic ideal makes it obvious that Nietzsche rules out this possibility, but not why. Even if, like Hume, they have heaped scorn on the "virtues of denial," it is not clear why they could not rethink their position once they recognize the dependence of the will to truth on the ascetic ideal, and affirm both will and ideal.

My suggestion is that if one accepts Nietzsche's full account of the will to truth, affirming the ascetic ideal is a logical, but not a psychological, possibility. Could beings who have rejected theism and all "other" worlds and who agree with Nietzsche that the only demonstrable reality is that revealed by empirical inquiry really embrace self-denial as their basic value? It does not seem that purely natural beings could be motivated to value self-denial, except as a means to the satisfaction of other desires. To endorse this answer, however, Nietzsche must argue that even those committed to truth have valued self-denial only as a means to something else. In the next chapter, I shall argue that he does. Self-denial has been valued, he thinks, because it gives a sense of power. I shall also argue that if this account of the underlying motivation is true, once its truth is accepted, it becomes psychologically impossible to affirm the ascetic ideal. Such affirmation would conflict not so much with what believers in truth believe but with getting what they want from the ascetic ideal.

What, then, is the fate of the will to truth? If believers in truth recognize the dependence of their commitment on an ideal they can no longer affirm, must they reject that commitment? If it seems obvious that they must, it is noteworthy that Nietzsche never refers to the self-overcoming of truthfulness, either in GM III or in the various other texts that refer to the self-overcoming of morality (the ascetic ideal) out of truthfulness (e.g., EH IV, 3; D P, 4). On the contrary, works before and (especially) after GM contain too many passages in which truthfulness or honesty, in the sense of the intellectual conscience, is presented as indispensable for the type of person Nietzsche admires, and perhaps even *the* measure of a person's value.

In a passage titled "The intellectual conscience" (GS 2), Nietzsche tells us that he feels the lack of one to be "contemptible":

> But what is goodheartedness, refinement, or genius to me, when the person who has these virtues tolerates slack feelings in his beliefs and judgments, when he does not count the *demand for certainty* his innermost desire and deepest need – as that which separates the higher human being from the lower!

Since he rejects Cartesian certainty, Nietzsche must mean that those he admires are committed to being as sure as they can that their beliefs are true. As Kaufmann emphasizes (against those who believe Nietzsche aims to overcome the will to truth), Nietzsche never gave up this attitude (1968a, 585). Consider what he says about the pursuit of truth in one of the books he wrote after GM. Asking whether "blessedness – or more technically speaking, *pleasure* – [would] ever be proof of truth," Nietzsche writes:

> The experience of all severe, of all profoundly inclined, spirits teaches the *opposite*. At every step one has to wrestle for truth; one has had to surrender for it almost everything to which the heart,

to which our love, our trust in life, cling otherwise. That requires greatness of soul: the service of truth is the hardest service (A 50).

There are two important passages from EH with the same message. One informs us that Nietzsche's most important reason for naming his fictional alter ego "Zarathustra" (Zoroaster) is

> that Zarathustra is more truthful than any other thinker. His doctrine, and his alone, posits truthfulness as the highest virtue; this means the opposite of the cowardice of the "idealist" who flees from reality; Zarathustra has more intestinal fortitude than all other thinkers taken together. To speak the truth and to *shoot well with arrows,* that is Persian virtue. – Am I understood? – The self-overcoming of morality out of truthfulness; the self-overcoming of the moralist into its opposite – into me – that is what the name of Zarathustra means in my mouth (EH IV, 3).

If this leaves open any possibility that Nietzsche might think the will to truth eventually overcomes itself, an earlier passage in EH closes it.

> How much truth does a spirit *endure,* how much truth does it *dare?* More and more that becomes for me the real measure of value. Error (faith in the ideal) is not blindness, error is *cowardice.*
>
> Every attainment, every step forward in knowledge, *follows* from courage, from hardness against oneself, from cleanliness in relation to oneself (EH, P 3).

Such passages led Kaufmann (1968a, 585 ff.) to conclude that Nietzsche objects not to the will to truth, but only to the unquestioning faith in (the overriding value of) truth. Many readers found this implausible. The failure to question the value of truth seems to be one last remnant of self-indulgence, whereas Nietzsche evidently objects to the whole ideal of self-denial of which the will to truth is an expression and to which Kaufmann's interpretation keeps Nietzsche committed. But both Kaufmann and his opponents assumed that the will to truth and the ascetic ideal went together, that if Nietzsche attacked one, he had to attack the other.[7] This made it impossible for either side to explain

---

7. Nietzsche does seem to support this in GM III, 25 when he claims that "a depreciation of the ascetic ideal unavoidably involves a depreciation of science." However, I take this to mean only that a depreciation of the ascetic ideal would make it impossible to take the value of truth for granted.

adequately both Nietzsche's obvious commitment to truth and his equally obvious attack on the ascetic ideal.

There is a way of accounting for both, of seeing the compatibility between Nietzsche's analysis of the will to truth as the expression, indeed kernel, of an ideal he rejects and his praise for the commitment to truth. We can suppose that Nietzsche remains committed to truth in the service of another ideal, a genuine alternative to the ascetic ideal – though he rejects, as even Kaufmann agrees, the unquestioning assumption of truth's overriding value.[8]

Given my interpretation of Nietzsche's analysis of the will to truth, it follows that he cannot advocate pursuing truth out of commitment to the ascetic ideal. But what are the alternatives? If we cannot pursue truth for its own sake, we must either give up the pursuit of truth altogether, or pursue it for the sake of something else. The former does not seem a serious option for the people Nietzsche has in mind. How could someone like Nietzsche, who devoted his life to the pursuit of truth, decide not to care about the truth anymore? Especially in view of Nietzsche's praise for the "intellectual conscience" (GS 2) and the "service of truth" (A 50), this is not a plausible reading of Nietzsche's hope for the "last idealists of knowledge in whom alone the intellectual conscience dwells and is incarnate today" (GM III, 24).

The second option admits of two different possibilities: to continue pursuing truth, but to abandon the commitment to it, or to find a new ideal for the sake of which one can remain committed to truth. To take the first option is to give up one's idealism regarding knowledge, to join the vast majority of scholars who either suffer from what Nietzsche calls "the unrest of the *lack* of ideals, the suffering from the *lack* of any great love" (GM III, 23), or who have learned to place their main interest "somewhere else" – in family, money, politics, reputation, etc. (BG 6). But this cannot be Nietzsche's recommendation to his "last idealists." The only alternative I can find is that he hopes the will to truth will lead these idealists to see the need for a new ideal, an

---

8. This unquestioning assumption of truth's overriding value is needed precisely because it keeps hidden from view the dependence of the commitment to truth on the ascetic ideal. Overcoming this faith in truth is therefore a necessary causal prerequisite for the overcoming of the ascetic ideal. But the will or commitment to truth may exist without the unquestioning aspect that would make it faith in truth.

ideal that requires the service of a commitment to truth. Unthinking faith in truth would be abandoned but not the commitment to truth.

This interpretation not only makes sense of what Nietzsche says about both the service of truth and the ascetic ideal, but is also supported by the whole point of his essay on the ascetic ideal. GM III's title asks "What is the Meaning of Ascetic Ideals?" As he begins his analysis of the will to truth, Nietzsche clarifies this question as follows:

> What is the meaning of the *power* of this ideal, the monstrous nature of its power? Why has it been allowed to flourish to this extent? Why has it not rather been resisted? The ascetic ideal expresses a will: *where* is the opposing will that might express an *opposing ideal*? (GM III, 23).

According to EH's account of the essay, GM III is designed to answer the above question as follows: "because it was the only ideal so far, because it had no rival." Nietzsche adds: "Above all, a *counterideal* was lacking – until Zarathustra" (EH III, GM). Nietzsche undoubtedly exaggerates in claiming that there has been no resistance, since GM itself (I, 16) suggests that the Renaissance provided an opposed ideal. But Nietzsche's main point remains: that we have had no culture-wide ideal that could function as an alternative to the ascetic ideal. The point of his analysis of the ascetic ideal is that we need a counterideal, that we need what Zarathustra provides (which Nietzsche alludes to at the end of GM II). His analysis of the will to truth is designed to show us *not* that we must overcome the will to truth, but that we need something that the will to truth cannot by itself provide, a new ideal for that will to serve.

> No! Don't come to me with science when I ask for the natural antagonist of the ascetic ideal, when I demand: "where is the opposing will expressing the *opposing ideal*?" Science is not nearly self-reliant enough for that; it first requires in every respect a value-creating power in the *service* of which it could *believe* in itself – it never creates values (GM III, 25)

This is no objection to science, but to stopping with science, to failing to realize the need for a new ideal.

I will examine Nietzsche's proposed ideal in my final chapter but will surprise few by suggesting in advance that it idealizes the affirmation rather than the denial of self and life. As I indicated above, Nietzsche seems to take as his measure of value what is "life-promoting, life-preserving, species-preserving, perhaps even species-cultivating" (BG 4). If his commitment to truth came into conflict with the affirmation of life or the promotion of its interests, Nietzsche would have to consider life the higher value. But it is difficult to see how his commitment to truth could conflict with his affirmation of life. One can only affirm life to the extent that one knows the truth about it – otherwise one affirms one's illusions about life, not life itself.[9] The most life-affirming person would therefore be the one who still finds life valuable in the face of the most truth about it. That he takes the affirmation of life as his ideal would therefore explain why the amount of truth one can endure has become Nietzsche's measure of value (EH P, 3).

Further, the hardness against oneself required by the will to truth need not be interpreted in an ascetic (i.e., life-devaluing) way. Consider the aphorism prefixed to GM III: "Unconcerned, mocking, violent, thus wisdom wants us: she is a woman, and always loves only a warrior." Without examining it in great detail, it seems safe to say that it offers a very unascetic characterization of the seeker of wisdom or truth. It is similar to the beginning of BG: "Supposing truth is a woman – what then? Are there not grounds for the suspicion that all philosophers, insofar as they were dogmatists – have been very inexpert about women?" (BG P). Both passages compare the seeker of knowledge to a lover, thus placing the pursuit of truth on a continuum with other recognizably natural activities of living beings. The analogy set up between the knower and the warrior should be compared to Nietzsche's wish for the "English psychologists" in the opening section of GM I:

> that these investigators and microscopists of the soul may be fundamentally brave, proud, and magnanimous animals, who know how to keep their hearts as well as their suffering in bounds and have trained themselves to sacrifice all desirability to truth, *every* truth, even plain, ugly, repellent, unchristian, immoral truth. – For such truths do exist.

---

9. John Wilcox (1974, 190) makes this point very forcefully.

Nietzsche here makes clear that those who pursue knowledge need much of what the ascetic ideal trains one for: hardness against oneself, willingness to sacrifice desirability, comfort, and comfortableness, for the truth. I denied in section 2 that Nietzsche believed philosophy requires any particular denial of sensuous impulses (i.e., any more than would be required by any other cultivated human activity). It should now be clear that the "self-denial" required by philosophy is intellectual rather than sensual and that one of the points of Nietzsche's distinction between the philosopher and the priest is that his ideal philosopher would not think of the intellectual self-mastery required by philosophy in ascetic terms, terms that idealize self-denial or devalue life. Accordingly, Nietzsche admires in the sacrifice of desirability for truth not the self-denial involved, but the courage and magnanimity.

Finally, although one can certainly promote the interests of life without knowing what one is doing, one can hardly be in a position to make decisions about these interests without enormous knowledge. This seems to be the role Nietzsche has chosen for himself and what he claims to be the role of the philosopher. His claim will have little popular appeal today, as he well knew, even among philosophers. But granting that it is his claim makes sense of both his continued commitment to truth, despite the apparent asceticism this requires, and his opposition to the ascetic ideal. I do not think anything else does.

This solution once again places my interpretation in disagreement with Nehamas who evidently denies that Nietzsche can consistently provide the kind of alternative to the ascetic ideal I have in mind. In addition to the points discussed in section 1, Nehamas seems to claim that anything of the same scope as the ascetic ideal, and even any explicit attack on it, would also embody what Nietzsche opposes in the latter, which Nehamas takes to be its dogmatism, its claim to be good for all. Nehamas believes that the basic problem posed for Nietzsche by his opposition to the ascetic ideal is how to "warn others against dogmatism without taking a dogmatic stand himself" (1985, 133–7). Part of the solution he offers is that Nietzsche exemplifies an ideal (by turning his own life into literature) but without making claims for it and certainly without commending it to "universal attention" (131). According to the interpretation offered here, in contrast, a philosopher can oppose the ascetic ideal only by commending an opposed ideal to universal attention. Otherwise, the philosopher will still be working in the service of the ascetic ideal. Nehamas' interpretation illustrates at least partially why this would be true. Why, after all, should Nietzsche be so concerned to avoid dogmatism?[10] Nehamas answers that dogmatism involves "contradictions and deceptions" (133). But if that were the bottom line, Nietzsche's basic commitment would be to truth. He would be engaging in a complicated exercise to avoid claiming truth for his ideal in order to avoid saying something false. In that case, Nietzsche's own analysis would require us to interpret his commitment to truth as an expression of the ascetic ideal.

My interpretation denies that Nietzsche is concerned to reject dogmatism in the sense that Nehamas means. In the preface to BG, Nietzsche compares "the dogmatist's philosophy" to astrology – as "only a promise across millennia" – and refers to the "dogmatist's error." I take him to be using "dogmatism" as Kant did, for the belief that pure reason can know things-in-themselves. Now Nietzsche did in fact reject this dogmatism because he believed that the very idea of the thing-in-itself involved "contradictions and deceptions." And the rejection of the thing-in-itself for this reason does reveal a commitment to truth. Further, this commitment, Nietzsche's analysis tells us, had its original source in the ascetic ideal. But, according to my interpretation, Nietzsche can escape the ascetic ideal and yet continue to reject the dogmatism (commitment to metaphysical realism) he originally rejected out of commitment to the ascetic ideal because he has a new ideal for the sake of which he remains committed to truth.

Whether human beings, and especially those who pursue truth, really do need an alternative to the ascetic ideal is not

10. Nehamas uses "dogmatism" in the colloquial sense of confidence that one possesses the truth, as when he says that "every effort to present a view, no matter how explicitly its interpretive nature is admitted, makes an inescapable dogmatic commitment. The point is not that the faith in truth is not questioned enough but that a view cannot be questioned at all while it is being offered. Even a view that denies that there is such a thing as truth must be presented as true" (131). I see no reason to think that Nehamas uses the term in this sense, and Nietzsche's protest against dogmatism therefore gives us no reason to agree with Nehamas' view of Nietzsche's basic problem: how to "warn others against dogmatism without taking a dogmatic stand himself" (137). Further, my whole interpretation is an argument against supposing that later Nietzsche has a problem with presenting views as true (hence with "dogmatic commitments" in Nehamas' sense).

something I feel confident about. But if we grant Nietzsche's assumption that we are natural beings without connection to a metaphysical world, GM III's argument for this claim is not easily dismissed. How can we explain the power of this life-inimical ideal among natural beings except by assuming that they really needed an ideal? How could it possibly have gained its enormous influence if it had not fulfilled life-enhancing needs? The state of the western world since the relative demise of the ascetic ideal – a world oriented largely to individual consumption and war – offers little reason to think that Nietzsche was wrong about what we need. Nor does the fact that interpreters have largely missed the point of GM III's analysis of the will to truth: the need for a new ideal. I myself missed this point repeatedly in reading and teaching this essay over many years and only recognized it in one of the last drafts of this chapter. But this is exactly what Nietzsche's argument should lead us to expect. If his interpreters still have faith in truth (however much they may deny the existence of truth, they may still do so from a will to truth), they will be under the dominance of the ascetic ideal, which will make it difficult for them to admit the need for, or the possibility of, a new ideal, and therefore to recognize the call for a new ideal in Nietzsche's admittedly indirect statements regarding the will to truth.

This last point fits well with what I take to be Nietzsche's final argument regarding the need for a new ideal. Quite apart from what the world needs, he argues that philosophers really have no choice, that philosophy always either creates ideals or serves pregiven ones. If we do not create new ideals, we will inevitably continue paying some sort of homage to the ascetic ideal. As I have reconstructed the argument, if we face up to the truth about the will to truth and philosophy, we must recognize the need to create new ideals if only to avoid service to an ideal we can no longer affirm. The account of philosophy needed for this argument will be presented in the next chapter.

7

THE WILL TO POWER

A remaining problem for my interpretation of Nietzsche's position on truth is its apparent incompatibility with two of his most important doctrines. As they are traditionally interpreted, the doctrines of will to power and eternal recurrence are metaphysical theories. According to my interpretation, Nietzsche rejects metaphysics. His denial of the thing-in-itself leaves no place into which a metaphysical theory could fit. My final two chapters interpret the doctrines of will to power and eternal recurrence so that they are fully compatible with this rejection of metaphysics.

The first section of this chapter gives reasons to interpret will to power as a metaphysical doctrine if it is supposed to be true. The remaining sections argue that Nietzsche's published works give us reason to deny that he regarded it as a truth.

1. Will to power as metaphysics

Most interpreters attribute to Nietzsche what I shall call the cosmological doctrine of will to power, the claim that the world, or at least the organic world, is will to power. The *Nachlass* provides ample evidence for doing so, including Nietzsche's answer to the question "Do you know what 'the world' is to me?": *"This world is the will to power — and nothing besides!* And you yourselves are also this will to power – and nothing besides" (WP 1067). The idea is that the world consists not of things, but of quanta of force engaged in something on the order of "universal power-struggle" (Schacht, 221), with each center of force having or being a tendency to extend its influence and incorporate other such centers. It certainly seems to be a metaphysical theory, comparable, for instance, to Leibniz' monadology. Heidegger seems right that will to power constitutes Nietzsche's answer to the metaphysical question concerning the essence of what is (see Chapter 1).

From the viewpoint of my interpretation, the main reason to take it as a metaphysical theory is that its basis appears to be *a priori* theorizing concerning the nature of reality. Although our empirical theories tell us otherwise, Nietzsche evidently provides us with *a priori* grounds for believing that the world is really will to power. My analysis in section 2 shows that Nietzsche's published argument for the cosmological doctrine of will to power begins from a premise that could only be known *a priori*, and I see no reason to believe that the arguments in Nietzsche's notebooks are any different in this regard. In that case, however, Nietzsche's theory is vulnerable to his own criticism of metaphysics, for he claims that only acceptance of the thing-in-itself creates room for *a priori* theorizing about the nature of reality.

One common strategy for reconciling Nietzsche's criticism of metaphysics with his doctrine of will to power is to claim that the former rejects only "true" or "other" worlds, whereas the latter gives Nietzsche's account of "this" world. This strategy seems to be Schacht's when he claims that will to power gives Nietzsche's account of "this" world (168). The problem is that we have no way of making the distinction between "this" world and the "other" one except in terms of the distinction between empirical and *a priori* knowledge. Nietzsche's insistence that "this" world is the only demonstrable one means that the only world of which we can have knowledge is the empirical world, the world accessible to empirical investigation (see Chapter 4, section 3). To claim knowledge of the world on the basis of an *a priori* theory therefore amounts to belief in a "true" world, and is precisely what Nietzsche rejects as metaphysical. According to Schacht's reconstruction of it, however, Nietzsche's argument for the claim that the world is will to power is *a priori*. None of its premises are presented as empirical ones. Its first premise, for instance, is that everything is in a state of becoming. This is not presented as a hypothesis we formulate on the basis of experience, but as a conclusion we must draw once we recognize, in effect, that any notion of stability, aim, or unity belongs to our merely human perspective, and that since we have projected permanence into the world, we must "pull it out again," thus leaving becoming as the only reality (206). This is an *a priori* argument that I have already criticized in my earlier treatment of Schacht as a violation of perspectivism (Chapter 5, section 5).

Another strategy for showing that will to power does not conflict with Nietzsche's rejection of metaphysics is to argue that it actually amounts to a rejection of metaphysics. Nehamas adopts this strategy, which he makes quite plausible in broad outline. He interprets the doctrine of will to power as a denial that a metaphysical theory "of the character of the world and the things that constitute it can ever be given" (1985, 80). He need not deny the doctrine's *a priori* character. Instead, he denies that will to power is a theory as to the nature of reality.

Identifying it with the claim (made in the *Nachlass*) that a thing is the sum of its effects, Nehamas takes the doctrine of will to power as equivalent to Nietzsche's denial of the thing-in-itself. As I have interpreted the latter, this would give reason to deny that the will to power is a metaphysical theory, for the denial of the thing-in-itself merely gets rid of an excuse for devaluing the empirical world. Nothing substantial follows from this about the nature of the world. We are told merely that we have no excuse for devaluing empirical knowledge in general, that is, no excuse for constructing *a priori* theories of the nature of reality. But in Nehamas' interpretation, it seems that something substantial does follow from Nietzsche's rejection of the thing-in-itself: for example, that nothing can exist by itself, that everything is interconnected, and that nothing can change without changing everything else (81–83). If there is a way to show that these are not really substantive claims about the nature of reality, Nehamas has not provided it. His use of the last of these claims to justify Nietzsche's doctrine of eternal recurrence (see Chapter 8, section 5) makes it especially difficult to see how he can deny that the doctrine of will to power says something about the way the world is. But since his account makes will to power an *a priori* theory derived solely from logical and conceptual considerations, Nehamas seems to commit Nietzsche to an *a priori* or metaphysical theory of the nature of reality.

His ultimate reason for denying this is his interpretation of Nietzsche's perspectivism. He thinks that because Nietzsche believes that the question as to what something is "can never have a single answer that holds good for everyone," his view that everything is essentially interconnected (the will to power) "is part of his effort to show that there is no ready-made world to which our views and theories could be true once and for all" (81). In other words, the will to power implies that what anything is depends on what everything else is, and perspectivism entails that the nature of everything else depends on one's perspective. I have already argued against Nehamas' interpretation of Nietzsche's perspectivism (Chapter 5, section 5). But even if I accepted it, I would not consider successful his attempt to deny metaphysical status to the doctrine of will to power. For perspectivism does all of the work in Nehamas' interpretation of Nietzsche's rejection of metaphysics. Contrary to what he implies, will to power has no essential role to play in it, for if perspectivism is true, he believes there is no ultimate truth about reality – whether or not everything is interconnected. Nehamas does not therefore give us sufficient reason to equate the doctrine of will to power with Nietzsche's rejection of metaphysics, nor therefore to deny what otherwise seems the case, that the doctrine makes a substantive *a priori* and therefore a metaphysical claim about the nature of reality.

Given my account of what for Nietzsche constitutes a "true" world, and therefore a metaphysical theory, Kaufmann offers the most promising way of rendering Nietzsche's theory of will to power consistent with his rejection of metaphysics. He claims that Nietzsche's will to power, unlike Schopenhauer's metaphysical will to existence, is "essentially an empirical concept arrived at by induction" (1968, 204). According to Kaufmann, the will to power first appears, in the aphoristic works prior to *Zarathustra*, as "a psychological drive in terms of which many diverse phenomena could be explained, e.g., gratitude, pity, self-abasement." Success in explaining such different types of behavior was the basis, Kaufmann believes, upon which Nietzsche then formulated the hypothesis that all human behavior could be explained in terms of the will (which I take to be equivalent here to a motivating desire) for power. This psychological doctrine is the core that Nietzsche then widened to include the behavior of all living beings, and that he generalized into "the still more extreme hypothesis that will to power is the basic force of the entire universe" (207).

According to Kaufmann's interpretation, then, Nietzsche's cosmological doctrine of the will to power is perfectly compatible with his perspectivism and rejection of metaphysics. In contrast to Schacht's version, for instance, Kaufmann's involves no *a priori* assumption that the human perspective on things is flawed. If the world is will to power, it follows that our common-sense view is flawed. But the claim that common-sense perspectives are flawed follows from the truth of the will to power rather than being its presupposition; therefore, Kaufmann's interpretation does not commit Nietzsche to a metaphysical theory. Nietzsche claims not that the world in itself is will to power, but that the latter is "the one and only interpretation of human behavior [and reality in general] of which we are capable when we consider the evidence and think about it as clearly as we can" (206). In other words, will to power is the theory that best accounts for the data available from the human perspective and is therefore the one we have reason to consider true.

In fact, Kaufmann thinks it obvious that the cosmological theory of the will to power is not true, and claims that it "need not be taken seriously, not even in an effort to understand Nietzsche" (1967, 510). Denying it any important role in Nietzsche's philosophy, he treats the cosmological theory as an over-enthusiastic and ill-advised extension of the psychological doctrine to which he does accord a central role. A major advantage of his interpretation is that it explains how Nietzsche could have arrived at the doctrine without violating minimal standards of consistency, that is, without violating his perspectivism or rejection of metaphysics, and it insulates the psychological doctrine of the will to power from the cosmological doctrine, so that we can legitimately regard the former as worthy of the serious consideration Kaufmann and I agree we should deny the latter.

From my viewpoint, Kaufmann's interpretation also has the advantage of fitting the published works much better than do Schacht's and Nehamas'. When Nietzsche first talks about the will to power, it is in psychological contexts. His point is to explain specific kinds of human behavior. There is no attempt to give a cosmological theory (either the will to power or anything else) in these works. Nietzsche's concern is the human world, not the cosmos. In Z, will to power first appears as a view of the cosmos, but even here the cosmological view is introduced by psychological considerations (Z II, 12). Further, the cosmology has more the character of a vision, a poetic conception of reality, than a cosmological theory, and Z is a work of fiction. It articulates Zarathustra's cosmological vision, which may or may not also be Nietzsche's. In BG, Nietzsche does give an argument – the only one in his published works – for the conclusion that the world is will to power (see section 2). But he also claims to understand psychology as the doctrine of the development of the will to power (BG 23). In his later works, for example, GM, the will to power seems to function largely as it did in the ones in which he first formulated it: to explain various human behaviors and tendencies in terms of the desire for a sense of power. It is difficult to deny therefore that the theory of will to power originated in attempts to account for various human behaviors.

Despite these advantages, I believe that Kaufmann's theory must be rejected. One of its major aims is to answer the objection that Nietzsche's doctrine of the will to power does not explain anything, that by finding the will to power at work everywhere, it empties it of all meaning and reduces it to a "mere phrase," devoid of explanatory power or cognitive significance. Kaufmann's answer is that "on the contrary, it is surprising how much of human behavior Nietzsche illuminates by calling attention to the will to power and its hidden workings" (1967, 511). One may agree with Kaufmann here, yet claim that the enlightening character of explanations of behavior in terms of the desire for power is dependent on an implicit contrast with other motives, and is therefore lost as soon as all other motives are interpreted as expressions of the will to power. The enlightening character of contemporary accounts of rape in terms of power, for example, seems dependent on the implied contrast between the desire for power and the desire for sex. What the rapist fundamentally wants is not sexual gratification but a sense of power. This explanation loses its enlightening character if one goes on to say that all behavior is motivated by a desire for power, for then the motive for rape has not been differentiated from any other motive.

The empiricist interpretation of Nietzsche's doctrine can be maintained in the face of this kind of objection only if the will to power is defined so that at least some possible motives are not instances of it, and the contrast between power and other possible motives is preserved. We can understand the will to power in such terms if we define "power" as the ability to do or get what one wants. The satisfaction of the will to power, a sense of power, has then nothing essential to do with power over others, but is a sense of one's *effectiveness* in the world. This understanding of the desire for power not only allows the possibility of other desires, but actually demands it, because it requires us to distinguish the desire for power – for the ability to satisfy one's desires – from the other desires one wants to be able to satisfy. It amounts to thinking of the will to power as a second-order desire for the ability to satisfy one's other, or first-order, desires (cf. Frankfurt).

This would not rule out by definition the truth of the claim that all behavior is motivated by a desire for power. For it is not impossible – in the sense of logically contradictory – to have a desire to be able to satisfy whatever first-order desire one might come to have even though one has never had a first-order desire. The existence of a second-order desire for power does not therefore entail the existence of any first-order desires, and is compatible with the empirical hypothesis that in the case of human beings, "whatever is wanted is wanted for the sake of power" (Kaufmann, 1967, 511). If there is nothing contradictory in this hypothesis, however, it is surely undeserving of serious consideration. It would make human life an attempt to gain the ability to satisfy first-order desires even though we have no such first-order desires, or only those first-order desires we have invented or created as an excuse for satisfying our second-order desire for power. It is not seriously entertainable that human beings would have developed a desire for power (or perhaps more accurately, for a sense of power) unless they already had other desires that they were sometimes unable to satisfy. It seems obvious that the desire or need for power develops on the foundation of other desires and needs, even though in human beings obsessed by power it may come to have more importance than any of them and may operate in all human beings in some contexts in which no first-order desire exists.

I conclude that Nietzsche's doctrine of will to power may be construed as an empirical hypothesis that all human behavior is motivated by a desire for power, but only at the cost of depriving it of all plausibility, which would mean that Nietzsche was less astute about psychological matters than many (including Freud) have thought. I agree with Kaufmann's suggestion that Nietzsche's doctrine of the will to power must be empirical if it is to cohere with his rejection of metaphysics and that it originated in his reflections on human motivation – in his recognition of the desire for power, or for a sense of power, as an important human motive. I also agree that in calling our attention to this motive, Nietzsche does illuminate large areas of human life and behavior. I resist, however, the idea that Nietzsche believed that all behavior is motivated by the desire for power because I do not see any way in which this could be a plausible or interesting hypothesis about human behavior. Of course, Nietzsche might have believed it anyway. But, if we confine ourselves to the works Nietzsche actually published, I will argue that we find little reason to believe he did, and quite a bit to think he did not.

2. The published argument for the world as will to power

For determining Nietzsche's published doctrine of the will to power, *Beyond Good and Evil* seems the most important source. Because Zarathustra's conception of life as will to power is too metaphorical and anthropomorphic to take seriously as a literal account of the essence of life and gives us no reason to assume that Nietzsche accepts it, we would naturally look for Nietzsche's own doctrine of the will to power in *Beyond Good and Evil*, the first book published after *Zarathustra*. BG does not disappoint in this regard. It not only contains the first articulation of the doctrine of will to power in Nietzsche's own voice, but its first two parts contain four relatively detailed sections that provide a more sustained reflection on the doctrine than we find in any of Nietzsche's other books (BG 9, 22, 23, 36). It also discusses the will to power by name in at least eight other sections (BG 13, 44, 51, 186, 198, 211, 227, 259), and in several others without mentioning it by name (BG 230, 257). The will to power is mentioned much less frequently in Nietzsche's later books, and it never again receives sustained discussion or explanation.

If we had to choose one of BG's passages on the will to power as the most important, 36 would be the obvious choice. It presents a detailed argument for the cosmological doctrine of will to power, and is the only passage in all of Nietzsche's published writings to do so. I will argue, however, that if we look at the argument carefully, we find overwhelming reason to deny that Nietzsche accepts it.

In the first place, he formulates both premises and conclusion in hypothetical form. He begins by asking us to "suppose nothing else is 'given' as real except our world of desires and passions, and we can not get down, or up, to any other 'reality' besides the reality of our drives." After a relatively long argument, he concludes that "the world viewed from inside, the world defined and determined according to its 'intelligible character' – it would be 'will to power' and nothing else" (BG 36). This passage certainly tells us how one could argue for the conclusion that the world is will to power. But it asserts neither the premises nor the conclusion. It tells us that *if* we accept a number of premises – that no reality is "given" to us except that of our passions or affects (i.e., our will), that the will is a causal power, and that our entire instinctive life can be explained as a development of one form of will, will to power – then we have a right to "determine *all* effective force univocally as *will to power*" and thus to regard will to power as the world's "intelligible character." At most, the passage itself gives us reason to believe that Nietzsche accepts the last of these premises, which he apparently calls "my proposition." But as he does nothing to assert any of the other premises, nothing in the passage commits Nietzsche to the argument. Of course, if the other premises are obviously true, or if Nietzsche claims they are true elsewhere, we would have strong reason to suppose that he accepted the argument. In fact, however, the other two premises I have mentioned have little plausibility, and Nietzsche argues against them in BG and other works.

The first premise – that only the world of our desires and passions is "given" as real, and that we cannot get up, or down, to any other "reality" than that of our drives – seems to mean that we have knowledge regarding the existence and nature of our drives, but not regarding anything else, that is, the external or material world. The basis for accepting this premise cannot be experience – for it challenges what experience has to teach us about the external world, but must be an *a priori* account of what constitutes "true knowledge," an account that gives the inner world priority over the outer. Why would anyone think we had reason to accept such a position?

The only plausible answer would have to be some variation on Descartes' granting of priority to the inner world because of its alleged indubitability. The reality of our own thoughts is "given" to us, immediately certain, according to Descartes, whereas the existence of the external world can be doubted. To make it even halfway plausible that we cannot get up or down to a "reality" other than the world of our drives, Nietzsche would have to offer a similar argument, with desires or drives playing the role Descartes gave to thoughts. He would have to claim, much as Schopenhauer did, that the fact that "I will" (effectively desire) is directly present to me, thus "given" or "immediately certain," whereas all knowledge of the external world is mediated by observation and is therefore dubitable. In that case, the first premise would openly conflict with Nietzsche's denial in BG 16 that there are any "immediate certainties," including "I think" or "I will." BG 34 returns to the issue of "immediate certainties," claiming that faith in them is "a moral naïveté that reflects honor on us philosophers," though "apart from morality, this faith is a stupidity that reflects little honor on us."

Even if we could find a way of defending the first premise of BG 36 without commitment to "immediate certainties," it would still be incompatible with BG 19's criticism of philosophers like Schopenhauer who "speak of the will as if it were the best-known thing in the world." For that is exactly what the premise asserts. The argument of BG 36 is, in effect, that because the will is the only thing we really know, we must make the experiment of explaining the rest of the world in terms of its type of causality. I do not see how we can seriously believe that Nietzsche accepted the doctrine of the will to power on the basis of this argument.

The second part of the argument – that we must attempt to explain the rest of the world in terms of the will's kind of causality – is even more obviously incompatible with Nietzsche's views than the first premise. For Nietzsche does not believe in the causality of the will. Consider GS 127:

> Every thoughtless person believes that will alone is effective; that willing is something simple, a brute datum, underivable, and intelligible by itself. He is convinced that when he does something – strikes something, for example – it is he that strikes, and that he did strike because he *willed* it. He does not see any problem here; the feeling of *will* seems sufficient to him not only for the assumption of cause and effect, but also for the faith that he *understands* that relation. He knows nothing of the mechanism of what hap-

THE WILL TO POWER

pened and of the hundredfold fine work that needs to be done to bring about the strike, or of the incapacity of the will in itself to do even the tiniest part of it. The will is for him a magically effective force; the faith in the will as the cause of effects is the faith in magically effective forces.

Nietzsche could not have made clearer that he denies the causality of the will. Later works refer to "the great calamity of an error that will is something which is effective," and insist that today we know it is "only a word" (TI II, 5), or only "a resultant" (A 14). His point is the same when he responds as follows to the "old belief" that we are "causal in the act of willing."

> Today we no longer believe a word of all this. The "inner world" is full of phantoms and will-o'-the wisps: the will is one of them. The will no longer moves anything, hence does not explain anything either – it merely accompanies events; it can also be absent (TI VI, 3).

In BG itself, Nietzsche explains that what we actually refer to when we talk of "the will" is a complex of sensation, thought, and the affect of command (the feeling of commanding an action). But because we use one word for this complex, and it appears, in the vast majority of cases, only when the action was to be expected, we are able to deceive ourselves into believing that "willing suffices for action" (BG 19), that is, that we experience in ourselves something that commands and thereby brings about actions. Nietzsche's problem with this seems clear from BG 3. He does not deny that something within us has causal power. But he denies that the ultimate causes of our actions are conscious: "most of the conscious thinking of a philosopher is secretly guided and forced into certain channels by his instincts" (BG 3). The ultimate causes of our actions, then, are not the conscious thoughts and feelings with which Nietzsche claims we identify the will.

Given these passages, we cannot reasonably attribute to Nietzsche the argument of BG 36. The problem is not that it makes use of the idea of will, but that it depends crucially on what Nietzsche has explicitly and repeatedly rejected, a belief in the causality of the will. "The question," according to this argument,

is in the end whether we really recognize the will as *efficient*, whether
we believe in the causality of the will: if we do – and at bottom our
faith in this is nothing less than our faith in causality itself – then
we have to make the experiment of positing the causality of the will
as the only one. "Will," of course, can effect only "will" – and not
"matter" (not "nerves," for example). In short, one has to risk the
hypothesis whether will does not affect will whenever "effects" are
recognized – and whether all mechanical occurrences are not, insofar as a force is active in them, will force, effects of will (BG 36).

This may give the impression that Nietzsche supports the causality of the will because otherwise he would have to give up something we cannot do without, "our faith . . . in causality itself." If
so, it seems to me that Nietzsche is playing with us, for he clearly
believes we can do without this faith. Consider TI VI, 3:

> People have believed at all times that they knew what a cause is;
> but whence did we take our knowledge – or more precisely, the
> faith that we had such knowledge? From the realm of the famous
> "inner facts," of which not a single one has so far proved to be
> factual. We believed ourselves to be causal in the act of willing: we
> thought here at least we caught causality in the act.

Nietzsche makes the point repeatedly that we have interpreted
causality in terms of our experience of willing (this would mean,
in particular, the feeling of commanding an action). Our "faith in
causality" is our faith in this interpretation of the causal relation.
    But BG 21 has already urged us to abandon this "faith": "one
should use 'cause' and 'effect' only as pure concepts, that is to say,
as conventional fictions for the purpose of designation and
commmunication." Nietzsche's formulations in this passage may
still belong to stage 5 of his tale of the "true world," because he
does not in any later book call causal concepts "fictions" or deny
their role in explanation. But his point in this passage – to rule
out "the prevailing mechanical doltishness which makes the
cause press and push until it effects its end" (BG 21) – does not
require these formulations. It is the same point Hume designed
his analysis of causality as constant conjunction to serve: as Nietzsche puts it, that the idea of an " 'unfree will' . . . amounts to a
misuse of cause and effect." In other words, our resistance to the
idea of human behavior as determined comes at least in part
from our misunderstanding of causal relations as involving "con-

straint, need, compulsion to obey, pressure, and unfreedom" (BG 21). Nietzsche differs from Hume only in claiming that our misunderstanding of determinism comes from our projection of our own experience of willing, and of being subject to the will of others, into our idea of causality.

I conclude from this that Nietzsche encourages us to continue to think in causal terms (going so far as to equate the "sound conception of cause and effect" with "science" and "knowledge" in A 49) but to abandon the interpretation of causality we derive from our experience of willing. BG 36 therefore gives us no reason to retain belief in the causality of the will, nor any way of reconciling its argument with Nietzsche's repeated rejection of that causality. Various means of reconciliation have been suggested, but none seem plausible. Schacht implies that the causality at issue in BG 36 is of the type Nietzsche was prepared to accept (185). However, this ignores the fact that Nietzsche explicitly makes the argument of BG 36 depend on the causality of the will, something he nowhere accepts. Schacht denies that Nietzsche's use of "will" to describe the world's "intelligible character" conflicts with his dismissal of will as "just a word" on the grounds that "will" is used here as a metaphor, with the conceptual content of "will to power" specified and exhausted through the idea of a tendency or disposition of forces "to extend their influence and dominate others" (220-2). But even if we accept this, it will not save the argument of BG 36. For the latter depends on an appeal to our intuition of ourselves as causal in the act of willing as a basis for interpreting the material world as will to power, and that is precisely the appeal for which Nietzsche accused Schopenhauer of enthroning a "primeval mythology" (GS 127).[1]

1. Two other strategies of reconciliation may seem promising. First, one could argue that Nietzsche rejects the causality of the will only in the sense of mental causes or conscious acts of will (TI VI, 3, e.g.). In that case, as long as willing is not interpreted so that it must be conscious, Nietzsche need not reject its causality. The problem is that if willing is not conscious, it becomes impossible to understand how BG 36 would support its first premise: that only willing is "given," and that we cannot get up or down to any world beyond our drives. Danto's reconstruction of Nietzsche's argument for the will to power suggests a second strategy (231): that Nietzsche rejects the will's capacity for acting on matter, but does not deny its ability to have an effect on other wills. "Will can only effect will, of course" (BG 36). The problem is that the idea that will affects only will is clearly part of the primitive mythology – "one can have an effect only on beings who will" – that Nietzsche claims Schopenhauer enthroned (GS 127).

Perhaps Nietzsche left us a different and better argument for interpreting the world as will to power in his notebooks. But BG 36 contains his only published argument for this interpretation, and it is a quite clear and extended argument, and it therefore deserves to be looked at in its own terms before we start deciding that we can understand it better in terms of the *Nachlass*. If what I have been arguing is correct – that Nietzsche gives us very strong reason to deny that he accepts the argument of BG 36 – it follows not that we should try to fix up the premises, but that we should try to understand why he presented us with *this* argument. Surely there is something in need of explanation here, if the only argument he published for the cosmological doctrine of will to power appears to depend on premises he rejects in the same work. I suggest that this is quite deliberate, and that Nietzsche is challenging us to look for an explanation. I am encouraged in this interpretation by a number of the passages that surround BG 36: by Nietzsche's praise of masks (BG 40), his stress on the importance of the distinction between the esoteric and the exoteric (BG 30), his admission that he does everything to be "difficult to understand" combined with expressed gratitude for "the good will to some subtlety of interpretation" (BG 27), and even by his claim that refutability is not "the least charm of a theory" (BG 18). The best place to look for an explanation is surely not the *Nachlass*, which only gets us sidetracked into more arguments of the same kind, but the surrounding material of BG.

3. Philosophy and the doctrine of will to power in *Beyond Good and Evil*

Nehamas aptly calls *Beyond Good and Evil* a work of "dazzling obscurity," insisting that individual sections dazzle with their brilliance, yet "we do not understand its structure, its narrative line" (1988, 46). I believe we may be able to get clearer on a major part of its structure, and at least one of its narrative lines, if we come to it with questions posed by section 36: Namely, what is the function of its argument in the larger work? And why does Nietzsche present to us in such detail an argument he does not accept?

Consider the characterization of philosophers in BG 5:

What provokes one to look at all philosophers half suspiciously, half mockingly, is not that one discovers again and again how innocent they are – how often and how easily they make mistakes and go astray; in short, their childishness and childlikeness – but that they are not honest enough in their work, although they make a lot of virtuous noise when the problem of truthfulness is touched even remotely. They all pose as if they had discovered and reached their real opinions through the self-development of a cold, pure, divinely unconcerned dialectic (as opposed to the mystics of every rank, who are more honest and doltish – and talk of "inspiration"); while at bottom it is an assumption, a hunch, indeed a kind of "inspiration" – most often a desire of the heart that has been filtered and made abstract – that they defend with reasons they have sought after the fact. They are all advocates who resent that name, and for the most part even wily spokesmen for their prejudices which they baptize "truths" – and *very* far from having the good courage of the conscience that admits this, precisely this, to itself; very far from having the good taste of the courage which also lets this be known, whether to warn an enemy or friend, or, from exuberance, to mock itself.

Given this criticism, we would expect Nietzsche to deny that he has arrived at his own philosophical views through a "divinely unconcerned dialectic" – that is, solely through rational considerations and concern for truth without regard to what he would like to be true – and to exhibit "the good taste of the courage to let this be known."

We can fit these expectations with the puzzling nature of BG 36. Its argument is exactly of the type one would expect Nietzsche to give for the cosmological doctrine of the will to power if he claimed to arrive at it through a "divinely unconcerned dialectic." I suggest that by constructing the argument so that it relies on premises he rejects earlier in the very same book, Nietzsche seeks to display the courage and self-knowledge to warn us that his doctrine is "a desire of the heart that has been filtered and made abstract," a "prejudice" he has baptized "truth."

It will seem strange that Nietzsche would construct an argument he does not accept to warn us of the motivation behind his doctrine. After all, whatever his motives for accepting it, his job as a philosopher is to explain the reasons anyone would have to accept it. The construction of an argument he knows is bad for his doctrine suggests he believes there are no good reasons to

accept it. But the motives philosophers have had for constructing their theories seem irrelevant to whether there are good
reasons for accepting them. To answer this objection, I will argue
that Nietzsche's claim in BG 5 concerns not merely the motivation of philosophers, but also the status of their doctrines. When
read in light of the sections that follow, BG 5 makes it reasonable
to conclude that Nietzsche denies the truth of the cosmological
doctrine of will to power and that he seeks to warn us of this by
constructing the argument of BG 36.

Consider BG 6, which I have already discussed in Chapter 6
(section 3). Nietzsche claims that the moral or immoral intentions
of a philosophy constitute "the real germ of life from which the
whole plant" grows. He illustrates what he means when he proceeds to treat Stoicism as a model of philosophy. You Stoics, he
writes, "pretend rapturously to read the canon of your law in
nature" (BG 9). That is, Stoics claim to derive from the study of
nature reasons for accepting the moral law "live according to
nature." After arguing against the plausibility of their claim, Nietzsche explains that the Stoics really "want something opposite."

> Your pride wants to impose your morality, your ideal on nature –
> even on nature – and incorporate them in her; you demand that
> she be nature "according to the Stoa" and you would like all
> existence to exist only after your own image – as an immense
> eternal glorification and generalization of Stoicism. For all your
> love of truth, you have forced yourselves so long, so persistently,
> so rigidly-hypnotically to see nature the wrong way, namely, Stoi-
> cally, that you can no longer see her differently. And some abys-
> mal arrogance finally still inspires you with the insane hope that
> *because* you know how to tyrannize yourselves – Stoicism is self-
> tyranny – nature, too, lets herself be tyrannized: is not the Stoic –
> a *piece* of nature?
>
> But this is an ancient, eternal story: what formerly happened
> with the Stoics still happens today, too, as soon as any philosophy
> begins to believe in itself. It always creates the world in its own
> image; it cannot do otherwise. Philosophy is this tyrannical drive
> itself, the most spiritual will to power, to the "creation of the
> world," to the *causa prima* (BG 9).[2]

2. I ignore the reference to the will to power in the last line of this passage for
   now, but discuss it in detail in section 4.

Nietzsche's point is that though philosophers claim otherwise, their theories are not even designed to arrive at truth. They are attempts to construct the world, or an image of the world, in terms of the philosopher's values. I have already interpreted Nietzsche as saying this about metaphysics (Chapter 6, section 3). The metaphysician is not, contrary to what he claims, driven by a desire for knowledge of ultimate reality, of things as they are themselves. Because we have no conception of any such thing, it could be of no cognitive interest to us, and Nietzsche does not believe that metaphysics has been based on a mere mistake about this. He believes that philosophers have used the idea of things-in-themselves to create the appearance of room for a "true" or metaphysical world, thus as an excuse for baptizing as the "truth" what is only their prejudices read into the world. In the passage I have just quoted, Nietzsche claims that this is true of all philosophy. If he is consistent about this, he must admit that his cosmological doctrine of the will to power is an attempt to read his values into the world and that he does not consider it to be true. His acceptance of it is inspired not by a will to truth, but by a will to construct the world in the image of his own values. The Stoics construct the world by picturing nature as subject to law. Nietzsche pictures the same nature as will to power.

He pretty much admits this in BG 22, a passage famous for its apparent admission that the doctrine of will to power is "only interpretation."

> Forgive me as an old philologist who cannot desist from the malice of putting his finger on bad modes of interpretation: but "nature's conformity to law," of which you physicists talk so proudly, as thought – why, it exists only owing to your interpretation and "bad philology." It is no matter of fact, no "text," but rather only a naively humanitarian emendation and perversion of meaning, with which you make abundant concessions to the democratic instincts of the modern soul! "Everywhere equality before the law; nature is no different in that respect, no better off than we are" – a fine instance of ulterior motivation . . . But as was said above, this is interpretation, not text; and somebody might come along who, with opposite intentions and modes of interpretation, could read out of the same "nature," and with regard to the same phenomena, rather the tyrannically inconsiderate and relentless enforcement of claims of power – an interpreter who would picture the unexceptional and unconditional aspects of all "will to

power" so vividly that almost every word, even the word "tyranny" itself would eventually seem unsuitable, or a weakening and attenuating metaphor – being too human – but he might, nevertheless, end by asserting the same about the world as you do, namely, that it has a "necessary" and "calculable" course, *not* because laws obtain in it, but because they are absolutely *lacking*, and every power draws its ultimate consequence at every moment. Supposing that this too is only interpretation – and you will be eager enough to make this objection? – well, so much the better (BG 22).

It is easy to misunderstand the kind of "interpretation" discussed in this passage. For Nietzsche, because all knowledge is interpretation, physics is interpretation too. As I have argued (Chapter 5), this amounts to anti-foundationalism and therefore to the claim that knowledge, and therefore physics too, is always subject to revision. But Nietzsche does not use "interpretation" in this sense in the above passage, as he shows by not including physics as interpretation (in contrast, e.g., to BG 14). Instead, the theories and mathematical formulas in terms of which the physicist calculates and predicts the relations between various phenomena here count as the "text," which Nietzsche claims can be interpreted in (at least two) different ways, as nature's conformity to law or as will to power. The interpretation one gives these mathematical formulas, he claims, depends on which moral values one reads into them. We regard the physicist's formulas as "laws" that nature must obey because we read democratic prejudices – that is, democratic values – into them (though BG 9 makes clear we might get the same result from the values of Stoicism). That is, we construct or use metaphors to imagine or "picture" the text provided by physics as analogous to something in our own experience, and which metaphors we use reflect and depend upon our moral values. The passage suggests that such metaphors have no cognitive function, but only extend to the universe our sense of morality, generalizing and therefore glorifying what we consider important. This in no way denies that physics provides knowledge or truth. Not physics itself, that is, physical theories, but the metaphors in terms of which we interpret them read moral values into nature.

When Nietzsche argues that "with opposite intentions and modes of interpretation," we could, in effect, construe the same nature as will to power, he means that we could arrive at the cosmological doctrine of the will to power by reading into the same text provided by physics values opposed to democratic ones. When he suggests that the will to power, too, is "only interpretation," therefore, he puts it on a par not with physics, but with a belief in nature's "conformity to law," which owes its existence to "bad 'philology'" and democratic values. I therefore take his "so much the better" as an admission that his doctrine of the will to power does read his values into nature, that he therefore does not regard it as any truer than the idea that nature conforms to law, but that this is fine with him since he thereby remains consistent with everything he has said about knowledge and philosophy.

Of course, if one believes that Nietzsche denies all truth, it will come as no surprise that he denies the truth of the cosmological doctrine of will to power. But my whole interpretation argues against the larger claim. I therefore interpret Nietzsche's admission in BG 22 that his doctrine is "only interpretation" as a warning that, in contrast to the claims he makes, he does not regard the cosmological will to power as true, or as belonging to the realm of knowledge. Although he does not mention "philosophy" in BG 22, the metaphor of nature's obedience to law is the very same one he stresses when presenting the projection of the Stoics' values into nature as the model of what philosophers always do. If my interpretation of it is correct, therefore, BG 22 implies that philosophical theories are not true, that they do not belong to the realm of knowledge. It suggests instead that philosophers always take a "text" provided by some form of knowledge and read values into it by constructing the appropriate metaphors.

It is not difficult to interpret the cosmological will to power so that it fits this pattern. In at least two passages of BG, the will to power is presented as if it had value implications. In BG 186, the fact that the essence of life is will to power is taken to show "how insipidly false and sentimental" Schopenhauer's basic principle of morality is. In BG 259, the fact that life is will to power is presented as showing the impossibility of overcoming exploitation, and therefore the life-negating character of the demand for its overcoming.

According to the usual interpretation and the one immediately suggested by these passages, Nietzsche gives reasons against certain value judgments (hurting anyone is wrong; exploitation is wrong) by appealing to the truth about life, that its essence is will to power. In that case, Nietzsche would be doing what the Stoics claimed to be doing, namely, basing value judgments on knowledge of nature. But if Nietzsche's own case fits what he claims about all philosophy, he has actually arrived at his characterization of nature by reading his values into it. He wants nature to live only after his own image, as an eternal generalization and glorification of what he finds valuable.

To pursue this line of interpretation, we must take the world as will to power as a generalization and glorification of *the* will to power, the psychological entity (the drive or desire for power) discussed in section 1. Because he considers this drive so important, I suggest, he glorifies it by picturing all human motivation, all of nature, and sometimes, all of reality, as its expression. When he appears to reject Schopenhauer's morality on the grounds that life is will to power (BG 186), we can read him as rejecting it instead because he values the will to power, which Schopenhauer's morality condemns. And when he rejects the demand for an end to exploitation on the grounds that life is will to power (BG 259), we can interpret this as a claim that the strengthening of the will to power, which he values, makes exploitation inevitable.

TI's comments on the Greeks support this reading. "I saw their strongest instinct, the will to power," Nietzsche writes, "I saw them tremble before the indomitable force of this drive." This implies that the Greeks had other instincts, thus that the will to power was one among other drives, albeit the most important one. Because the passage proceeds to identify this drive with "inner explosives" and a "tremendous inward tension" that "discharged itself in terrible and ruthless hostility to the outside world," one may doubt that Nietzsche values it so highly as to generalize and glorify it in his picture of the world as will to power. But the same passage gives an indication of why he would, by presenting the will to power as responsible for the Greeks' political institutions and other cultural achievements. Their political institutions grew out of preventative measures taken to protect each other against the will to power, Nietzsche claims, "and with festivals and the arts they also aimed at nothing other than to feel on top, to show themselves on top" (TI X, 3). Further, the beginning of *The Antichrist* leaves no doubt that

Nietzsche did place the highest value on this drive when it gives this answer to the question "what is good?": "Everything that heightens the feeling of power in man, the will to power, power itself." What Nietzsche here puts forward as the good seems to be exactly what he found in such abundance among the Greeks: the will to power – a psychological entity, one drive among others (though in the Greeks, the strongest drive) – and the satisfaction of this drive, "the feeling of power in human beings" and "power itself." It is clearly a particular component of human life, rather than life or the world as a whole, that Nietzsche here values under the title of "the will to power." It is this component of human life, I am claiming, that Nietzsche "generalized and glorified" in his picture of life and the cosmos as will to power.

In addition to its line of argument about the nature of philosophy, BG offers more specific support for my reading in the first section after BG 36 to mention "will to power." After describing those who call themselves "free spirits" but want only "security, lack of danger, comfort, and an easier life for everyone," Nietzsche writes that "we with opposed feelings" (*wir Umgekehrten*)

> having opened our eyes and conscience to the question where and how the plant "man" has so far grown most vigorously to a height – we think that this has happened every time under the opposite conditions, that to this end the dangerousness of a situation must grow to the point of enormity, his power of invention and simulation (his "spirit") had to develop under prolonged pressure and constraint into refinement and audacity, his life-will had to be changed into an unconditional power-will (BG 44).

The distinction drawn here between a "life-will" and a "power-will" constitutes very strong evidence for the interpretation I have suggested. It amounts to an admission that life itself is not will to power, because it says that a power-will does not automatically come with life, but must be developed by enhancing one's life-will.[3] The passage also shows that Nietzsche believes there is rea-

---

3. Nietzsche suggests the same point in the passage in which he explains the Greeks' will to power. He writes that "one needed to be strong; danger was near, it lurked everywhere. The magnificent physical suppleness, the audacious realism and immoralism which distinguished the Hellene constituted a *need,* not 'nature.' It only resulted, it was not there from the start" (TI X, 3). This means that certain effects of the will to power were not there from the start, and it implies that the will to power itself was something that grew

son to value the will to power that has nothing to do with cosmology (or metaphysical biology/psychology), namely, that every enhancement of the human type depends on a strengthening of the will to power. Nietzsche evidently finds in the will to power the source of everything "for whose sake it is worthwhile to live on earth, for example, virtue, art, music, dance, reason, spirituality – something transfiguring, subtle, mad, and divine" (BG 188). He believes that these enhancements of the human type require "the craving for an ever new widening of distances within the soul itself, the development of ever higher, rarer, more remote, further-stretching, more comprehensive states" (BG 257), and that this would have been impossible without that "*pathos of distance*" that grows out of the "ingrained difference between strata" that one finds in an aristocratic society. The idea seems to be that the desire for, hence the development of, such higher states of soul requires a spiritualized version of the will to power.

This claim requires much more explanation and examination than I can give it within the scope of this book. But the passages I have discussed provide strong evidence that Nietzsche gives a reason for valuing the will to power that in no way implies that the world or life is will to power, or that human beings want only power, namely, that this drive is the source of what is most valuable in human life, the activities and states of soul that make life worth living. They also help us to see the following passage, which begins with a description of psychology as the "doctrine of the forms and development of the will to power," as a partial explanation of why Nietzsche was not more forthright about his position:

> The power of moral prejudice has penetrated deeply into the most spiritual world, which would seem to be the coldest and most devoid of presuppositions, and has obviously operated in an injurious, inhibiting, blinding, and distorting manner. A proper physio-psychology has to contend with the unconscious resistance in the heart of the investigator, it has "the heart" against it: even a doctrine of the reciprocal dependence of the "good" and the "wicked" drives, causes (as refined immorality) distress and aversion in a still hale and hearty conscience – still more so, a doctrine of the derivation of all good impulses from wicked ones. If, however, a person should regard even the affects of hatred, envy,

stronger under the conditions of Greek life, that it was not their "strongest instinct" as a matter of "nature."

covetousness, and the lust to rule as conditions of life, as factors which, fundamentally and essentially, must be present in the general economy of life (and must, therefore, be further enhanced if life is to be further enhanced) – he will suffer from such a view of things as from seasickness (BG 23).

Finally, the passages discussed here allow us to see how Nietzsche's cosmological doctrine of will to power fits the characterization he gives of philosophy in his discussion of the Stoics: He pictures life as will to power because he values the will to power, not because he has reason to believe that life is will to power (or that power is the only human motive). The argument of BG 36, in the context of the account of philosophy in part one of BG, can therefore be read as Nietzsche's way of letting it be known – "whether to warn an enemy or friend" (BG 5) – that his doctrine of the will to power is a construction of the world from the viewpoint of his moral values.

4. The psychology of the will to power and its relation to the will to truth

I have argued that Nietzsche's doctrine of will to power is not a doctrine at all. Although Nietzsche says that life is will to power, he also gives us clues that he does not regard this as a truth or a matter of knowledge, but as a construction of the world from the viewpoint of his values. However, this is only half the story, for it is not plausible to interpret everything Nietzsche says about power in this way. He clearly claims all sorts of knowledge of the human desire for power, for example, and this is the other side of the story.

What Nietzsche claims knowledge of, I suggest, is *the* will to power, a second-order drive that he recognizes as dependent for its existence on other drives, but which he generalizes and glorifies in his picture of life as will to power. The knowledge Nietzsche claims of the will to power belongs to psychology rather than to metaphysics or cosmology. In BG 23, he writes that he understands psychology as "*the doctrine of the forms and development of the will to power,*" identifies this psychology as a "proper physio-psychology," to differentiate it, I assume, from anything metaphysical, and asserts that psychology is "the path to the fundamental problems." Interpreting the will to power as a second-order drive allows us to see that Nietzsche's claims to knowledge of it are perfectly compatible with his claims about knowledge. His psychology of the will to power does not depend on denying the relevance of sense testimony, or on the assumption of a thing-in-itself, and is therefore not a metaphysical doctrine or a violation of his perspectivism. Although I cannot undertake a systematic exploration of Nietzsche's psychology here, I will examine enough of it to explain why he considers it "the path to the fundamental problems."

I will focus on Nietzsche's psychology of the will to truth in its relation to his claim that philosophy is the "the most spiritual expression of the will to power" (BG 9). This claim about philosophy has a prominent place in the treatment of the will to power in both BG and Z. BG first mentions the will to power to characterize the drive responsible for philosophy (BG 9). Z introduces it to characterize what lies behind a people's values – what the people call "good and evil," Zarathustra says, reflects their "will to power" (Z I, 15) – but mentions it next to claim that the people's values reflect the will to power of the wisest (Z II, 12), among whom philosophers are at the very least included. In the same section, Zarathustra calls the will to power of the wisest their "danger." He then proceeds to formulate the cosmological version of will to power, in the obviously metaphorical and anthropomorphic language mentioned earlier. An interpretation of these claims about values, philosophy, and the will to power will help to explain why Nietzsche considers knowledge of the will to power "the path to the fundamental problems" (BG 23) and why he generalizes and glorifies this drive in his cosmological doctrine of will to power.

First, why does Zarathustra portray values as the voice of a people's will to power (Z I, 15)? The point does not seem to be to explain the act of valuing. About that, Zarathustra says merely that a people could not survive without esteeming. The will to power is introduced to explain why a people esteems as it does. Zarathustra has already said that a people must not esteem as its neighbor esteems, presumably because it would then have no identity as a separate people. So what a people values depends in part on what its neighbor values. The other major factor that determines values, he suggests, is what gives a people the greatest sense of its power or effectiveness. But that depends on several other factors. Because power is a second-order desire, it depends, to begins with, on their first-order desires. If there is no perceived need or desire for something, the ability to do or get it will not give a sense of power, and therefore, according to Zarathustra's account, it will not be esteemed. A second factor he mentions is what they find difficult. If something comes easy, the ability to do it will not give much sense of power either. Finally, Zarathustra says a people value what makes them "rule, and triumph, and shine to the envy of their neighbor" (Z I, 15). Various forms of winning in competition with others – including ruling over them – provide very obvious ways of confirming one's power in the world. Zarathustra's stress on this factor seems to show that Kaufmann's account of the will to power is too moralistic when he says (1958, 119) that what is meant by "power" in this context "is clearly power over self," or, as he calls it elsewhere, "self-overcoming." Nothing Zarathustra says in this first passage on the will to power suggests the possibility that power over oneself would satisfy the will to power, much less that it has the kind of privileged status Kaufmann gives it. What the will to power aims at is evidently a sense of effectiveness in relation to the world, a sense of one's ability to have the world satisfy one's (first-order) will.

Self-overcoming is not connected to the will to power until Zarathustra claims in part 2 that the people's values reflect the will to power of the wisest. This means that the people's values are determined by what gives those they recognize as the wisest (priests and philosophers) the greatest feeling of power or effectiveness. Because Nietzsche argues in GM that priests and philosophers have been proponents of the ascetic ideal, this seems to mean that the self-overcoming or self-denial required by the ascetic ideal has given priests and philosophers the greatest sense of their power or effectiveness. This suggests that priests and philosophers connected the will to power to self-overcoming, diverting it away from more obvious ways of acquiring a sense of power.

This connection to the ascetic ideal also explains why Zarathustra warns the wise that the will to power is their "danger." For this ideal appears to turn the activity of valuing, which Zarathustra presents as necessary for, and directed by, life, against life itself. Both Zarathustra and Nietzsche turn to the psychology of the will to power to understand how this is possible.

Nietzsche explains asceticism as an internalization of the will to power. In BG 51, he tells us it was the " 'will to power' that made [the most powerful human beings] stop before the saint" (BG 51).

> Why did they bow? In him – and as it were behind the question mark of his fragile and miserable appearance – they sensed the superior force that sought to test itself in such conquest, the strength of will in which they recognized their own strength and delight in dominion: they honored something in themselves when they honored the saint. Moreover, the sight of the saint awakened a suspicion in them: such an enormous amount of denial, of anti-nature will not have been desired for nothing, they said to themselves and asked themselves. Perhaps there is a reason for it, some very great danger about which the ascetic, thanks to his secret comforters and visitors, might have inside information?

That is, the powerful perceived the saint's asceticism as an expression of his will to power, even though he turns this will against his own impulses. In his discussion of the bad conscience, Nietzsche makes it explicit that this self-denial expresses an internalized will to power (GM II, 18). He claims that "the *delight* that the selfless man, the self-denier, the self-sacrificer feels . . . is tied to cruelty," and that the force involved is the same force that is "at work on a grander scale in those artists of violence and organizers who build states":

> namely, the *instinct for freedom* (in my language: the will to power); only here the material upon which the form-giving and ravishing nature of this force vents itself is man himself, his whole ancient animal self and *not*, as in that greater and more obvious phenomenon, some *other* man, *other* men (GM II, 18).

The will to power described here expresses itself by disciplining, castigating, forming, and otherwise getting power over the self. How did this come about? Nietzsche evidently believes that one condition for this internalization of the will to power is that "outward discharge was *inhibited*" (GM II, 16). He traces the bad conscience to the change that occurred when human beings were "finally enclosed within the walls of society and peace," and the bulwarks of political organization kept them from satisfying the "instincts of wild, free, prowling man." These instincts – "hostility, cruelty, joy in persecuting, in attacking, in change, in destruction" – could be satisfied only by being turned back against their possessors. Given that Nietzsche explicitly claims that this is a matter of internalizing the will to power, he must count the instincts civilization suppressed as external expressions of the will to power. When such external expression was blocked, human beings got their sense of power by directing the same instincts against the self – by hurting and persecuting themselves rather than others. In this project, they had help from the priests who invented the ascetic ideal.

Nietzsche treats the priests as the real experts in the internalization of the will to power. In their case, it is internal rather than external barriers that kept them from directing the will to power outward. There is "from the first something *unhealthy* in such priestly aristocracies and the habits ruling in them which turn them away from action and alternate between brooding and emotional explosions" (GM I, 6). The priests are the "*most evil enemies,*" Nietzsche claims, "because they are the most impotent," i.e., the ones who have the greatest problem giving direct or external expression to their will to power. "It is because of their impotence that in them hatred grows to monstrous and uncanny proportions, to the most spiritual and poisonous kind of hatred" (GM I, 7). The priests' inability to exercise their will to power in direct ways strengthens it, so that it requires for its satisfaction incredible acts of "spiritual revenge," and is "ultimately satisfied with nothing less than a radical revaluation of their enemies' values" (GM I, 7).

The priests' asceticism is another way in which their strong will to power is expressed. Nietzsche makes clear that the priest's self-denial aims for power not merely over the self, but also over life:

> here rules a *ressentiment* without equal, that of an insatiable instinct and power-will that wants to become master not over something in life but over life itself, over its most profound, powerful, and basic conditions; here an attempt is made to employ force to block up the wells of force; here physiological well-being itself is viewed askance, and especially the outward expression of this well-being, beauty and joy; while pleasure is felt and *sought* in ill-constitutedness, decay, pain, mischance, ugliness, voluntary deprivation, self-mortification, self-flagellation, self-sacrifice. All this is to the highest degree paradoxical: we stand before a dis-

cord that *wants* to be discordant, that *enjoys* itself in this suffering and even grows more self-confident and triumphant the more its own presupposition, its physiological capacity of life, *decreases* (GM III, 11).

But, contrary to what the ascetic believes, Nietzsche claims that asceticism is itself "an artifice for the *preservation* of life" (GM III, 12). The ascetic ideal "indicates a partial physiological obstruction and exhaustion against which the deepest instincts of life, which have remained intact, continually struggle with new expedients and devices." The ascetic ideal is one such expedient, and it engages human beings in a "physiological struggle against death (more precisely: against disgust with life, against exhaustion, against desire for the 'end')." This means that the ascetic ideal actually promotes the affirmation of life – by which I mean the sense of life's value, the feeling that life is worth living – even though its message is precisely that life itself has no value. And it does this, according to Nietzsche's theory, because it gives its followers a sense of power.

I believe we find throughout GM the view that a sense of power promotes, and is perhaps necessary for, the affirmation of life. Nietzsche gives his most explicit statement of this view when he calls the will to power the "most life-affirming drive" (GM III, 18). I take this to mean that the best way to promote the affirmation of life – to overcome depression or disgust with life, to boost one's willingness to go on, to keep acting, willing, changing – is to satisfy the need for a sense of power or effectiveness.

In the same passage, Nietzsche also makes clear that the priest provides the people with alternatives to the more obvious ways of satisfying their will to power that involve hurting each other. An alternative is necessary because the more obvious expressions of the will to power threaten to "blow up herd and herdsmen" (GM III, 15), whereas the inability to express it at all threatens human beings with depression or sickness of the will (e.g., GM II, 16; III, 28). The point seems to be that without a sense that our will matters, that we can be effective in the world, it will be difficult to work up a great deal of enthusiasm for living and doing.[4] The ascetic ideal evidently works to provide a sense of

4. My formulations in this paragraph may distort the causal picture somewhat if the feeling of power belongs to the level of consciousness, because Nietzsche denies that the ultimate causes of our actions are found at that level. It would

power, thereby promoting such enthusiasm for living, as Nietzsche suggests in the following account of the asceticism of early philosophers:

> cruelty towards themselves, inventive self-castigation – this was the principle means these power-hungry hermits and innovators of ideas required to overcome the gods and tradition in themselves, so as to be able to *believe* in their own innovations. I recall the famous story of King Vishvamitra, who through millennia of self-torture acquired such a feeling of power and self-confidence that he endeavored to build a new heaven (GM III, 10).

Nietzsche thus explains asceticism as an "artifice for the preservation of life" (GM III, 12). But why was the ascetic ideal needed for this? That is, why couldn't ascetics just internalize their will to power and gain a sense of power without denying the value of human life? The problem seems to be that an ascetic who believed he engaged in asceticism simply in order to get a sense of power would no longer be able to get a sense of power from it. As Nietzsche presents him, the priest is not satisfied simply by having a sense of power over his other instincts; he needs a feeling of power over life itself. This he gets by interpreting the

then be more in accord with Nietzsche's views on these matters to think of a sense of power as a phenomenological or epiphenomenal reflection of our actual doings rather than a cause of them. In other words, we will have a sense of power sufficient for enthusiasm in living and doing if there are no obstructions to acting, whereas we will suffer from physiological depression and its psychological or conscious reflection, a sense of powerlessness, if such obstructions do block our path(s) to action. This fits Nietzsche's physiological emphasis in his description of the ascetic ideal's fight against life. He claims that the ascetic ideal fights "profound physiological depression" (GM III, 17) by allowing otherwise blocked impulses to be expressed against the self. As a result "[t]he old depression, heaviness, and weariness were indeed *overcome* through this system of [ascetic] procedures; life again became *very* interesting: awake, everlastingly awake, sleepless, glowing, charred, spent and yet not weary" (GM III, 20). The connection to a sense of power seems to be that the latter is the reflection in consciousness of success in satisfying one's impulses. The ascetic ideal evidently works to promote a sense of power and the affirmation of life by providing alternate ways of satisfying impulses. If this is correct, we should formulate Nietzsche's general thesis about the will to power as a claim that a satisfaction of this drive, namely, a sense of power, is the reflection in consciousness of whatever is necessary for the affirmation of life. The ascetic ideal saved the will – fought depression, which amounts to promoting the affirmation of life – by providing a way to satisfy otherwise blocked impulses by directing them against the self, and the reflection in consciousness of its success is a sense of power. I ignore this complication in the remainder of my discussion.

denial of his other instincts as a triumph over life. This is what the ascetic ideal allows him to do, by holding out self-denial as the ideal, and life itself as without value unless it turn against itself. The ascetic needs the valuation and interpretation of life offered by the ascetic ideal in order to get a sense of power from self-denial. It would not work to say to himself "I value self-denial only because I get a feeling of power from it." Because the will to power is a second-order drive, being able to do something furnishes a sense of power only if there is some independent reason to want to be able to. Nietzsche says that the powerful people who honored the ascetic thought that he must have some "inside information" precisely because they could not interpret his self-denial as a sign of strength or power unless they believed he got something out of it besides a sense of power (BG 51). Thus ascetics needed a way of interpreting their activity of self-denial that gave it value quite apart from any sense of power they got from it, which is what the ascetic ideal provided.

This explains why Nietzsche thinks that the will to truth overcomes the ascetic ideal (Chapter 6, section 5). If his psychology of asceticism is correct, once the will to truth exposes it, ascetics can no longer get what they wanted from the ideal except by denying or ignoring the truth. To believe fully that asceticism is an expression of the same impulses that the ascetic ideal condemns, that is, the will to power, would make it impossible to get a sense of power from ascetic practices, since it would make it impossible to interpret them as a triumph over life. Nietzsche's psychology makes them appear instead as "an artifice for the preservation of life," a way in which life detains "its creatures in life and compels them to live on" (BT 18). Rather than giving mastery over life, asceticism amounts to being outsmarted or mastered by life. This explains why Nietzsche considers psychology the "path to the fundamental problems" (BG 23). Those with the will to truth cannot go back to explicit acceptance of the ascetic ideal once they accept Nietzsche's claim that their will to truth is itself an expression of the ascetic ideal. The difficulty here is psychological: one would feel foolish rather than powerful embracing a life-devaluing ideal if one accepted Nietzsche's theory that one's motive was to get a sense of power necessary for feeling better about life. I have argued in the previous chapter that those with the will to truth must therefore create a new ideal. An examination of Nietzsche's psychology of the will to truth will reinforce this point, and will help us to see the grounds he has – in addition to his belief that the world needs such an ideal – for thinking that philosophers need to create one.

Nietzsche claims, of course, that the will to truth is itself the latest expression of the ascetic ideal. This means that the will to truth expresses the will to power, as BG 230 also makes clear. In the previous section, Nietzsche has explained that all of higher culture is a spiritualization of cruelty, and that

> even the seeker after knowledge forces his spirit to recognize things against the inclination of his spirit, and often enough against the wishes of his heart – by saying No where he would like to say Yes, love, and adore – and thus acts as an artist and transformer of cruelty. Indeed, any insistence on profundity and thoroughness is a violation, a desire to hurt the basic will of the spirit which unceasingly strives for the apparent and superficial – in all desire to know there is a drop of cruelty.

This suggests that in the case of knowing, the will to power is directed back against the knower. The knower gets a sense of power by hurting "the basic will of the spirit." But this seems strange. If knowing is motivated by the desire for power, one would expect it to be a desire for power over the objects of knowledge.

In fact, the next section, which sets out to explain Nietzsche's claim about the "basic will of the spirit" because it "may not be readily understood," seems to admit that knowledge is first directed by the need for a sense of power in relation to the external world.

> That commanding something which the people call "the spirit" wants to be master in and around its own house and wants to feel that it is master; it has the will from multiplicity to simplicity, a will that ties up, tames, and is domineering and truly masterful.

In thus explaining the will to knowledge in its first stage, Nietzsche ignores an earlier stage, where "knowing" is directed by more immediately practical needs, the need to know how to build a fire, kill an animal, bake bread, and so on. His concern in this passage is to explain what motivates knowledge when we get to a more theoretical level, where knowledge is wanted quite apart from the obvious practical purposes it serves. The original intent in such knowing, Nietzsche suggests, is to "appropriate the foreign," that is, "to assimilate the new to the old, to simplify the manifold, and to overlook or repulse whatever is totally contradictory." What it is after is growth, "or, more precisely, the *feeling* of growth, the feeling of increased power" (BG 230).

On Nietzsche's view, then, the desire for theoretical knowledge is not originally directed by a will to truth. What the knower wants is not truth, but the feeling of intellectual appropriation or command over the world. Therefore, "an apparently opposite drive serves this same will" (the will to power that intellectual appropriation of the world serves):

> a suddenly erupting decision in favor of ignorance, of deliberate exclusion, a shutting of one's windows, a kind of state of defense against much that is knowable, a satisfaction with the dark, with the limiting horizon, a Yea and Amen to ignorance – all of which is necessary in proportion to a spirit's power to appropriate, its "digestive capacity," to speak metaphorically – and actually "the spirit" is relatively most similar to a stomach (BG 230).

Thus, the intellectual appropriator is too easily satisfied with a feeling of command over the world to count as having a will to truth. Of course, intellectual appropriation may happen upon the truth, but Nietzsche claims that the will behind it is the same will that lies behind avoidance, ignorance, masks, and so on. What follows is a point already made in Chapter 6, that the will to truth – the commitment to truth at any price – is a late development. Originally, the discoverer of theoretical truths is satisfied at least as much by simplification, falsification, flight into ignorance (as Nietzsche seems to think the history of philosophy attests).

How to explain the emergence of a will to truth is the question with which Nietzsche begins BG: "*What* in us really wants 'truth'?" He gives his most direct answer in BG 230.

> *This* will to mere appearance, to simplification, to masks, to cloaks, in short, to the surface – for every surface is a cloak – is *countered* by that sublime inclination of the seeker after knowledge who insists on profundity, multiplicity, and thoroughness, with a *will* which is a kind of cruelty of the intellectual conscience and taste. Every courageous thinker will recognize this in himself, assuming only that, as fit, he has hardened and sharpened his eye for himself long enough and that he is used to severe discipline, as

well as severe words. He will say; "there is something cruel in the inclination of my spirit"; let the virtuous and kindly try to talk him out of it.

This is the psychological side of the analysis of the will to truth as the latest expression of the ascetic ideal. Nietzsche claims that a will to knowledge or truth, as opposed to a will to what I have called "intellectual appropriation," requires the internalization of the will to power, the ability to get a sense of power out of denying oneself the satisfaction of interpretations one would like to be true because of what one actually has reason to believe.

But how does this occur? Nietzsche does not answer this question here, but the answer suggested by both BG and GM is that it developed out of philosophers' commitment to the ascetic ideal.

Zarathustra's talk to the wisest suggests that philosophy involves two different orientations expressive of the will to power.

> A will to the thinkability of all beings; this I call your will. You want to *make* all being thinkable, for you doubt with a well-founded suspicion that it is already thinkable. But it shall yield and bend for you. Thus your will wants it. It shall become smooth and serve the spirit as its mirror and reflection. This is your whole will, you who are wisest: a will to power – when you speak of good and evil too, and of valuations. You still want to create a world before which you can kneel: that is your ultimate hope and intoxication (Z II, 12).

Zarathustra here attributes two different desires to philosophers, first, the desire for the intellectual appropriation of the world, a desire to make the world fit into its categories. Secondly, there is the desire "to create a world before which [they] can kneel," that is, to construct a picture of the world that reflects the philosopher's values. The first of these tendencies or desires differentiates philosophers from mythmakers. But BG 5 makes clear that in the case of philosophers, the desire for knowledge or intellectual appropriation is subordinate to the second desire, of constructing the world in the image of its values. This means that the categories into which philosophers have attempted to force the world have been determined by the ascetic ideal. For, as I have already argued in detail, Nietzsche thinks philosophy has been an expression of that ideal.

Consider again GM's claim that the typical doctrines of dogmatic or metaphysical philosophy are exactly what one would expect if the ascetic priest, "this incarnate will to contradiction and antinaturalness[,] is induced to philosophize."

> Upon what will it vent its innermost contrariness? Upon what is felt most certainly to be real and actual: it will look for error precisely where the instinct of life most unconditionally posits truth. It will, for example, like the ascetics of the Vedanta philosophy, downgrade physicality to an illusion; likewise pain, multiplicity, the entire conceptual antithesis "subject" and "object" – errors, nothing but errors! To renounce belief in one's ego, to deny one's own "reality" – what a triumph! not merely over the senses, over appearance, but a much higher kind of triumph, a violation and cruelty against *reason* – a voluptuous pleasure that reaches its height when the ascetic self-contempt and self-mockery of reason declares: "*there is* a realm of truth and being, but reason is *excluded* from it!"
> (GM III, 12)

The philosophical doctrines mentioned here are ones BG counts as projections of the philosopher's values. We see from this passage one of Nietzsche's reasons for thinking that this philosophy expresses a spiritual will to power – like the ascetic, the philosopher's desire for a sense of power or effectiveness turns against the self, forcing it to give up the satisfaction of its natural inclinations (e.g., by reducing physicality to an illusion, or renouncing belief in one's ego). Because Nietzsche explicitly calls this philosophy a way in which the spirit has "raged against itself," it seems clear that he considers it an internalization of the will to power. But it also is a will to power directed against the world. For the world is forced to accept categories that devalue it, allow it value only as a means to, or condition of, something that is its own negation. As in the case of more obvious ascetics, the philosopher's internalized will to power is evidently interpreted in a way that gives a sense of power in relation to the world.

When the ascetic priest is induced to philosophize, he is induced to use the means for intellectual appropriation, the resources of logic, concepts, thinking, for carrying out ascetic projects. Some independent development of thinking, that is, of intellectual appropriation, is necessary, but it is taken over by the ascetic ideal for its own purposes (to devalue the empirical world). Yet, the ascetic ideal ultimately pushes the spirit far enough in its asceticism that the will to intellectual appropriation becomes a will to truth.

This is why Nietzsche suggests in BG 2 that the will to truth grew out of the will to deception. We are liable to misunderstand this claim – in ways that support radical interpretations of Nietzsche's position on truth – if we do not recognize that Nietzsche means by the "will to truth" the commitment to truth at any price and that he considers this a late and rare development. His suggestion in BG 2 is not that one who wants truth really wants to be deceived, or wants something that does in fact deceive, or that such a person is bound to find illusion rather than truth. The point is rather that the commitment to truth that we find in Nietzsche's own writings, for instance, grew out of the ascetic ideal's use of the will to intellectual appropriation and the will to deception this involved. This deception was the pretense that what was actually a matter of reading their own ascetic values into the world was instead devotion to truth. Nietzsche claims that an actual will to truth grew out of this pretended will to truth.

Nietzsche admits, therefore, that his own will to truth is an expression of the will to power, but this introduces no paradoxes into his position. To say that the will to truth is an expression of the will to power is not to deny that it is a will to truth or that it arrives at truth. The will to truth expresses an internalized will to power, after all. It makes the knower give up comforting or desirable views precisely because they conflict with what there is reason to believe. It is quite different in the case of the externalized will to power with which Nietzsche first identifies philosophy (BG 9): the desire to create the world in the image of one's values. The latter will is not constrained by considerations of truth, but constructs the world to fit its own will, though it pretends to be concerned only with truth.

The main question for understanding Nietzsche's view of the future of philosophy concerns what happens to this externalized will to power, the will to construct the world in its own image, when the will to intellectual appropriation becomes the will to truth. Several passages of BG indicate that when the will to intellectual appropriation becomes the will to truth, it belongs to science or scholarship rather than to philosophy (consider the contrast between philosophy and science or scholarship·in BG 6, and throughout part 6). Thus Nietzsche's will to truth is displayed in his psychology of the will to power, for instance, not in his philosophical "doctrine" of will to power. It is certainly clear that the will to construct the world in the image of the philosopher's values can no longer pretend to be a will to truth. Nehamas has argued in effect that we must go further and say that Nietzsche has no place for this will with which he identifies philosophy (1988, esp. 56 ff.). According to Nehamas, BG eschews argument and merely exemplifies Nietzsche's own values in order to avoid doing that for which he criticizes other philosophers, namely, reading his own values into the world. The interpretation I have offered suggests a quite opposed answer. What Nietzsche objects to in previous philosophers is not that they read their values into the world, but that they pretended to be doing something else, that they were not "honest enough in their work" (BG 5). If my interpretation is correct, what BG attempts to exemplify is precisely the compatibility between the will to impose the philosopher's values on the world and the will to truth. The cosmological doctrine of the will to power is the kind of construction of the world Nietzsche claims philosophers have self-deceptively engaged in. The difference is that Nietzsche knows perfectly well it is not the truth and that he gives us the clues we need to figure out that it is actually a projection of his life-affirming (and self-affirming) ideal.

Nietzsche suggests not only that the will to truth can coexist with the philosopher's will to impose values on the world, but that the former may actually require the latter. Consider BG 230's account of the task of those with a will to knowledge or truth. After claiming to find in every courageous thinker "a *will* that is a kind of cruelty of the intellectual conscience," Nietzsche writes that it would "sound nicer . . . to be distinguished not by cruelty but by 'extravagant honesty,' we free, *very* free spirits – and perhaps *that* will actually be our – posthumous reputation." But Nietzsche claims that "we hermits and marmots have long persuaded ourselves in the full secrecy of a hermit's conscience" that such "moral tinsel words" belong to "the gold dust of unconscious human vanity, and that under such flattering colors and make-up the basic text of *homo natura* must again be recognized."

> To translate human beings back into nature; to become master
> over the many vain and overly enthusiastic interpretations and

connotations that have so far been scrawled and painted over the eternal basic text of *homo natura;* to see to it that we henceforth stand before human beings as even today, hardened in the discipline of science, we stand before the *rest* of nature, with intrepid Oedipus eyes and sealed Odysseus ears, deaf to the siren songs of old metaphysical bird catchers who have been piping at us all too long, "you are more, you are higher, you are of a different origin" – that may be a strange and insane task, but it is a *task* – who would deny that? Why did we choose this insane task? Or, putting it differently, "why have knowledge at all?"

Everyone will ask us that. And we, pressed this way, we have put the same question to ourselves a hundred times, we have found and can find no better answer ——— (BG 230).

The ultimate task of those committed to truth is evidently to "become master over the many vain and overly enthusiastic interpretations" of their own will to truth, to recognize the latter as an internalized will to power, a matter of cruelty against the self. We can explain why this might appear as an "insane task" to Nietzsche in terms of the fact that it undermines the ascetic ideal that is responsible for the existence of the will to truth. So why this task? Because Nietzsche does not fill in this blank, he evidently wants the reader to do so on the basis of the surrounding material. Alderman suggests that the next section shows the task has not been chosen but given, for Nietzsche writes that "at the bottom of us, really 'deep down,' there is, of course, something unteachable, some granite of spiritual *fatum*, of predetermined decisions and answers to predetermined selected questions" (BG 231). But then the question is: What is it about us that gives us this task, and why can we not simply abandon it? It seems to me that Nietzsche must expect us to fill in the blank at least partly from what he has been saying in this section about cruelty: that what has given us this task is a tremendous and tremendously internalized will to power. This will has put the whole of our ability for intellectual appropriation in the service of the truth. In BG 227, he even refers to "us" as "we last Stoics." And he calls on "us" to "remain *hard*" should our honesty, the "virtue from which we cannot get away" and "the only one left us" (the last virtue we share with traditional morality?), "grow weary one day" and want things "better, easier, tenderer." To do this, we must "come to the assistance of our 'good' with our 'devils,' " namely, "our adventurous courage, our seasoned and choosy curiosity, our subtlest, most disguised, most spiritual will to power and overcoming of the world."

This "most spiritual will to power and overcoming of the world" cannot refer to our will to truth, because it is supposed to keep the will to truth from growing "weary." Nietzsche's wording suggests that the will to truth requires the aid of an externalized will to power, one that provides a sense of power in relation to the world. Such a will always accompanies an internalized will to power in Nietzsche's account of philosophers. The internalization of the will to power was promoted by the ascetic interpretation of existence, which gave philosophers a way of overcoming the world by devaluing it. As one would expect of the successors to the ascetic priest, Nietzsche's philosophers need a sense of power in relation to the world, not just in relation to themselves. I suggest that this is Nietzsche's final argument for why we must propose new ideals. As BG 10 suggests, if they are going to live "vigorously and cheerfully," philosophers cannot confine themselves to the truth, to what science and scholarship can reveal. Philosophers need to be able to "create values," to put their stamp on the world. They have done this through their adherence to the ascetic ideal, by devaluing the world, making it accept the philosopher's devaluing categories. But this required a certain self-deception, a failure to understand their own psychology. They cannot both face up to the truth about themselves and get a sense of power over the world from the ascetic ideal. Hence, the necessity of inventing a new ideal – if we agree with Nietzsche that we cannot pursue truth simply for its own sake. The creation of an alternative to the ascetic ideal would give philosophers a sense of power in relation to the world insofar as they get to decide what is valuable, but it would also give them an ideal in whose service they could pursue truth. An externalized will to power could thus come to the aid of the will to truth.

I assume that Nietzsche himself has brought to the aid of his own will to truth his doctrine of life as will to power. For though he presents it as if it were true (perhaps exemplifying the suggestion of BG 4 to "recognize untruth as a condition of life"), it is actually his "creation of the world," a construction of the world from the viewpoint of his own ideal. I will discuss this ideal in my final chapter, but have already made clear that it is Nietzsche's alternative to the ascetic ideal. It should therefore be easy to see why Nietzsche would regard the world as will to power as an alternative to the ascetic ideal's interpretation of life (which he sometimes calls the "moral world-view"). According to Nietzsche's theory, the ascetic interpretation of life is a construction of the world from the viewpoint of the ascetic ideal. Since it idealizes the denial both of life and of the value of life, the ascetic ideal gives us an interpretation of life that deprives it of value. I have argued that Nietzsche also considers the world as will to power a construction of life from the viewpoint of an ideal. He believes this construction of the world expresses an opposed ideal, I suggest, because it glorifies the will to power, a drive he thinks aims at what is necessary for affirming or finding value in life.

This line of interpretation also helps to explain the embarrassing material of part 6 of BG in which Nietzsche suggests that philosophy should "dominate" (BG 204) and that "*genuine philosophers are commanders and legislators*" (BG 211). The point is not to denigrate the "objective person," who is called a "mere instrument" (BG 207), or the scientists, scholars and "philosophical underlaborers" who are supposed to be "servants" of philosophy (BG 211) – for these are clearly components of the philosophical soul. Nietzsche's point is that knowledge is not enough for ascetic priests who have been "induced to philosophize." Even when they have developed a real will to truth, and have therefore pursued knowledge rigorously, they have done so in service to an ideal that gives them a sense of power in relation to the world, and they cannot pursue it rigorously without commitment to some ideal that establishes the value of a commitment to truth. Because they can no longer pursue truth in service to the ascetic ideal, they must, if they are to remain truthful, invent a new ideal to serve. But this is clearly not "pure invention," as Nietzsche's ideal philosopher is constrained by a commitment to truth, and the truth destroys the old ideal and shows us the form that a new ideal must take. If there is still room for decision or "commanding" here, it is because rational considerations alone cannot tell us that we ought to pursue the truth or affirm life, and in any case, we might choose instead to be "puritanical fanatics of conscience who prefer even a certain nothing to an uncertain something to lie down on – and die" (BG 10). But if philosophers are to continue the vigorous pursuit of truth, Nietzsche's claim seems to be that they must do so in service to a new ideal.

Nietzsche does not deny therefore that philosophers could

abandon the will to truth. But it seems unlikely that those with such a strong and strongly internalized will to power could live "vigorously and cheerfully" by simply relaxing the demands of their will to truth. What is more likely for philosophers who refuse to invent a new ideal, I think Nietzsche would say, is that they will continue to serve the ascetic ideal in various disguised forms (for instance, devoting their work to showing that philosophers cannot do what they have wanted, namely, to establish *a priori* the truth about reality and to provide a rational foundation for values). As my next chapter will show, Nietzsche was very aware of the possibility of serving the old ideal while claiming devotion to a new one.

8

———————————————————— ❧ ❧ ————————————————————

ETERNAL RECURRENCE

It is certainly not the least charm of theory that it is refutable; it is precisely thereby that it attracts subtler minds. It seems that the hundred-times-refuted theory of the "free-will" owes its persistence to this charm alone; again and again someone comes along who feels he is strong enough to refute it (BG 18).

Substantial agreement exists that Nietzsche considered the eternal recurrence his most important teaching. He calls it the "fundamental conception" of *Zarathustra,* which he celebrates as "the highest book there is . . . also the deepest, born out of the innermost wealth of truth" (EH III, Z 1; P 4). And he identifies himself in a special way with its teaching when summing up his philosophical intentions and achievements in one of his last books: "I, the last disciple of the philosopher Dionysus – I, the teacher of the eternal recurrence" (TI X, 5). If it is his central teaching, however, it is also the most frequently and effectively criticized of Nietzsche's doctrines. The body of philosophically sophisticated and interesting criticism of the doctrine of eternal recurrence remains unmatched by the literature on any other aspect of Nietzsche's philosophy. I will organize my interpretation of eternal recurrence as a response to the most important objections that have been raised against it.

The most common objection to eternal recurrence is that we have no reason to accept its truth. The doctrine is apparently a cosmological theory, taught by Zarathustra and formulated by his animals in the following terms:

"Behold, we know what you teach; that all things recur eternally, and we ourselves too; and that we have already existed an eternal number of times, and all things with us. You teach that there is a great year of becoming, a monster of a great year, which must, like an hourglass, turn over again and again so that it may run down and run out again; and all of these years are alike in what is greatest as in what is smallest; and we ourselves are alike in every great year, in what is greatest as in what is smallest.

"And if you wanted to die now, O Zarathustra, behold, we also know how you would speak to yourself. . . . 'Now I die and vanish,' you would say, 'and all at once I am nothing. The soul is as mortal as the body. But the knot of causes in which I am entangled recurs and will create me again. I myself belong to the causes of eternal recurrence. I come again, with this sun, with this earth, with this eagle, with this serpent – not to a new life or a better life or a similar life: I come back to this same, self-same life, in what is greatest as in what is smallest, to teach again the eternal recurrence of all things.' " (Z III, 13)

Zarathustra's animals thus believe that everything – Zarathustra, his identical life, and the identical history of the cosmos (the knot of causes in which he is entangled) – literally recurs. The issue is whether this is also Nietzsche's teaching.

Until recently at least, interpreters have assumed it is. Nietzsche's posthumously published notebooks contain arguments for the truth of the theory described by Zarathustra's animals. From the premises of an infinite amount of time and a finite amount of the basic stuff of the universe, Nietzsche apparently concludes that the identical history of the universe repeats itself eternally. Interpreters have therefore assumed that the "fundamental conception" of *Zarathustra* and the main content of Nietzsche's teaching of eternal recurrence is a cosmological theory.

However, the cosmological arguments from the *Nachlass* have been analyzed in depth and found wanting on a number of different counts (e.g., Simmel, 172–73; Danto, 204–9). I cannot review the extensive literature here, but shall assume it shows that Nietzsche's arguments fail to establish a recurrence cosmology and that no plausible changes could rehabilitate them for this purpose. Many interpreters have found it troubling that Nietzsche's central doctrine should be so easily defeated and have taken the criticism of eternal recurrence as an incentive to free Nietzsche's doctrine from dependence on the *Nachlass* arguments.

For the purposes of the present study, it is even more troubling that the cosmological arguments in Nietzsche's notebooks are of an *a priori* nature. The only premise Nietzsche uses that could plausibly be considered empirical is that the history of the universe has not yet come to an end. Nietzsche's "proofs" otherwise appeal exclusively to *a priori* considerations regarding the nature of time, force, necessity, and probability. Kaufmann stresses Nietzsche's claim that eternal recurrence is the "most scientific of all possible hypotheses" (WP 55), but does nothing to make evident its scientific or empirical character. On this point, it seems we must agree with Heidegger (I, 371) that the considerations at the heart of Nietzsche's "proofs" have a metaphysical rather than a scientific character. I have interpreted Nietzsche as rejecting the pursuit of substantive *a priori* truths. I can regard Nietzsche's mature philosophy as consistent on the topic of truth, then, only if his doctrine of eternal recurrence can be freed from dependence on the cosmological arguments found in his notebooks.

Recent interpreters have made substantial progress towards this goal by interpreting eternal recurrence as a practical doctrine, a directive concerning how to live, rather than a theory concerning the nature of the universe. Not that traditional interpreters have ignored the doctrine's practical aspect. The standard interpretation has been that Nietzsche's doctrine tells us to live in such a way that we would be willing to live again – but that his reason is that we will live again (an infinite number of times) exactly the same lives we now lead. Recent defenders of what I call the practical interpretation of recurrence, on the other hand, claim that it is only a practical doctrine, to which cosmological considerations are completely irrelevant.

Although I share the aspirations of these interpreters, I do not believe they have established the irrelevance of cosmological considerations. I explain why in the first section below and argue for a different way of establishing the practical interpretation of eternal recurrence throughout this chapter.

1. The irrelevance of the truth of recurrence

GS 341 introduces the eternal recurrence in a way that supports the practical interpretation of the doctrine.

The greatest Weight. What if some day or night a demon were to steal after you into your loneliest of loneliness and say to you: "This life as you now live it and have lived it, you will have to live once more and innumerable times more; and there will be nothing new in it, but every pain and every joy and every thought and everything unutterably small and great in your life will return to you, all in the same succession and sequence. . . ."

Would you not throw yourself down and gnash your teeth and curse the demon who spoke thus? Or have you once experienced a tremendous moment when you would have answered him; "You are a god and never have I heard anything more divine?" If this thought were to gain possession of you, it would change you as you are, or perhaps crush you. The question in each and every thing: "Do you want this once more and innumerable times more?" would lie upon your actions as the greatest weight. Or how well-disposed would you have to become to yourself and life *to crave nothing more fervently* than this ultimate confirmation and seal? (GS 341)

In this central passage, Nietzsche shows no interest in the truth of the recurrence cosmology, and apparently uses it only to formulate a practical doctrine. I will argue later in this section that this practical doctrine is an ideal for human beings: to become the kind of person who, in the situation described, would consider the demon's message divine. Some have interpreted it instead as a decision criterion or imperative: perform only those actions you can will to repeat eternally. In either case, however, it is difficult to see how cosmological considerations can be relevant to it – unless the cosmology constitutes Nietzsche's theoretical grounding for the practical doctrine. But if it does, why would he introduce the practical doctrine without mentioning the cosmology? Why would he withhold his proofs of recurrence from publication?

Ivan Soll began the recent trend in the interpretation of eternal recurrence by answering that Nietzsche did not consider the proofs of recurrence essential to the doctrine's significance. The passage quoted above shows, according to Soll, that Nietzsche's main concern is not the truth of recurrence, but the psychological consequences of accepting it (322–3). Accepting recurrence is supposed to crush us or change us, on this view, but need not involve believing in its truth. Soll treats the practical doctrine of recurrence as a decision criterion – we are to perform only those actions we would be willing to perform eternally – and finds evidence in the *Nachlass* that Nietzsche considered the mere possibility of recurrence sufficient motivation for accepting it (324–5). In other words, Nietzsche thought that a belief that our lives may recur eternally would be sufficient to crush or change us – and, in the latter case, would provide sufficient motivation to live in a way we would be willing to live eternally. This could explain why he was willing to introduce the doctrine of eternal recurrence without the cosmological arguments worked out in his notebooks. Although a cosmological proof would seem a powerful tool for bringing about the psychological consequences in which Nietzsche was interested, Soll argues that it would not seem necessary if Nietzsche believed that the mere possibility of recurrence could have the same effect, because he probably supposed that his description of recurrence was enough to establish that. Soll suggests that his analysis greatly diminishes the importance of cosmological arguments for the evaluation of Nietzsche's doctrine and requires us to shift the focus of evaluation to issues concerning the doctrine's practical import.

However, Soll's focus on the putative effects of accepting recurrence only postpones the question as to whether we have any reason to accept a recurrence cosmology. Even if we grant that cosmological considerations would provide a reason for accepting the practical doctrine, it seems false that the mere possibility of recurrence would suffice. Whatever Nietzsche may have believed, it seems unlikely that many people would, or should, be crushed or scared into living as they would be willing to live again by the belief that recurrence is one among a large number of equally possible theories, or worse, that it is a possible, but physically improbable, cosmology. Although Soll takes an important step towards the practical interpretation of recurrence, he does not establish the irrelevance of cosmological considerations to the evaluation of Nietzsche's doctrine.

For that purpose, Bernd Magnus' approach seems more promising. Attempting to make eternal recurrence "utterly indifferent to the truth value of the doctrine," he construes the cosmology as a heuristic device that allows us to understand the life-affirming attitude of Nietzsche's *Übermensch* (1978, esp. 111–54). Magnus interprets this overman as a person who follows Nietzsche's imperative to live as one would be willing to live again. To understand this imperative, Magnus suggests, we must consider our own reactions when we imagine a proposed action recurring eternally. But to imagine our life recurring, we need not believe it will, or even consider this possible (see section 3). Further, cosmological considerations – the truth or even possibility of actual recurrence – have no role in the justification of Nietzsche's imperative. According to Magnus, Nietzsche instead offers as justification the importance of overcoming nihilism, – the sense of the meaninglessness of human life that follows upon the loss of faith in God and other transcendent sources of value – and the effectiveness of his imperative for combatting nihilism. Because historical and psychosocial hypotheses justify the doctrine of recurrence, cosmology is completely irrelevant.

Unfortunately, Magnus' account of how eternal recurrence combats nihilism does not sustain the irrelevance of cosmological considerations. Eternal recurrence is said to combat nihilism by intensifying the dynamics of choice: Our decisions and actions have a point because what we choose to be we shall be for eternity. Further, according to Magnus' essentially Heideggarian interpretation, nihilism is ultimately rooted in kronophobia, fear or hatred of time, inability to accept or find value in the merely finite. Eternal recurrence strikes at the root of nihilism by attaching "eternalistic predicates" to our lives. It eternalizes the moment, transforming the aimlessness of becoming into a fated eternity.

But Magnus does not explain how recurrence can have such effects unless one accepts the cosmology as true (or at least probable). He assigns these effects to the "myth" of eternal recurrence, which he claims Nietzsche invented as a countermyth to the Platonic myth of another or "true" world. By making this world eternal, he claims, the myth of recurrence counters the Platonic devaluation of this world. But how can it do this if it is recognized as a myth? Heaven and hell certainly lose their psychological effects when regarded as myths. In the end, Magnus seems to resort to a position like Soll's. "Even as a 'mere possibility,'" he writes, eternal recurrence "exalts *this* world against all 'beyonds,' religious or metaphysical," and "seems to demand a Sisyphus who is jubilant in the affirmation of his fate as its response" (154).

But the mere possibility of recurrence seems to require about as much response as the possibility that the sun will not rise tomorrow. Logical possibility is clearly too weak to demand any response – much less to eternalize the moment. If anything stronger is claimed for eternal recurrence, however, Nietzsche's doctrine is made dependent on cosmological argumentation. We cannot establish the irrelevance of cosmological considerations if we focus on the putative transformational effects of the eternal recurrence cosmology. If Nietzsche is concerned to produce such effects, he must convince us to accept the cosmology. If we are rational, we will ask what reason exists for accepting the cosmology. Focus on the consequences of accepting the cosmology as a possibility or a myth leads straight to the proofs for recurrence in Nietzsche's notebooks.

The alternative is to recognize that Nietzsche's published works show no concern with bringing about such consequences. He refers to them in the passage quoted above, but only to formulate a test for the affirmation of life. He asks how we would react or what the psychological consequences would be, if a demon sneaking into our "loneliest of loneliness" proclaimed the eternal recurrence. The quoted phrase suggests a situation of vulnerability to suggestions one would otherwise dismiss, a situation in which critical powers are at a minimum. Nietzsche may describe the idea of recurrence as "being there" and "gain-[ing] possession of you" *not*, as Soll suggests (324 ff.), to include its acceptance as a mere possibility, but because "belief" is too weak to convey the uncritical acceptance of recurrence built into the situation to which he asks our reaction.

I interpret Nietzsche as taking our hypothetical reaction to the demon's message – how we would react if we accepted the message uncritically – to reflect our actual attitude towards ourselves and our lives. A joyful reaction would indicate a fully affirmative attitude towards one's (presumably, nonrecurring) life, whereas gnashing of teeth, and the need to ask "do you want this once more and innumerable times more?" would indicate a negative attitude. There can be no doubt that Nietzsche wants to promote the former attitude. I thus agree with Magnus that the recurrence cosmology provides a device for articulating Nietzsche's ideal of the life-affirming person. This ideal person satisfies what Nietzsche calls "the idea of eternal recurrence," the "highest formula of affirmation that is at all attainable" (EH II, Z1). The formula of affirmation provided by eternal recurrence is that of being a person who would respond joyfully to the demon's message if she accepted it uncritically as the truth. I will call this "affirming eternal recurrence," and I interpret Nietzsche's doctrine of eternal recurrence as the presentation of such affirmation as an ideal for human beings. Affirming eternal recurrence depends in no way on believing recurrence to be true, probable, or even logically possible. It requires the willingness to live one's life again, not the belief that one will, even as a "mere possibility."

Although Soll and Magnus seem to recognize the use of eternal recurrence as a test for Nietzsche's ideal person, they do not accord this ideal the centrality I think it deserves, perhaps because they see no way of explaining why Nietzsche would have considered it so important. To explain its importance to Nietzsche, they interpret the practical doctrine of recurrence as a criterion – "do you want this once more and innumerable times more?" – designed to add weight or significance to our decisions. What adds weight to decisions, however, can only be the threat that recurrence is or may be true.

We can avoid thus making Nietzsche's doctrine ultimately dependent on cosmological support if we interpret his doctrine of recurrence as the ideal of affirming eternal recurrence. We can also explain why Nietzsche considered it so important. Magnus seems correct to focus on the importance of eternal recurrence for combatting nihilism, but it is the ideal of affirming eternal recurrence, not the recurrence cosmology, even in mythical form, to which that role belongs. More generally, Nietzsche offers eternal recurrence as the necessary alternative to the ascetic ideal.

As I discussed in Chapter 6, Nietzsche believes that the ascetic ideal originally closed the door to "suicidal nihilism." It did so by explaining human suffering as punishment for sin and by providing a goal: the overcoming of one's attachment to life, which the great ascetics carried to extremes of self-torture. This explanation and the related goal saved the will, making it possible for human beings to affirm life, to find living and the pursuit of other goals worthwhile. However, the cost was a devaluation of human life. The ascetic ideal's answer to nihilism made later outbreaks of nihilism inevitable because it deprived human life of intrinsic value, treating it as valuable only as a means to its own negation: nirvana, heaven, for example. When the *honesty* promoted by the ascetic ideal eventually casts doubt on all transhuman sources of value, human life is once again without a goal and in even more danger of appearing devoid of value.

Nietzsche identified his own aspirations with overcoming the nihilism conditioned by the ascetic ideal. Consider, for instance, his characterization of the "human being of the future"

> who will redeem us not only from the hitherto reigning ideal but also from what was bound to grow out of it, the great nausea, the will to nothingness, nihilism; this bell-stroke of noon and of the great decision that liberates the will again and restores its goal to earth and his hope to man; this antichrist and antinihilist; this victor over God and nothingness – *he must come one day* (GM II, 24).

This "human being of the future" is clearly Zarathustra (GM II, 25). Through the character of Zarathustra, therefore, Nietzsche aims to provide an alternative to the ascetic ideal, something that would play its role of combatting nihilism, but without devaluing human life. Nietzsche explains (EH III, GM) the ascetic ideal's tremendous power in terms of the fact that "a *counterideal* was lacking – until Zarathustra!" I can find only two serious candidates for the counterideal Zarathustra teaches: the Übermensch and the ideal of affirming eternal recurrence. In section 4 I argue that the Übermensch ideal is still too closely tied to the ascetic ideal, and that, in the course of Z, affirming eternal recurrence replaces it as the true alternative to the ascetic ideal. Because this makes the affirmation of eternal recurrence Nietzsche's proposed solution to the problem of nihilism, we can explain why Nietzsche accorded it central place in his own thought without any reference to cosmology.

We do not, therefore, need cosmology to explain the justification Nietzsche offers for his practical doctrine of recurrence. Nietzsche's basic argument for his ideal is that we need a counterideal to the ascetic ideal, and that affirming eternal recurrence is the only candidate that fits the bill. The considerations he offers to support his ideal are genealogical (historical and psychosocial) hypotheses concerning the origins of nihilism and the ways in which ideals work to combat it. The truth claims Nietzsche makes in support of his ideal cohere fully therefore with the view of truth I find in his later works. Like Magnus', my interpretation places the theoretical backing for the practical doctrine of recurrence completely outside the sphere of *a priori* theorizing. But because I find Nietzsche's prime concern to be the transformative effects of accepting the ideal of affirming eternal recurrence rather than the cosmology (even in epistemologically attenuated or mythical form), I do not reintroduce cosmological considerations.

My interpretation relies so far largely on GS 341 and the desirability of making the doctrine of recurrence independent of the cosmological arguments in Nietzsche's notebooks. The next section argues that it also coheres fully with the other texts on eternal recurrence that Nietzsche actually published.

2. The published texts

Apart from *Zarathustra*, Nietzsche mentions eternal recurrence in only three books: TI, GS, and EH. TI's single reference, Nietzsche's identification of himself as the "last disciple of the philosopher Dionysus" and "the teacher of the eternal recurrence" (TI XI, 5), fully supports interpreting his teaching as the ideal of affirming recurrence since the surrounding material contains nothing even vaguely cosmological but focuses instead on "saying Yes to life even in its strangest and hardest problems."

In GS's major passage on recurrence (341), I have already argued, Nietzsche uses the demon's proclamation of eternal recurrence to formulate his ideal of affirmation and shows no concern with its truth. This interpretation also fits the only other explicit reference to eternal recurrence in GS: "you will the eternal recurrence of war and peace" (GS 285). Several other passages in this work are usually considered allusions to recurrence. Of these, only GS 109 could present a problem for my interpretation: "and the whole music box eternally repeats its tune." But this is easily interpreted as a metaphor, and by itself, certainly provides no basis for a cosmological construal of eternal recurrence.

Ecce Homo mentions the eternal recurrence in three different passages. That it presents the idea of eternal recurrence as the "fundamental conception" of *Zarathustra* constitutes important evidence for my interpretation since it also identifies the idea as "this highest formula of affirmation that is at all attainable" (EH, Z 1). Two other passages in this work require more attention.

In his comments on *The Birth of Tragedy* in *Ecce Homo*, Nietzsche writes:

The doctrine of the "eternal recurrence," that is, of the unconditional and infinitely repeated circular course of all things – this doctrine of Zarathustra *might* in the end have already been taught by Heraclitus. At least the Stoa has traces of it, and the Stoics inherited almost all of their principle notions from Heraclitus (EH III, BT 4).

Here, finally, eternal recurrence certainly sounds like a cosmological theory. But two considerations leave room for doubt. First, the context is a discussion of the tragic, in which Nietzsche identifies tragedy with Dionysus and, echoing the passage from TI cited previously, with "saying *yes* to life even in its strangest and hardest problems." Claiming the right to consider himself "the first *tragic philosopher*," the first to transpose "the Dionysian into a philosophical pathos," Nietzsche then names Heraclitus as the only philosopher who might provide reason to doubt his priority. He mentions that Heraclitus might have taught Zarathustra's doctrine of recurrence to underline the similarity between their two philosophies. The context thus suggests that this similarity lies in the Dionysian or life-affirming character of the two philosophies. Cosmology seems beside the point.

Second, how we should interpret this passage depends on the doctrine Zarathustra actually teaches. If, as I shall argue, the text of *Zarathustra* shows him teaching the affirmation of eternal recurrence but not a recurrence cosmology, this passage can provide no basis for changing our interpretation.

In the third passage from EH (III, Z 6), Nietzsche describes Zarathustra as he who has "the hardest, most terrible insight into reality, who has thought the 'most abysmal thought,' " yet

> nevertheless does not consider it an objection to existence, not even to its eternal recurrence – but rather one more reason for being himself the eternal Yes to all things, "the tremendous, unbounded saying Yes and Amen."

This passage stresses Zarathustra's Dionysian affirmation, his willingness to have life recur eternally. It would support the cosmological interpretation only if we had reason to accept the traditional interpretation of Zarathustra's "most abysmal thought" as the belief that things recur eternally. However, as Nehamas argues (1985, 148), this would make nonsense of the passage. Nietzsche would be saying that Zarathustra does not consider the eternal recurrence an objection to eternal recurrence. To understand Zarathustra's "abysmal thought," and to interpret this passage, we must turn to *Zarathustra*.

This fictional work is therefore the crucial text for determining which doctrine(s) of recurrence Nietzsche actually taught. He tells us that eternal recurrence is the "fundamental conception" of *Zarathustra*, and, except for GS 341, provides no other independent basis for interpreting it. His other references to recurrence support the idea that Zarathustra teaches the affirmation of eternal recurrence, but tell us nothing about whether he also teaches a recurrence cosmology. The clearest suggestion that he does teach a cosmology (EH III, BT 4) is ambiguous and is formulated so that how we should interpret it depends on our interpretation of *Zarathustra*.

However, even unambiguous evidence that Zarathustra teaches a recurrence cosmology would not be sufficient evidence that Nietzsche believed in it or taught it. Nietzsche might well have created a character who believed in eternal recurrence to illustrate or teach something else, for instance, the ideal of affirming eternal recurrence. How better to portray concretely the complicated idea of a person who *would* respond affirmatively to the demon's message if he accepted it as the truth than by a person who does respond affirmatively to belief in recurrence?

It is therefore particularly noteworthy that, although Nietzsche sometimes suggests that Zarathustra believes in recurrence, he nowhere gives him an unambiguous statement of belief. Only the animals express belief in recurrence. Zarathustra responds to their version of his teaching by calling them "buffoons and barrel-organs" and telling them they are making his experience into a *Leier-Lied* (literally, a lyre-song, a trivial and repetitive, or, as Kaufmann has it, "hurdy-gurdy," song). We certainly never hear Zarathustra teaching a recurrence cosmology. According to the higher men (Z IV, 19), Zarathustra taught them to say to death, "Was that life? Well, then, once more!" – not a recurrence cosmology, but the affirmation of recurrence.

Zarathustra apparently teaches eternal recurrence as a doctrine of redemption. "To redeem all who lived in the past and to recreate all 'it was' into a 'thus I willed it,' " he says in one of Z's main passages on eternal recurrence, "that alone would I call redemption." Some suppose that a recurrence cosmology is to bring redemption, by insuring future existence to those who lived in the past. But *Ecce Homo* gives a quite different meaning to the definition of redemption just quoted.

> Zarathustra once defines, quite strictly, his task – it is mine, too – and there is no mistaking his meaning: he says Yes to the point of justifying, of redeeming even all of the past (EH III, Z 8).

Zarathustra redeems the past by "saying Yes" to it, that is, by affirming its eternal recurrence. Belief in recurrence would have no redeeming effect in the absence of such affirmation. Further, Nietzsche says nothing to suggest that belief in recurrence is necessary for redemption of the past – it is Zarathustra's affirmation that redeems. If, as I have argued, the affirmation of recurrence does not require belief in recurrence, the belief is evidently neither sufficient nor necessary for Zarathustra's redemptive task.

We reach the same conclusion by considering Zarathustra's account of why this task is necessary. In "On Redemption" (Z II, 20), he tells us that the need for redemption stems from the problem posed by "time and its 'it was.' " Having taught for most of the book that willing (or creating) liberates from suffering, Zarathustra now informs us that the will itself needs liberation.

> " 'It was' – that is the name of the will's gnashing of teeth and most secret melancholy. Powerless against what has been done [*gegen das, was getan ist*], it is an angry spectator of all that is past. The will cannot will backwards; and that it cannot break time and time's covetousness, that is the will's loneliest melancholy.
>
> "Willing liberates; what means does the will devise for itself to get rid of this melancholy and to mock its dungeon? Alas, every prisoner is a fool and the imprisoned will redeems itself foolishly. That time does not run backwards, that is its wrath; 'that which was' is the name of the stone it cannot move. And so it moves stones out of wrath and displeasure, and it wreaks revenge on whatever does not feel wrath and displeasure as it does. Thus the will, the liberator, took to hurting; and on all who can suffer it wreaks revenge for its inability to go backwards. This, indeed, this alone, is what revenge is: the will's ill will [*Widerwille*] against time and its 'it was.'
>
> "Verily, a great folly dwells in our will; and it has become a curse for everything human that this folly has acquired spirit. The Spirit of revenge, my friends, has so far been the subject of man's

best reflections; and where there was suffering, one always
wanted punishment too.
"For punishment is what revenge calls itself; with a hypocritical
lie, it creates a good conscience for itself.
"Because there is suffering in those who will, inasmuch as they
cannot will backwards, willing itself and all life was supposed to
be – a punishment. And now cloud upon cloud rolled over the
spirit, until eventually madness preached, 'Everything passes
away; therefore everything deserves to pass away. And this too is
justice, the law of time that must devour its own children.' Thus
preached madness."

In opposition to Heidegger's influential reading of this passage
(Allison, 71 ff.), I shall offer a psychological interpretation, one
that takes "the will" to refer only to human willing (or human
beings insofar as they will), and "revenge" to be an appropriate
object of psychological investigation.

According to Zarathustra, willing has redemptive force. If we
suffer from the way things are, we can attempt to change them.
Willing and creating – imagining differences we can make, setting goals, and working towards them – can liberate us from our
suffering. But if we suffer from what has already happened, we
can do nothing but gnash our teeth. In relation to the past,
willing is completely powerless – there is nothing we can even try
to do about it. Suffering from the past therefore induces what
Zarathustra here calls the will's "melancholy" or "affliction"
(*Trübsal*), or what Nietzsche elsewhere (GM III, 17) calls "depression" (*Depression*). Revenge can be understood as an attempt to
overcome such depression by recovering the will's sense of
power (cf. GM II, 6). In the usual case, the sufferer's sense of
power is restored (perhaps only momentarily) by hurting the
person perceived as the cause of the suffering. Zarathustra is
claiming that thinkers, and especially inventors of redemptive
doctrines, have employed a spiritualized version of this same
strategy. They interpret life as a punishment and devalue time
relative to eternity, he suggests, to get revenge against, to achieve
a sense of power relative to, the perceived sources of their own
suffering: not a particular past event, but time itself and the life
characterized by time.

"On Redemption" goes on to present eternal recurrence as
liberation from both revenge and the doctrines inspired by it.

"I led you away from these fables when I taught you, 'The will itself is a creator.' All 'it was' is a fragment, a riddle, a dreadful accident – until the creative will says to it, 'But thus I willed it.' Until the creative will says to it, 'But thus I will it; thus shall I will it.'

"But has the will yet spoken thus and when will that happen? Has the will been unharnessed yet from its own folly? Has the will yet become his own redeemer and joy-bringer? Has it unlearned the spirit of revenge and all gnashing of teeth? And who taught it reconciliation with time and something higher than any reconciliation? For that will which is the will to power must will something higher than any reconciliation; but how shall this be brought about? Who can teach it also to will backwards?" (Z II, 20)

The kind of "willing backwards" Zarathustra here equates with redemption must be the affirmation of eternal recurrence. Again, without the affirmation, belief in recurrence would not address the problem Zarathustra wants to solve. Acceptance of a recurrence cosmology could provide a solution *if* the problem with time stemmed from an inability to accept transience, change, and passing away. Because Magnus accepts this Heideggerian explanation for the problem with time (Magnus, 1978, 190 ff.), he considers the recurrence cosmology, though in mythical form, Nietzsche's proposed solution. By making things eternal, according to Magnus, the myth of recurrence overcomes the will's depression at the fact of transience. But Zarathustra's words make clear that our problem with time is our complete powerlessness in relation to the past. It is because they cannot will backwards that thinkers have devalued this life as a punishment. And because the fact of recurrence would not make us able to will backwards (i.e., change the past), belief in it would not liberate the will.[1] If we

---

1. Sartre (346 ff.) claims that Nietzsche needed the dogma (cosmology) of eternal recurrence to try to cope with his unacceptable present, that it justified his pretense that he was the "legislator of a pre-established order" and thus that he actually willed the misery of his own life. But this makes little sense. As Sartre recognizes, if recurrence is true, Nietzsche is forced to undergo it, and is not the creator of it. Sartre responds that the "secret mechanism of the stratagem" is that Nietzsche does not know it is true, that by believing it (or pretending to believe it) anyway, he can therefore convince himself that he chooses it to be true, and can thus pretend that he wills his present, even while he "hates it in his heart" (349). I see no justification for using this kind of psychologizing to interpret Nietzsche's text. If we reject the idea that the truth of recurrence has anything to do with it, we can interpret the text quite plausibly without taking it to involve pretense. Sartre thinks that Nietzsche's point is to be able to *will the present as future* (347), and ignores Zarathustra's

cannot affirm recurrence, belief in it can only make things worse. If we can affirm recurrence, however, belief in it seems unnecessary since we should have no need for revenge against either our particular past or temporality in general.

Consider our relation to past events that were exactly as we wanted them to be and would still want them to be if given a choice. Although we are powerless to change them, they do not make us feel powerless or in need of revenge. The idea of eternal recurrence formulates for us the same possibility in relation to those parts of the past that did contradict our will. If we would now be willing to go through all over again whatever we did not like when it happened (and would not like while we were going through it again), we should no longer be reduced to melancholy or depression by our inability to change our particular past, nor therefore by the fact of temporal existence. Recurrence can thus be used to formulate a kind of choice we have in relation to the past. We can change neither the past nor how we felt about it. But instead of grinding our teeth or taking revenge, we can attempt to reconcile ourselves to it in the form of affirming its eternal recurrence. I can find nothing in this passage that makes belief in recurrence necessary for the development of such affirmation.

However, several passages do suggest that Zarathustra also believes in recurrence. In the first (Z III, 2), Zarathustra relates the tale of his journey up a steep mountain path while weighed down by a dwarf, the spirit of gravity who symbolizes his weariness with life. He says that courage finally allowed him to get the dwarf off his back, "courage which attacks, which slays even death itself, for it says 'Was that life? Well, then! Once More!' " This suggests that the spirit of gravity can be defeated by affirming eternal recurrence (certainly not by believing in it). But Zarathustra succeeds in getting this spirit of gravity off his back by insisting that it could not bear his "abysmal thought." He begins formulating this thought as an argument, very similar to the ones in Nietzsche's notebooks, for a recurrence cosmology, and ends with the question, "must we not eternally recur?" When he becomes afraid of this thought, and, hearing a dog howl nearby, takes pity, the dwarf

own emphasis on the past. It seems to me instead that affirming eternal recurrence provides Nietzsche with a formula for what it is to affirm the past – to affirm or will the past as future – and that a person who would really be happy about the eternal recurrence really does accept or affirm a past that was unacceptable at the time it occurred.

disappears along with thoughts of eternal recurrence, and Zarathustra has his vision of the shepherd who bites off the head of the "heavy black snake" of nausea. The passage suggests that Zarathustra manifests his courage by starting to face up to the truth of recurrence, by formulating grounds for accepting a recurrence cosmology, until his pity gets in the way. This reading is supported by the later passage (Z III, 13) in which Zarathustra finally confronts his "most abysmal thought." Overcome by great nausea and disgust, he needs seven days to recover from the experience. His animals celebrate his recovery by reciting as Zarathustra's teaching the cosmological version of recurrence. The "most abysmal thought" obviously has something to do with eternal recurrence, and Zarathustra's nausea would not seem to make sense unless we suppose that he recognizes it as the truth. The mere thought that life *might* recur eternally seems unlikely to produce such a violent reaction.

Further, Zarathustra himself explains his nausea as a response to the recurrence of the small man:

> "The great disgust with man – *this* choked me and had crawled into my throat; and what the soothsayer said: 'All is the same, nothing is worthwhile, knowledge chokes.' A long twilight limped before me, a sadness, weary to death, drunken with death, speaking with a yawning mouth. 'Eternally recurs the man of whom you are weary, the small man' – thus yawned my sadness and dragged its feet and could not go to sleep . . . 'Alas, man recurs eternally! The small man recurs eternally!' . . . All-too-small, the greatest! that was my disgust with man. And the eternal recurrence even of the smallest – that was my disgust with all existence."

The implication that Zarathustra's disgust results from finally facing up to the truth of eternal recurrence is difficult to explain away. It must be noted, however, that Nietzsche still does not straightforwardly commit Zarathustra to belief in recurrence. Zarathustra never says that everything recurs, but only that he is disgusted at the thought of the recurrence of the small man. If we can explain this disgust without assuming that he accepts recurrence as a truth, we need not attribute belief in recurrence to Zarathustra.

Nehamas attempts such an explanation. After arguing on the basis of EH (III, Z 6) that Zarathustra's "abysmal thought" cannot be the cosmological version of recurrence, he attempts to explain Zarathustra's nausea as a response to the thought that if anything recurs, everything must recur. For this means that if Zarathustra is to exist again, everything else, "the small man included, would also have to exist again" (1985, 148). But it is difficult to see why the thought that his own recurrence requires the recurrence of the small man would induce nausea unless Zarathustra believes that he will recur. Therefore Nehamas' interpretation cannot explain his nausea without committing him to belief in recurrence.

Nehamas seems to think that the abysmal point for Zarathustra is that he cannot affirm the recurrence of his own life unless he affirms the recurrence of the small man. (This is precisely what he thinks follows from the doctrine of will to power.) But why should he affirm his own recurrence? Nehamas (who writes of wanting life to recur rather than affirming recurrence) says that this "is the desire he is trying to make his own" (148), but does not explain why. The answer I would give is one Nehamas would not accept (see Chapter 6): that Zarathustra is committed to the affirmation of life in opposition to the ascetic ideal's devaluation of it, and he has come to realize that the highest affirmation of life is the affirmation of eternal recurrence.

Given my answer, we can interpret Zarathustra's "abysmal thought" as the realization that to affirm life is to affirm the eternal recurrence of everything, including the small man. We can then explain Zarathustra's nausea in the following way. Zarathustra is committed to the affirmation of life; he has preached it from the beginning of the book (in accord with the suggestion of GM II, 24–25). But he has avoided the realization that affirming life requires affirmation of eternal recurrence because he cannot affirm the recurrence of the small man (section 3 explains why). Zarathustra need not believe even in the possibility of recurrence, then, to be choked by the thought of the small man's recurrence. Finally realizing that the affirmation of life requires affirmation of eternal recurrence, he must determine what his reaction would be if he did believe in recurrence. In discovering that he would be choked by nausea at the recurrence of the small man, he realizes his own distance from the ideal he has been preaching.

A final passage that seems to imply his belief in recurrence occurs after Zarathustra's successful confrontation with his "most abysmal thought." Zarathustra sings "the other dancing song" to life, who responds in the following way.

> "O Zarathustra, you are not faithful enough to me. You do not love me nearly as much as you say; I know you are thinking of leaving me soon. There is an old, heavy growl-bell that growls at night all the way up to your cave; when you hear this bell strike the hour at midnight, then you think between one and twelve – you think, O Zarathustra, I know it, of how you want to leave me soon."
>
> "Yes," I said hesitantly, "but you also know – "and I whispered something into her ear, right through her tangled yellow foolish tresses.
>
> "You *know* that, O Zarathustra? Nobody knows that." And we looked at each other and gazed on the green meadow over which the cool evening was running just then, and we wept together. But then life was dearer to me than all my wisdom ever was (Z III, 15).

What Zarathustra whispers to life surely concerns eternal recurrence, probably whatever he has just learned in his confrontation with the "most abysmal thought." Nehamas' suggested reading of this thought – that if anything recurs, everything must recur – cannot be what Zarathustra whispers since it would not be an appropriate reaction to life's worry that Zarathustra plans to leave her soon. On the other hand, the traditional interpretation – Zarathustra tells life that although he plans to leave, he will return to her as part of the eternal recurrence of the same – makes sense, and even seems demanded by the passage.

There is, however, an alternative interpretation of what Zarathustra tells life, namely, that to affirm life, one must affirm the eternal recurrence of everything, including death. The topic of the conversation, after all, is Zarathustra's love of life. Life accuses him of not loving her enough on the grounds that he wants to leave her, which could mean simply that he is willing to die. He could quite reasonably respond that love of life requires affirmation of death, affirmation of the eternal recurrence of both life and death.

This second interpretation fits the stated topic of the exchange better than does the traditional interpretation. It also makes more sense of its final two sentences. What Zarathustra says to life apparently makes both of them somewhat sad. If their tears resulted instead from joy (or from being deeply moved), the "but" in the final line would make little sense. The "but" suggests that although one might expect what has happened (or what has been said) to lessen Zarathustra's love of life – it does, after all, make them both sad – it does not have that effect. If Zarathustra responded to life's accusation by insisting that he will return to her, their sadness would be inappropriate. The fact of Zarathustra's return should constitute a consolation, something to be happy about in this context. On the other hand, if Zarathustra tells life that his love of her must include the acceptance of death, we can consider their sadness appropriate. In that case, Zarathustra offers life no consolation for his death, but merely answers her accusation that he does not love her enough. Zarathustra's doctrine would be ridiculous if he claimed that a love of life precludes sadness at the necessity of death. The point of this passage seems to be instead that such (perhaps momentary) sadness is compatible with the highest affirmation of life. The "but" of the last line indicates that Zarathustra does not turn his sadness about the connection between life and death into an objection to life.

The passages on recurrence in *Zarathustra* therefore allow us to conclude either that Zarathustra teaches only the affirmation of recurrence or that the text is essentially ambiguous. It certainly suggests at several points that he teaches a recurrence cosmology in addition to the ideal of affirmation. But the cosmology adds nothing to the ideal, and Nietzsche goes out of his way to avoid giving Zarathustra a direct expression of belief in it. Why the ambiguity? Why does Zarathustra whisper his doctrine to life instead of telling us what it is? Nietzsche seems to set the reader up to assume the cosmological interpretation, while leaving open the possibility of recognizing an alternative, and ultimately more plausible, interpretation of the whispered message.

To what point? To begin with, the strategy coheres with Nietzsche's praise for the distinction between the esoteric and the exoteric, especially in relation to "our highest insights" (BG 30), which the subtitle of Z, "A Book for All and None," also suggests. He may have thought that the cosmological version of the doctrine provided a kind of protective shield which would help protect the esoteric doctrine from being reduced to the level of those who would otherwise appropriate it. After all, superficial talk about affirming life might well drive serious thinkers back to the ascetic ideal. Further, Nietzsche may have thought that to replace the ascetic ideal, his ideal would need a two-level interpretation. Some may find sufficient reason for accepting and teaching it in Nietzsche's hypotheses regarding nihilism, the ascetic ideal, the will to power, and the nature of religious teachers and philosophers. But surely most people will not. To accept the ascetic ideal, people certainly needed a more compelling reason than its suitability for overcoming nihilism: for example, the promise of heaven and the threat of hell. Here talk of the "myth" of eternal recurrence may have some point. What Nietzsche may have regarded as a myth, that is, a lie or a mere possibility, he may also have considered an important instrument for bringing about acceptance of his ideal of affirming recurrence – in people who did not regard it as a myth. If so, Soll and Magnus are correct in taking Nietzsche to be interested in the psychological effects of accepting the recurrence cosmology. However, if I am correct, the important effect of accepting the cosmology is the motivation it gives one for accepting the ideal of affirming recurrence, and this motivation would be necessary only for those who cannot appreciate sufficiently and act upon the other reasons Nietzsche gives to support his ideal. Those prepared to think seriously about psychology, history, philosophers, and ascetics will find in Nietzsche's published works an argument for accepting the ideal of affirming eternal recurrence that depends on neither cosmology nor metaphysics.

These speculations concerning Nietzsche's intentions are not essential to my interpretation. Even if we say that Zarathustra's teaching of eternal recurrence is ambiguous, we need not make the same claim about Nietzsche's. Nietzsche did not call himself "the teacher of the eternal recurrence" on the basis of what his notebooks contained. To identify the doctrine of recurrence he actually taught (the one he refers to when he calls himself "the teacher of eternal recurrence"), we must look to the texts he published on the topic. These texts leave no doubt that Nietzsche taught the ideal of affirming eternal recurrence. They also suggest a justification for this practical doctrine that explains why Nietzsche accorded it such importance without making it dependent on cosmology. On the other hand, the published texts reveal no unambiguous commitment to a recurrence cosmology, much less arguments for one. Unless the practical doctrine of recurrence would receive stronger support from Nietzsche's cosmological arguments than it does from his genealogical hypotheses – and my argument in the next section shows it would not – no plausible principle of interpretation justifies saddling Nietzsche's doctrine of eternal recurrence with the cosmological argumentation found in his notebooks. Although these arguments might be relevant for biographical speculation concerning what Nietzsche believed, they remain completely irrelevant to the philosophical question concerning the doctrine he actually presented in his books. We might be justified in saying that he also taught a cosmological doctrine of recurrence in his notebooks. But then he taught two different doctrines of recurrence, and we have no justification for conflating the two or for burdening the evaluation of the doctrine Nietzsche identified as his central teaching with the cosmological doctrine he played with in his notebooks.

3. Does it matter if we recur?

A second major objection to eternal recurrence is that it would have no practical significance even if it were true. Originally formulated by Simmel (173–4), this objection has influenced recent discussion in the form of Soll's insistence that the recurrence of one's life "should actually be a matter of complete indifference" (339). Nietzsche thought recurrence should be a matter of momentous concern, Soll argues, because it would increase infinitely the amount of pain in one's life. However, recurrence requires the qualitative identity of a life in each cycle of cosmic history and thus precludes memory links and therefore the accumulation of experience or any continuity of consciousness between cycles. Soll concludes that it thereby precludes the kind of identity between me and my double in later cycles "necessary for me to view his experiencing pain tantamount to my experiencing further pain" (340).

Whereas Simmel's formulation of this objection presupposes that personal identity requires continuity of consciousness (174), Soll attempts to sidestep such metaphysical issues. He claims that whatever constitutes personal identity, I have reason for special concern about the pain I may experience later in life because of the continuity of consciousness between myself and the person who will experience the pain. However, no such continuity exists between me and my double in the next cycle of the eternal recurrence. It therefore appears that I have no reason for any special concern (any more concern than I would have for any other human being). Only if I misconstrue the recurrence of my life on the model of occurrences later in my present life, that is, only if I presuppose a continuity of consciousness, would the extreme reactions to the demon's proclamation of eternal recurrence (despair or elation) described in GS 341 make sense.

This argument threatens the use of recurrence as a test and means of formulating Nietzsche's ideal. If Soll is correct, even accepting recurrence as the truth would give one nothing to overcome – in which case, affirming the eternal recurrence cannot provide an alternative to the ascetic ideal. Further, everyone should be able to pass the test if it requires only a lukewarm willingness to have recurrence be true. If, on the other hand, only those who respond with elation pass it, the test picks out not those who have achieved the highest affirmation of life, but those who misunderstand what eternal recurrence really involves.

I agree with Soll that the recurrence of my life should be a matter of relative indifference. His argument may require slight modification because some will find it as reasonable to have a special concern for the destiny and suffering of the person qualitatively identical to myself in the next cycle as to have such concern for the person I would be after an operation or accident that removed all memory connection to my present self. But if there is not continuity of consciousness in the latter case, there is a kind of continuity. It still makes sense to think of my present life as in some (perhaps limited) kind of continuity with my life after the memory loss. In the case of eternal recurrence, on the other hand, no continuity exists. There is neither continuity of consciousness nor any kind of continuity or traceability through time and space.

My life must recur at the same time and place as my present life relative to everything else in its cycle of cosmic history, or the lives would not be qualitatively identical. But something must differentiate my life from its recurrence. Otherwise, as Magnus has argued effectively, there is no recurrence but only two different names for the one numerically identical occurrence of my life. Only a difference in temporal position fits the bill – the recurrence of my life must be part of an earlier or later cycle of cosmic history than my present life (which is, of course, also a recurrence). So I live and die, and eons later someone is born whose life has exactly the same characteristics as mine, including temporal/spatial relation to everything else in its cycle. No connection exists between the two lives, nothing carries over from my death to the birth of my double in the later cycle. A clear conception of this lack of connection should reduce a person's concern for her double in the next cycle to the level of concern one would have for any human being. It might be argued that this is not any human being, for what you decide to do now determines what that human must do. But then one should also believe that what you will do is already determined by what someone did in an earlier cycle, so one's feeling of responsibility for the person in the later cycle is also undermined by the clear conception of what eternal recurrence involves.

This point can be strengthened by considering a spatial analogy to recurrence suggested by both Simmel and Magnus. Suppose the demon, instead of announcing the eternal recurrence, proclaims that there now exist an infinite number of duplicates of our solar system and therefore an infinite number of individuals qualitatively identical to myself. Although this might arouse much amazement and even interest, few people would perceive the existence of such duplicates as adding infinitely to the suffering or joy of their own lives. But how is there any stronger basis for such perception in the case of eternal recurrence? The only important difference I can see between the two cases is that the lack of connection between qualitatively identical individuals is clearer if they exist simultaneously than if they exist successively. It would be easier to fall into using the wrong model in the latter case, to think of the life of one's duplicate as in continuity with, hence as a continuation of, one's life, thus as increasing its pain or joy, and as trapping one forever in the cycle of existence. If this is correct, a clear conception of the lack of connection involved in eternal recurrence would remove the practical significance it would seem to have on the personal level. It would certainly remove all reason for adopting recurrence as a decision criterion. More to the point of my interpretation, it should render eternal recurrence equally a matter of indifference to individuals with quite opposed attitudes towards their lives, thereby undermining its use as a test of affirmation and means of formulating an ideal of affirmation.

Despite several recent attempts (Magnus and Nehamas), the literature on eternal recurrence contains no adequate answer to this objection. I suggest that we can answer it only if we incorporate an unrealistic or uncritical model of recurrence into our formulation of Nietzsche's ideal of affirmation. To see the plausibility of doing so, compare Nietzsche's question – would you be willing to live this same life eternally? – with a question people do in fact ask each other: if you had it to do all over, would you marry me again? The way in which members of a couple respond to the latter question is usually taken to reflect their true feelings about their marriage. Whether they would marry each other again is taken to reflect their true feelings about having married each other once. Yet, answering the question seems to involve them in a confusion. It requires the use of a contradictory or unrealistic model: you, knowing what you do now, going through an experience identical to one in which you knew much less. But no one would seriously argue that this prevents the question from testing one's attitudes towards one's marriage. Getting an honest answer is, of course, another matter. But if an honest answer would reveal one's underlying attitude, and one can adopt the unrealistic model it presupposes through imagination, the model is the right one for the purpose. Refusal to adopt it would show evasion, not intellectual honesty.[2]

I believe we should interpret Nietzsche's use of eternal recurrence in similar terms. It seems quite plausible for him to take the willingness to re-live one's life as a measure of the affirmation (positive valuation) of one's nonrecurring life. What Soll's objection makes clear is that this willingness cannot function as a measure of affirmation unless one imagines recurrence unrealistically, on the model of a later occurrence in one's present life. But we certainly have reason to make this unrealistic model part of Nietzsche's test of affirmation. As I have argued, Nietzsche's use of the demon to proclaim recurrence suggests that passing his test depends on one's uncritical response to recurrence. He asks how we would react to its proclamation in a situation that is hardly conducive to questioning either its truth or conceivability, a situation that would force us to imagine it as a reality in whatever way we could. But to imagine eternal recurrence at all puts one in danger of misconstruing it. I can only imagine recurrence as it would appear to a continuing consciousness for whom the cycles of world history were temporally distinguishable – a consciousness whose existence is ruled out by the eternal recurrence of lives identical in each cycle. It would be

2. I owe several of the formulations in this section to Claudia Card's helpful comments on an early version of this chapter.

natural to conflate this continuing consciousness with my own individual consciousness and therefore, even if I recognized the absence of memory links, to imagine recurrences of my life as continuous with, thus adding to the experienced content (joy or suffering, e.g.) of my present life. I agree with Soll that this distorts what eternal recurrence would actually amount to. But it does not vitiate Nietzsche's use of eternal recurrence as a test of affirmation because it is precisely thereby that recurrence becomes useful for testing what Nietzsche wants to test: one's affirmation of life.

To use eternal recurrence as a test of affirmation, one must be willing to "play the game," to imagine eternal recurrence in an uncritical or preanalytical manner, suspending all doubts concerning its truth or conceivability. As in the case of the "marriage test," one may refuse to play and analyze the test instead. The absence of memory links and continuity will then make indifference seem rational. But if one plays the game and imagines the recurrences of one's life as continuous with and therefore as adding suffering and joy to one's present life, the extreme reactions Nietzsche describes – gnashing of teeth or calling the demon divine – make sense and complete indifference would seem psychologically impossible.

To satisfy the ideal of affirming eternal recurrence is thus to be a person who would respond joyfully to the demon's proclamation of eternal recurrence if she accepted it as the truth, interpreted it in the uncritical or preanalytic manner I have described, and responded honestly. This interpretation of Nietzsche's ideal seems demanded by the principle of charity since it allows us to answer an otherwise unanswerable objection and fits perfectly the demon situation Nietzsche describes. I argue below that it also allows us to understand how Nietzsche's formula for the highest affirmation of life excludes two ways of affirming life we have reason to think he would want to rule out, namely, those dependent on valuing life only as a means or on taking revenge against life.

4. Meaning, revenge against life, and the Übermensch

Soll offers a second objection to Nietzsche's assumption that recurrence should drive some to despair. Apart from the pain it would add to one's own life, Nietzsche evidently thought eternal recurrence would be a source of despair because it precludes a final state for the universe and therefore amounts to "the meaningless" eternally (WP 55). Of course, Nietzsche believed, and Zarathustra illustrates, that such despair can be overcome. Nietzsche presents this overcoming as an arduous process, however, for which traditional tools (traditional philosophical theories certainly) are inadequate. Soll argues to the contrary that recurrence is quite compatible with history reaching an ideal state or goal at the end of each cycle, and that "one might derive great metaphysical comfort from the thought of the successful pattern of fulfillment displayed and repeated in each cycle" (338). Recurrence therefore allows the meaningful to be repeated eternally.

Zarathustra's problem with the recurrence of the small man, which is his problem with recurrence in general, does seem related to the issue of meaning. Zarathustra's life is directed towards the creation of the Übermensch, to such an extent that he would not "know how to live if [he] were not a seer of what must come" (Z II, 20) – that is, of the Übermensch. The small man, however else we understand him, is the man overcome by the overman. To preach the overman ideal is to preach the overcoming of the small man. This explains why Zarathustra would perceive the eternal recurrence of the small man as depriving his life of meaning: it would amount to the impossibility of reaching his goal, of overcoming the small man. At this point, Soll's objection seems relevant. Eternal recurrence does not preclude either the creation of the overman or even the complete overcoming of the small man within each cycle, perhaps at the end of each cycle, of world history. If Nietzsche considered this unlikely or impossible, eternal recurrence, which is compatible with any pattern of progression or regression within each cosmic cycle, provides no basis for this position. Whatever gives the single occurrence of a life meaning is merely repeated if life recurs. Why, then, does Nietzsche present eternal recurrence as making a difference to Zarathustra? Why can't he devote his life to creating the overman, and find meaning and consolation in the thought (or hope) that each cycle of world history will exhibit the meaningful progress from small man to overman?

I agree that eternal recurrence should not make any difference to the meaningfulness of Zarathustra's life, if he construes it realistically. If he imagines it in the uncritical manner described in section 3, however, the situation changes radically. Imagining his life as going on and on, Zarathustra cannot imagine his goals as ever really achieved. Whatever he achieves will come undone, and he will need to redo it. As he imagines it, eternal recurrence is incompatible with ever establishing the overman or overcoming the small man. Whatever he accomplishes in this regard, the small man will return and Zarathustra will have to resume the fight against him. The unrealistic model of recurrence makes Zarathustra's position like Sisyphus', and makes impossible the metaphysical consolation Soll prescribes for his despair.

Not that it makes it impossible to affirm (find value or meaning in) one's life, but it does preclude one way of doing so. If one values life only as a means to something beyond the process itself – heaven, nirvana, the rock sitting on top of the mountain, the existence of the realm of right and justice or any other kind of utopia – belief in eternal recurrence (imagined uncritically) makes the affirmation of life impossible. The point is not that the ideal of affirming eternal recurrence makes having goals problematic. Nietzsche clearly thinks we need goals. Without goals, there is no activity, no life, only depression and nihilism. By providing a goal, the ascetic ideal gave life meaning and saved the will. But it did so in a way that deprived life of intrinsic value, that accorded it value only as a means to its own negation. When it is construed unrealistically, belief in eternal recurrence makes this strategy impossible. Finding intrinsic value in life itself, that is, valuing the process of living as an end, becomes the only alternative to despair.

But what is it to value life intrinsically (as an end, or for its own sake) if human life is largely goal-directed activity, and we undertake the activities we do only because we perceive them as necessary (or helpful at least) for the establishment of these goals? I am suggesting that Nietzsche's answer is: to be joyfully willing to engage in the same activities again and again, even if one had no hope of the goal being finally achieved, that is, to affirm the eternal recurrence, unrealistically construed. This unrealistic construal of eternal recurrence gives Nietzsche a formula for what it is to value living for the sake of the activity itself, to value the process of living as an end and not merely as a means. It allows his formula for the highest affirmation of life to rule out finding life valuable only because one sees it as a means to an end beyond the process.

Zarathustra certainly seems to value human life as a mere means for most of the book. Although he preaches the affirmation (positive valuation) of "this" life, as opposed to the "next" one, he appears to value human life only as a means to a superhuman life. His demand that the Übermensch be the meaning of our lives establishes human life as something to be overcome. What is important about human beings, he says, is that they are "a bridge and not an end [Zweck]" (Z P, 4). The value of human life therefore derives completely from its status as a means to the Übermensch, the negation or overcoming of the merely human. Here we have the same pattern we find in the case of the ascetic ideal: Human life is accorded value as a means to something that is its own negation. Further, Zarathustra evidently values his own life only as a means to the Übermensch because he says that he cannot endure the past or present and would not know how to live were he not a seer of what must come. Under these circumstances, his inability to affirm the eternal recurrence is hardly surprising. Able to consider human life valuable only because he considers it a means to something of intrinsic value, the existence of the Übermensch, he cannot affirm it once eternal recurrence rules out the establishment of the Übermensch. For Zarathustra, eternal recurrence (unrealistically construed) means that his goal will never be fully achieved and that it cannot therefore confer meaning or value on a human life that would otherwise be the means to it. Given Zarathustra's way of valuing or affirming it, the eternal recurrence – but only if construed unrealistically – leaves human life unredeemed and without value, because it cannot be absorbed in a transhuman life.

But why is Zarathustra unable to find intrinsic value in the process of living itself? Why is he unable to value human life as an end? Two chapters in part 2 of Zarathustra suggest that the answer lies in Zarathustra's need for revenge against life.

"On Redemption" implies that recurrence is needed as an alternative to revenge against time (i.e., against what has already been), to teach us "reconciliation with time and something higher than reconciliation" (Z II, 20). Because Zarathustra still cannot affirm eternal recurrence at this point, we must assume that he has not yet learned this alternative to revenge.

In "The Tomb Song," we have already learned of a part of

Zarathustra's own past with which he sounds less than reconciled. He says to his enemies: "What is all murder of human beings compared to what you have done to me?" But it is somewhat unclear exactly what his enemies have done.

> You murdered the visions and dearest wonders of my youth. My playmates you took from me, the blessed spirits. In their memory I lay down this wreath and this curse. This curse against you my enemies! For you have cut short my eternal bliss . . .
> Thus spoke my purity once in a fair hour: "All beings shall be divine to me." Then you assaulted me with filthy ghosts; alas, where has this fair hour fled now?
> "All days shall be holy to me" – thus said the wisdom of my youth once; verily, it was the saying of a gay wisdom. But then, you, my enemies, stole my nights from me and sold them into sleepless agony; alas, where has this gay wisdom fled now? (Z II, 11).

I interpret Zarathustra as bewailing the loss of his original and nonreflective affirmation of life, an affirmation similar to that exemplified by the nobles of GM I. I cannot believe that Nietzsche has Zarathustra say that depriving him of this affirmation is worse than murdering human beings because he believes it. Nietzsche celebrates a very reflective affirmation of life and claims (GM I, 6) that human beings became interesting animals only through what amounts to the overcoming of the nobles' unreflective affirmation of life at the hands of the priests' revaluation of values. We can more plausibly interpret Zarathustra's extreme expression as indicating his lack of reconciliation with the past and the source of his need for revenge against it. Additional support comes from the fact that the very next section, "On Self-overcoming," contains the first reference in Z to the will to power and the claim that this will is the danger of those who create values.

Consider now the connection between "On Redemption" and "The Tomb Song." At the end of the latter, Zarathustra says that the visions and hopes of his youth remained "unredeemed" in him and that only his will allowed him to endure it and to overcome the suffering inflicted by his enemies. Because Zarathustra equates willing and creating, this means that he has been able to endure the loss of his affirmation of life through what he has created, namely, the overman ideal, the ideal of someone who fully affirms life. I have already argued that the Zarathustra's teaching of the overman ideal deprives human life of intrinsic meaning. "On Redemption" (discussed in more detail in section 2) can be read as an explanation for this. After repeating his teaching that willing and creating liberate from suffering, Zarathustra adds a major qualification: that the will itself needs liberation and that its redemptive doctrines have therefore redeemed only foolishly. This means that redemptive doctrines have been inspired by revenge and have therefore been able to redeem only in an ultimately self-defeating way. Because Zarathustra still needs redemption, we must assume that this applies to his own creation, the overman ideal. We must therefore consider whether Nietzsche gives us the means to understand how the overman ideal expresses Zarathustra's own need for revenge.

I have argued that for Nietzsche the affirmation of life depends on a sense of power (Chapter 7) and that revenge attempts to restore this prerequisite for affirming life by hurting the perceived cause of one's suffering and powerlessness (section 2). GM I suggests that the inventors of slave morality are better able to affirm their own lives because their moral condemnation of the life-affirming nobles (whose power and easy affirmation of life is a source of suffering and resentment for the priests who invent the good/evil mode of valuation) gives them an imaginary revenge against the nobles, a spiritualized version of burning them in effigy. "On Redemption" suggests that traditional redemptive doctrines function in an analogous way, that they allow their creators to affirm life because they condemn life, and this condemnation provides a sense of revenge against the aspects of life, for example, temporality, that they perceive as the cause of their suffering. If Zarathustra's case is similar, the doctrine of the Übermensch has allowed him to endure his suffering (to affirm life despite his suffering) because it gives him a sense of revenge against those he perceives as its cause. This makes perfect sense if Zarathustra's enemies, who destroyed the visions of his youth, are equivalent to the small men whose overcoming Zarathustra has been preaching and whose eternal recurrence nauseates him.

We have reason to believe they are. Contrary to usual assumptions (Nehamas, 1985, 148, e.g.), the small man does not seem so closely related to the "last man" of the prologue who is "happy" knowing nothing of love, longing, or creation. Explaining his nausea at the thought of eternal recurrence, Zarathustra first refers to the small man in the context of the claim that man is the cruelest animal. The "small man, especially the poet – how eagerly he accuses life with words. Hear him, but do not fail to hear the delight [*Lust,* and a few lines later, *Wollust,* or voluptuous delight, in the same context] in all accusation." The small man is not the pathetic last man, but rather those who formulate doctrines that accuse life. The admonition to hear the pleasure in his accusations suggests that the small man achieves his own affirmation of life by accusing and condemning life. But this fits the enemies Zarathustra cannot forgive. They attained their affirmation of life in ways that made life seem ugly and that deprived Zarathustra of his affirmation. This suggests strongly that what deprived Zarathustra of his original affirmation of human life – his vow that "all beings shall be divine to me" (Z II, 11) – was recognizing the extent to which human beings use doctrines that devalue life and deprive others of the ability to affirm it in order to find their own lives worth living. This is, of course, something Zarathustra might learn from reading Nietzsche's *Genealogy of Morals.* It therefore seems reasonable to assume that Zarathustra's need for revenge is directed not merely against something that happened in his past but also against what Nietzsche regards as an important aspect of human life itself, an aspect Zarathustra cannot accept.

We can now understand the implication of "On Redemption," that his Übermensch ideal expresses Zarathustra's own need for revenge. His teaching of that ideal implies that human life has value only as a means to a life that overcomes all trace of the small man. The overman ideal therefore negates the value not only of the small man, but also of any life contaminated by him. Teaching this ideal can therefore be seen as an act of spiritual revenge against those who deprived Zarathustra of his unreflective affirmation of life, and also against life itself. Zarathustra's Übermensch ideal functions very much like the moral doctrines of the ascetic priests of GM. By their moral condemnation, the priests strip the nobles of value in their own imagination. But they condemn the nobles precisely on the grounds of their affirmation of life (this is the interpretation they give of sin, Nietzsche's analysis suggests). They deny the nobles' value by means of an ascetic doctrine that deprives life itself of value (except as a means to its own negation). This gives the priest an imaginary revenge against life that allows him to affirm his own life, to feel good about it, to treat it as valuable. Likewise with Zarathustra. By preaching the Übermensch, he denies value to the small man, but also to human life itself, except as a means to its own negation. This means – assuming, as "On Redemption" suggests, that Zarathustra achieves his own affirmation of life in this way – that his way of handling his own suffering is a variation on the strategy he despises. The self-defeating character of his strategy also parallels that of the ascetic ideal. Given the ascetic ideal, life itself must be perceived as devoid of value once the truth is apparent: that there is no God, nor any transcendent realm to which this life can be construed as a means. And if Zarathustra comes to perceive the truth about his own motivation, he must, given his own ideal, perceive his own life as devoid of value for he contains the small man within himself.

Zarathustra's nausea at the thought of eternal recurrence can now receive additional explanation. As the passage itself makes clear, nausea is the opposite of affirmation. Zarathustra had been able to overcome the nausea induced by his "enemies" and affirm life because his preaching of the Übermensch gave him a sense of revenge against his enemies for what they had done to him, and against life itself, against the life he had to lead as a result. Revenge helps one to affirm life, I presume, because it gives one a sense of power relative to what has caused one suffering. Zarathustra's doctrine could give him a sense of power over what has caused him suffering because, like the priest's moral condemnation, it says no to it, tells it that it ought not be. However, when he imagines his enemy, the small man, coming back over and over again, his sense of power in relation to life is lost, and nausea overcomes him. The point is that if one has to imagine the object of one's condemnation returning eternally, no matter how much one condemns it, no matter how much one fights to eradicate it, an affirmation of life based on revenge becomes psychologically impossible. The unrealistic construal of eternal recurrence therefore gives Nietzsche a formula that excludes from the highest affirmation of life one based on revenge against life.

5. The evaluation of Nietzsche's ideal

If the interpretation I have offered is correct, work on the evaluation of Nietzsche's central doctrine has barely begun. The doctrine of eternal recurrence has been kept at the center of philosophical interest in Nietzsche by subtle work on the *Nachlass* arguments for a recurrence cosmology and on questions concerning whether the cosmology has any practical significance. I have argued that this work provides no relevant objections to the doctrine Nietzsche actually taught. Relevant objections must be objections to the ideal Nietzsche formulates with the help of eternal recurrence or to the helpfulness of eternal recurrence for formulating that ideal.

Several arguments of this type can be reconstructed from the literature, that is, disentangled from assumptions I reject concerning the interpretation of the doctrine. When I refer in what follows to objections to the ideal of affirming the eternal recurrence, I refer to the objections that the relevant opponents of eternal recurrence would have a basis for formulating if they accepted my interpretation of the doctrine.

A first objection is suggested by Heidegger's claim that the doctrine of eternal recurrence expresses Nietzsche's own resentment against time (in Allison, 76–7). Like the metaphysicians he criticizes, Heidegger claims, Nietzsche devalues the finite temporal world relative to the eternal world. Although Heidegger presupposes Nietzsche's acceptance of a recurrence cosmology, his objection seems worth consideration even if Nietzsche teaches only the affirmation of eternal recurrence. In idealizing the desire for eternity – "joy wants eternity," Zarathustra repeatedly proclaims – does not Nietzsche idealize the eternal at the expense of time? Does this not express another refusal of finitude and therefore another expression of resentment against time? If we have no reason to believe our life recurs, why isn't our affirmation of life best tested by reaction to a demon who tells us that we will live and die, and that will be it for us? As Magnus formulates this objection, why not a finitude test?

My interpretation offers the following answer. Nietzsche attempts to formulate what it is to find intrinsic value in a temporal, finite life, a life that will come to an end. This includes articulating what it is to accept death in a way that does not vitiate one's affirmation of life. The finitude test is not a good alternative to eternal recurrence. A response of unadulterated joy at the thought that one will not live forever seems incompatible with the highest affirmation of life, and even less enthusiastic but still positive responses would be compatible with welcoming death out of dislike of life or out of boredom. Someone with the attitude of "eat, drink, and be merry, for tomorrow we die" could easily pass the finitude test. But if their merry attitude is a cover for despair, they would not pass the eternal recurrence test. For them, death is a way of dealing with despair. As Nietzsche himself wrote: "the thought of suicide gets one through many a dreadful night" (BG 157).

Magnus has recently suggested a different argument against Nietzsche's ideal. He actually denies that Nietzsche offers a normative ideal, arguing that if it were an ideal, the eternal recurrence would require us to love unconditionally and for its own sake each and every single moment of our lives and of world history. This, he rightly claims, is impossible and/or monstrous: How can one affirm the painful experiences of one's life for their own sake? How can one idealize affirming Hitler's atrocities unconditionally? This interpretation, he claims, agrees with Nietzsche's own characterization of eternal recurrence as Zarathustra's "most abysmal thought." For those who believe that Zarathustra eventually embraces that thought and teaches the affirmation of eternal recurrence, Magnus' interpretation becomes the objection that Nietzsche's ideal is both an impossible and an abysmal one for human beings.

The interpretation stems in part, I believe, from the failure to distinguish affirming an event merely as an unwelcome detour "on the way to a Neil Simon happy ending" (Magnus, 1988, 171) and affirming it only as part of a whole process. We can agree that Nietzsche's ideal precludes affirming painful, horrible, and obscene events merely as means to ends beyond themselves, while denying that we are to love them "unconditionally" or "for their own sake." Nietzsche's ideal is to love the whole process enough that one is willing to relive eternally even those parts of it that one does not and cannot love. To defend this interpretation, however, one must also reject a crucial assumption Magnus makes: that affirming eternal recurrence amounts to preferring the exact recurrence of history to any variation on it. To prefer a history including all the pain and horror to an otherwise identical one minus the pain and horror amounts precisely to valuing the pain and horror "for its own sake."

Although no one has drawn out its implications so clearly, Magnus is far from alone in his assumption that Nietzsche's ideal person prefers the exact repetition of her life and world history to any alternative. Nehamas seems to share it, for instance, and his recent interpretation of eternal recurrence seems motivated in large part by the desire to answer the problems it raises. Why, Nehamas wonders, does not Nietzsche give us a choice other than to accept or reject the exact recurrence of our lives? Why don't we get the choice of an emended version? Attempting to provide Nietzsche with a reasonable answer here, Nehamas attributes to him the metaphysical theory of will to power described in Chapter 7: Everything is so intertwined that if anything recurs, everything must recur; if anything had been different, everything would be different. According to Nehamas, this leaves only two alternatives: affirming the exact repetition of my life and all of history or "rejecting my entire life and the whole world with it" (156). I cannot recur unless everything else recurs "all in the same succession and sequence" (GS 341). But even if the metaphysical theory in question were sound, it would not answer Magnus' objection.

In the first place, the theory of "internal relations," that a thing is constituted by its relation to everything else, does not preclude the future occurrence of variations on our present history. It entails only that the occupants of such histories would not be identical with the occupants of our present history. If Hitler had not existed, I could not have existed, for the same reason that the Buddha could not have existed: The persons with our otherwise identical characteristics would not also have had the characteristic of bearing a relationship to Hitler. But this does not preclude the future occurrence of what I would much prefer to my identical recurrence, the existence of someone exactly like me except that she does not live in the same chain of events as Hitler. To say that this person would not be me but only someone very like me has no force when the only difference is the absence of a characteristic I would prefer to be without. Therefore, attributing to Nietzsche a metaphysical theory of internal relations will not explain why he does not offer us the choice of an emended version of our lives. To make Nehamas' explanation more plausible, we must suppose that Nietzsche posits a more substantial connection between things, so that the existence of everything is *causally* dependent on the existence of everything else. My existence might depend on Hitler's in this way, for instance, if my parents would not have met but for World War II. If this kind of connection exists between all things, then nothing in our present history could recur unless everything did, and affirming my own recurrence without the recurrence of all the horrors of human history would be "metaphysically incoherent" (Soll, 335). However, even if it were plausible that everything is causally dependent on everything else, this would not explain why Nietzsche does not offer us the choice of an emended version of our lives when formulating his test for the affirmation of life. Why cannot I affirm life precisely by preferring a history stripped of its horrors to the exact recurrence of my life? Why isn't it a greater affirmation of life to want the repetition of the past without the bad things? That I cannot recur unless all of the horrors do too does not seem like a very good or a very Nietzschean answer.

What Nietzsche may have believed about the necessary interconnection of all things will not help to explain why he identifies the affirmation of life with affirming eternal recurrence. We can answer Magnus' objection, I believe, only by denying that affirming eternal recurrence amounts to preferring the exact recurrence of our lives and world history to any variation thereof. Why, to repeat Nehamas' question, does not Nietzsche offer us an alternative other than the acceptance or rejection of the exact recurrence of our lives? Because if he did, he would be committing himself to precisely the ideal Magnus so ably criticizes. Suppose the demon of GS 341 gave us a choice between different courses of history, and Nietzsche wrote: "How well disposed would you have to become to yourself and to life to choose the exact course you have already lived?" In that case, as Magnus argues, only God or a Leibnizian could pass Nietzsche's test of affirmation. But the demon does not give you a choice. He does not ask you whether you would live your life the same way if you had to do all over again. To say yes to that test is to have learned nothing from life.

The demon says you are going to relive eternally this exact life. The affirmer of eternal recurrence is a person who would experience joy at this prospect. But that is perfectly compatible with preferring a world that is just like ours except for the absence of Hitler if given the choice. We can designate the affirmer of eternal recurrence as one who would choose this exact life again if given the choice, but against what alternatives? Certainly the choice between recurrence and heaven, recurrence and nirvana, recurrence and nothing. But I see no evidence that Nietzsche's ideal person would have to choose this exact life over a similar one in which Hitler was aborted. Calling the demon's message divine (even saying "never have I heard anything more divine") does not commit one to denying that a slightly different life would be even better, though it does preclude yearning for it, or spending much time thinking about it.

Magnus finds evidence to the contrary in Nietzsche's well-known "formula for greatness":

> *Amor fati:* that one wants nothing to be different, not forward, not backward, not in all eternity. Not merely bear what is necessary, still less conceal it – all idealism is mendaciousness in the face of what is necessary – but love it (EH II, 10).

Reading this passage in the most literal sense would make *amor fati* the attitude of wanting nothing to be different than it is right now. But this quietist doctrine is completely incompatible with Nietzsche's emphasis on change and creation and the connection between creation and destruction. It therefore seems reasonable to interpret *amor fati* as the attitude of one who affirms eternal recurrence. Not wanting anything different in the past means accepting the past in the sense of affirming its eternal recurrence. The passage thus gives us no independent basis for interpreting the affirmation of eternal recurrence, and does not override the reason we have for denying that it means preferring the exact repetition of human history to *any* alternative, namely, that this would saddle Nietzsche with an obviously objectionable ideal.

The strongest evidence for Magnus' interpretation comes from the end of GS 341: "Or how well disposed would you have to become to yourself and to life to *crave nothing more fervently* than this ultimate confirmation and seal?" To crave nothing more fervently than eternal recurrence may seem to mean preferring the exact repetition of history to any variation. But there are two considerations on the other side. First, craving nothing more fervently than X does not preclude preferring Y to X if given the choice. I would say that I now crave nothing more fervently than finishing this book, even though there are many things I would prefer to it (e.g., finishing my second or third book) if given the choice. Secondly, if we take into account the context of the above quotation – the question: How would you react if a demon proclaimed eternal recurrence to you? – we see that affirming eternal recurrence is not a matter of craving eternal recurrence, but of being a person who would come to crave it under certain conditions that need never obtain, namely, if one accepted and interpreted the doctrine uncritically, but was initially put off by it. The end of GS 341 suggests two opposed directions that life might take for those who initially gnash their teeth instead of calling the demon's message divine. They might be crushed by the question "do you want this once more?" which would "lie upon [their] actions as the greatest weight." Or they might change with a view to being able to bear their fate, becoming so well disposed to themselves and to life that they could be said to crave nothing more than eternal recurrence. This does not seem incompatible with being a person who would choose some variation on the exact recurrence of actual history *if* that were presented as an option.

A final objection to the ideal of affirming eternal recurrence can be extracted from Magnus' attempt to show that eternal recurrence is not a normative ideal, namely, that it does not require the kind of moral self-overcoming many (especially Kaufmann) have considered Nietzsche's ideal (Magnus, 1988, 173). Magnus presents affirming eternal recurrence as requiring only a yes-saying attitude towards life, and claims that this entails "no specifiable behavioral norm at all" (1988, 170). We can formulate this as two different objections to Nietzsche's ideal, first, that even moral barbarians might live up to it, and second, that it requires nothing but a certain attitude and is therefore an empty ideal that cannot possibly provide guidance concerning how to live.

As to the first objection, I believe Magnus is right, that the ideal of affirming eternal recurrence does not by itself demand moral self-overcoming. The nobles of the first essay of GM seem to be Nietzsche's paradigm of people who could affirm eternal recurrence. Yet, Nietzsche portrays them as without much tendency to moral self-overcoming (the internalization of the will to power) when he describes them, for instance, as emerging from "a disgusting procession of murder, arson, rape, torture, exhilarated and undisturbed of soul, as if it were no more than a student's prank, convinced that they have provided the poets with a lot more material for song and praise" (GM I, 11). I agree with those who deny that Nietzsche holds out such barbaric behavior as his ideal. I assume his concern is to foster the nobles' self- and life-affirmation in those who are already expert in the self-overcoming of the moral tradition. I see him as offering his ideal of affirming eternal recurrence primarily to the teachers of the purpose of existence (GS 1), that is, to priests and philosophers. These are the experts in moral self-overcoming whose resentment against life has created and furthered the adoption of the ascetic ideal. Zarathustra offers them the ideal of the Übermensch, and Kaufmann seems right to link this to self-overcoming. However, in accord with GM II, 24, the overcoming Zarathustra encourages is directed not against one's animal passions, but against one's all-too-human condemnation of life and everything that stands in the way of affirming life (pity, resentment, e.g.). It turns out, as I have argued, that the Übermensch ideal is itself motivated by resentment against life and is therefore replaced by the ideal of affirming eternal recurrence. This ideal requires all the self-overcoming that the Übermensch ideal promotes, but it does not condemn its own opposite, the small man who can affirm life only by condemning it and depriving other people of their affirmation. The eternal recurrence (unrealistically construed) gives Nietzsche a formula for what it is to promote an ideal without condemning those who fail to live up to it.

The problem Magnus points out is, in effect, that the barbarian nobles of GM I, do live up to it. My response is that being like them is not a real possibility for those to whom the ideal is offered, and Nietzsche therefore has no need to formulate an ideal that would rule out the possibility. On the other hand, there is no reason to think of affirming eternal recurrence as a complete ideal, one that entails all the values Nietzsche promotes. This ideal tells us not what all of our values should be, but only that whatever they are, they should be rooted in gratitude and service to life rather than resentment against it. I suspect that Nietzsche thought that if teachers of the value of existence could get over their resentment against life and affirm eternal recurrence, they would be liberated from the ascetic ideal at last, and able to create new ideals. He might consider eternal recurrence the form, as it were, of all such ideals (all that are not variations on the ascetic ideal), but I do not see that it has to supply all of the content.

On the other hand, in response to the second objection, I certainly believe that the ideal of affirming eternal recurrence supplies some content. Although it does not supply a decision criterion for specific actions, it does require something of us, namely, whatever is necessary to affirm eternal recurrence. To understand what this demands of us, we need to understand human psychology in general, and our own psychology in particular. One might be required by the ideal to get out of one's present situation (say, a situation of oppression), for instance, precisely because it prevented getting a sufficient sense of power in relation to life except by devaluing it. Zarathustra's own adherence to the ascetic ideal after he had already formulated a life-affirming ideal gives some indication of the kind of self-overcoming Nietzsche thought affirming eternal recurrence required in philosophers and other "teachers of the value of existence." My study suggests that Nietzsche also knew something of this from his own philosophical development.

In addition to all of the self-overcoming the Übermensch ideal requires, affirming eternal recurrence seems to require the overcoming of moral condemnation (especially in its many disguised forms, which means that it also requires the overcoming of a great deal of self-deception). I have argued that we do not have to affirm Hitler unconditionally, or for his own sake. On the other hand, Nietzsche's ideal surely requires us to affirm him, and much else we find abhorrent, in some important sense, and I think that sense is one that excludes moral condemnation. To show why Nietzsche believes this would require an exploration of GM's account of morality – an account of what moral condemnation involves and its connection to a whole set of moral attitudes and judgments. This is a huge task that requires another whole study. But the conclusion to which I am led by my consideration of Nietzsche's ideal of affirming eternal recurrence, and my study of Nietzsche on truth, is that we need such a study. I have tried to show that the obvious objections to Nietzsche's ideal can be answered, and in particular that considerations of truth and his view of truth do not raise unanswerable objections. But this still leaves the question: Is it a good ideal? The issue, Nietzsche says in effect, is whether one considers Hitler or anything else an objection to the rest of life – whether one is well enough disposed towards life that one would be willing to have the whole thing repeat itself eternally including the most horrible parts. But why should one be so well disposed to life? Why wouldn't it be better to say no, refuse to repeat the whole thing, if it included the morally awful things? That in fact seems to be the proper moral attitude, at least as Nietzsche sees it. The moral attitude is that the value of the whole is vitiated by its moral failures, and the whole process is in need of redemption by some morally better future to which it leads. This is also Zarathustra's doctrine before he is able to affirm eternal recurrence. His doctrine afterwards is that the whole needs no redemption or is redeemed by recognizing it needs no redemption, that is, by affirming it.[3]

If this is correct, the evaluation of eternal recurrence would involve deciding between the moral point of view and Nietzsche's standpoint beyond good and evil. Nietzsche's ideal is, contrary to Magnus, neither empty nor banal if it requires us to overcome the former. On the other hand, it seems to me that there is much work for philosophical underlaborers to do before we can understand well what our choices are and what reasons can be given on either side. One point my present study should suggest in that regard is that the kinds of reasons Nietzsche has to offer in support of his ideal are not metaphysical ones, but empirical claims, especially psychological ones, concerning human beings, their needs, and their values.

---

3. This formulation sounds like Magnus who says that the only glad tiding is that there are no religious or philosophical glad tidings, and that there has never been a need for them (1988, 177). The difference is that I think Nietzsche believes that there is a need for ideals, because there is a need for the internalization of the will to power, and that the role of philosophers is to provide them.

BIBLIOGRAPHY

Alderman, Harold. *Nietzsche's Gift.* Athens: Ohio University Press, 1977.

Allison, David B., ed. *The New Nietzsche.* New York: Delta, 1977.

Allison, Henry E. *Kant's Transcendental Idealism.* New Haven: Yale University Press, 1983.

Austin, J. L. *Philosophical Papers.* 2d ed. Oxford: Oxford University Press, 1970.

Bird, Graham. *Kant's Theory of Knowledge.* London: Routledge & Kegan Paul, 1962.

Blanshard, Brand. *The Nature of Thought.* Vol. 2. London: Allen & Unwin, 1939.

Breazeale, Daniel, ed. and trans. *Philosophy and Truth: Selections from Nietzsche's Notebooks of the 1870's.* New Jersey: Humanities Press, 1979.

Clark, Maudemarie. "Nietzsche's Attack on Morality." Unpub. diss. Madison: University of Wisconsin, 1977.

———. "On 'Truth and Lie in the Extra-Moral Sense.' " *International Studies in Philosophy* 16, no. 2 (1984): 57–66.

———. "Nietzsche's Perspectivist Rhetoric." *International Studies in Philosophy* 18, no. 2 (1986): 35–83.

———. "Deconstructing *The Birth of Tragedy.*" *International Studies in Philosophy* 19, no. 2 (1987): 67–75.

———. "Language and Deconstruction: Nietzsche, de Man, and Postmodernism," in *Nietzsche as Postmodernist: Essays Pro and Contra.* Edited by Clayton Koelb. Forthcoming from SUNY Press.

Danto, Arthur C. *Nietzsche As Philosopher*. New York: Macmillan, 1965.

Davidson, Donald. *Inquiries into Truth and Interpretation*. Oxford: Oxford University Press, 1984.

——. "A Coherence Theory of Truth and Knowledge." In Henrich, *op. cit.*: 423–38.

Deleuze, Gilles. *Nietzsche and Philosophy*. Translated by Hugh Tomlinson. New York: Columbia University Press, 1983.

de Man, Paul. *Allegories of Reading*. New Haven, Conn.: Yale University Press, 1979.

Derrida, Jacques. *Speech and Phenomenon*. Translated by David Allison. Evanston: Northwestern University Press, 1973.

——. *Writing and Difference*. Translated by Alan Bass. Chicago: The University of Chicago Press, 1978.

——. *Spurs. Nietzsche's Styles*. Translated by Barbara Harlow. Chicago: The University of Chicago Press, 1979.

——. *Margins of Philosophy*. Translated by Alan Bass. Chicago: The University of Chicago Press, 1982.

Descartes, René. *The Philosophical Works of Descartes*, Vol. 1. Translated by Elizabeth S. Haldane and G.R.T. Ross. Cambridge University Press, 1968.

Draine, Betsy. "Writing, Deconstruction, and Other Unnatural Acts." *Why Nietzsche Now? A Boundary 2 Symposium* 9–10 (Spring/Fall 1981): 425–36.

Dummett, Michael. *Frege: Philosophy of Language*. 2d edition. Cambridge, Mass: Harvard University Press, 1981.

Fink, Eugen. *Nietzsches Philosophie*. Stuttgart: Kohlhammer, 1960.

Frankfurt, Harry G. "Freedom of the Will and the Concept of a Person." *The Journal of Philosophy* 68 (January 14, 1971): 5–20.

Galileo. *Discoveries and Opinions of Galileo*. Edited by Stillman Drake. New York: Doubleday (Anchor Books), 1957.

Gram, Moltke S. "Things in Themselves: The Historical Lessons." *The Journal of the History of Philosophy* 18 (October 1980), 407–31.

Grimm, Ruediger Hermann. *Nietzsche's Theory of Knowledge*. Berlin: Walter de Gruyter, 1977.

Guyer, Paul. *Kant and the Problem of Knowledge*. Cambridge University Press, 1987.

Haack, Susan. *Philosophy of Logics*. Cambridge University Press, 1978.

Harper, William L. "Kant on Space, Empirical Realism and the Foundations of Geometry." *Topoi* 3 (December 1984): 143–62.

Heidegger, Martin. *Nietzsche*. 2 vols. Pfullingen: Neske, 1961. Where a translation is cited, it is volume 4 of the English translation by David Krell. New York: Harper & Row, 1982.

——. *Sein und Zeit*, 15th ed. Tübingen: Niemeyer, 1984. Translated by Macquarrie and Robinson. *Being and Time*. New York: Harper & Row, 1962.

"Who is Nietzsche's Zarathustra?" in Allison, *op. cit.*: 64–79.

Henrich, Dieter, ed. *Kant oder Hegel?* Stuttgart: Klett-Cotta, 1984.

Higgens, Kathleen. *Nietzsche's Zarathustra*. Philadelphia: Temple University Press, 1987.

Hoy, David. "Philosophy as Rigorous Philology? Nietzsche and Poststructuralism." *New York Literary Forum* 8–9 (1981): 171–85.

Review of Alexander Nehamas' *Nietzsche: Life as Literature. London Review of Books* 9 (January 8, 1987): 15 ff.

James, William. *The Writings of William James*. Edited by J. McDermott. New York: Random House (Modern Library), 1968.

Kant, Immanuel. *Kritik der reinen Vernunft*. Edited by R. Schmidt. Hamburg: Felix Meiner, 1966. Translated by Norman Kemp Smith. *Critique of Pure Reason*. New York: St. Martin's, 1961.

Kaufmann, Walter. *Nietzsche: Philosopher, Psychologist, Antichrist*. 4th ed. Princeton, N.J.: Princeton University Press, 1974. Third ed. 1968.

"Nietzsche" entry in *Encyclopedia of Philosophy*. Vol. 5, 505–14. Edited by Paul Edwards. New York: Macmillan, 1967.

Translation and Notes to *On the Genealogy of Morals*. In *Basic Writings of Nietzsche*, 439–599. New York: Random House (Modern Library), 1968a.

Translation and Notes to *Thus Spoke Zarathustra*. In *The Portable Nietzsche*. New York: Viking, 1958.

Kofman, Sarah. *Nietzsche et la métaphore*. Paris: Payot, 1972. Where a translation is cited, it is the selection (pp. 16–37) translated in David Allison, *op. cit.*, 201–14.

Kuenzli, Rudolf E. "Nietzsche's Zerography: *Thus Spoke Zarathustra.*" *Why Nietzsche Now? A Boundary 2 Symposium* 9–10 (Spring/Fall 1981): 99–117.

Kuhn, Thomas S. *The Structure of Scientific Revolutions*. 2d ed. enlarged. Chicago: University of Chicago Press, 1970.

Lampert, Laurence. *Nietzsche's Teaching. An Interpretation of Thus Spoke Zarathustra*. New Haven: Yale University Press, 1986.

Lange, Friedrich Albert. *Geschichte des Materialismus und Kritik seiner Bedeutung in der Gegenwart*. 1875. Frankfort: A. Schmidt, 1974.

LePore, Ernest, ed. *Truth and Interpretation: Perspectives on the Philosophy of Donald Davidson*. Oxford: Blackwell, 1986.

Levi, Isaac. *The Enterprise of Knowledge*. Cambridge, Mass.: MIT Press, 1980.

Magnus, Bernd. *Nietzsche's Existential Imperative*. Bloomington: Indiana University Press, 1978.

"Nietzsche Today: A View from America." *International Studies in Philosophy* 15, no. 2 (1983): 95–104.

"The Deification of the Commonplace: *Twilight of the Idols.*" In Solomon and Higgins, *op. cit.* (1988), 152–81.

"The Use and Abuse of *The Will to Power*." In Solomon and Higgins, *op. cit.* (1988), 218–35.

McGinn, Colin. "Truth and Use." In Platts, *op. cit.*, 19–41.

Megill, Allan. "Nietzsche as Aestheticist." *Philosophy and Literature* 5 (Fall 1981): 204–225.

Müller-Lauter, Wolfgang. *Nietzsche: Seine Philosophie der Gegensätze und die Gegensätze seiner Philosophie.* Berlin: Walter de Gruyter, 1971.

Nehamas, Alexander. *Nietzsche: Life As Literature.* Cambridge, Mass.: Harvard University Press, 1985.

Review of Richard Schacht's *Nietzsche. Philosophical Review* 93, no. 4 (October 1984): 641–46.

"Who are 'the Philosophers of the Future'?: A Reading of *Beyond Good and Evil.*" In Solomon and Higgins, *op. cit.* (1988), 46–67.

O'Brien, Conner Cruise. "The Gentle Nietzscheans." *The New York Review of Books* 15, no. 8 (Nov. 5, 1970): 12–16.

Parsons, Charles D. "Infinity and Kant's Conception of the 'Possibility of Experience.' " *Kant: A Collection of Critical Essays.* Edited by Robert Paul Wolff. 88–133. New York: Doubleday (Anchor Books), 1967.

Plato, *The Collected Dialogues.* Edited by Edith Hamilton and Huntington Cairns. Princeton, N.J.: Princeton University Press, 1961.

Platts, Mark, ed. *Reference, Truth and Reality.* London: Routledge & Kegan Paul, 1980.

Prauss, Gerold. *Kant und das Problem der Dinge an sich.* Bonn: Bouvier, 1974.

Putnam, Hilary. *Meaning and the Moral Sciences.* London: Routledge & Kegan Paul, 1978.

Reason, Truth and History. Cambridge University Press, 1981.

Quine, W. V. O. *From a Logical Point of View.* New York: Harper & Row (Harper Torchbook), 1961.

Rescher, Nicholas. *The Coherence Theory of Truth.* Oxford: Oxford University Press (Clarendon Press), 1973.

Rorty, Richard. *Philosophy and the Mirror of Nature.* Princeton, N.J.: Princeton University Press, 1979.

Consequences of Pragmatism. Minneapolis: University of Minnesota, 1982.

"The Contingency of Selfhood" and "The Contingency of Language." *The London Review of Books* 8 (May 8, 1986): 11–15 and (April 17, 1986): 3–6.

Contingency, Irony, and Solidarity. Cambridge University Press, 1989.

Sartre, Jean-Paul. *Saint Genet: Actor and Martyr.* New York: Braziller, 1963.

Schacht, Richard. *Nietzsche.* London: Routledge & Kegan Paul, 1983.

Schopenhauer, Arthur. *The World as Will and Representation.* Vol. 1. 1st ed. 1813. Translated by E. F. J. Payne. Mineola, N.Y.: Dover, 1969.

On the Fourfold Root of the Principle of Sufficient Reason. 1st ed. 1819. Translated by E. F. J. Payne. Lasalle, Ill.: Open Court, 1974.

Simmel, Georg. *Schopenhauer and Nietzsche.* German edition 1923. Translated by H. Loiskandle, D. Weinstein, and M. Weinstein. Amherst: The University of Massachusetts Press, 1986.

Soll, Ivan. "Reflections on Recurrence: A Re-examination of Nietzsche's Doctrine, *die ewige Wiederkehr des Gleichen.*" In Solomon, *op. cit.:* 322–42.

Solomon, Robert, ed. *Nietzsche: A Collection of Critical Essays.* Garden City, N.Y.: Doubleday (Anchor Books), 1973.

and Higgins, Kathleen, eds. *Reading Nietzsche.* Oxford: Oxford University Press, 1988.

Stack, George J. *Lange and Nietzsche.* Berlin: de Gruyter, 1983.

Strawson, P. F. *Logico-Linguistic Papers.* London: Methuen, 1971.

Tarski, Alfred. "The Semantic Conception of Truth." In *Semantics and the Philospohy of Language.* Edited by L. Linsky. 13–49. Urbana: The University of Illinois Press, 1952.

Vaihinger, Hans. "Nietzsche and His Doctrine of Conscious Illusion." From *The Philosophy of As-If.* In Solomon, *op. cit.,* 83–105.

Van Straaten, Zak, ed. *Philosophical Subjects: Essays Presented to P. F. Strawson.* Oxford: Oxford University Press (Clarendon Press), 1980.

Wallace, John. "Only in the Context of a Sentence Do Words Have Any Meaning." *Midwest Studies in Philosophy* 2 (1977): 144–67.

West, Cornell. "Nietzsche's Prefiguration of Postmodern American Philosophy." *Why Nietzsche Now? A Boundary 2 Symposium* 9–10 (Spring/Fall 1981): 241–70.

Westphal, Kenneth R. "Was Nietzsche a Cognitivist?" *Journal of the History of Philosophy* 23, no. 1 (January 1985): 343–63.

Wilcox, John. *Truth and Value in Nietzsche.* Ann Arbor: The University of Michigan Press, 1974.

"Nietzsche Scholarship and 'the Correspondence Theory of Truth': the Danto Case." *Nietzsche-Studien* 15 (1986): 337–57.

Williams, Michael. "Coherence, Justification, and Truth." *Review of Metaphysics* 37, no. 2 (December 1980): 243–72.

Zanardi, William. Comments on Maudemarie Clark's "On 'Truth and Lie in the Extra-Moral Sense.' " *International Studies in Philosophy* 16, no. 2 (1984): 67–70.

INDEX